CHAPPO

FOR THE SAKE OF THE GOSPEL

CHAPPO: FOR THE SAKE OF THE GOSPEL
John Chapman and the Department of Evangelism

Michael Orpwood

Eagleswift Press

A book by
Eagleswift Press
42 Hampden Rd, Russell Lea, Australia. 2046

Published August 1995
Reprinted October 1995
Copyright © Michael Orpwood

Scripture taken from the HOLY BIBLE. Copyright © 1973, 1978, 1984, by the International Bible Society. Used by permission of Zondervan Publishing House. All rights reserved.

Every effort has been made to trace the original source material contained in this book. Where the attempt has been unsuccessful, the publisher would be pleased to hear from the author/publisher to rectify any omission.

National Library of Australia Cataloguing-in-Publication data:
Orpwood C M (Christopher Michael), 1944–
Chappo: for the Sake of the Gospel: John Chapman and the Department of Evangelism.
Includes index.
ISBN 1 875981 00 4
1. Chapman, John 1930–.
2. Anglican Church of Australia, Diocese of Sydney. Dept of Evangelism - History.
3. Anglican Church of Australia - Clergy - Biography.
4. Evangelists - Australia - Biography. I. Title
    283.092

Front cover photograph by permission of
Sydney Missionary and Bible College, Croydon.
Back cover photograph by Stephen Toomey.

Designed and printed by Bell Graphics,
7 McCauley St, Alexandria, Australia. 2015

Foreword

This book is a fine and deserved tribute to John Chapman as he retires from the Sydney Diocesan Department of Evangelism. I consider it an honour to contribute a Foreword to it.

My first duty is to reassure his world-wide circle of friends that John is not thereby retiring from the fray but simply from his responsibilities in the Department, where, for so many great years, he has been its leader and its heart and soul. This inveterate traveller, whose phenomenal work-rate is a continual marvel, is, I am pleased to report from observation, still going strong. Long may it be so.

The work of an itinerant evangelist is not an easy one. But in the deepest sense of the words, John was made for it. For one thing he has a quite unique capacity (at least I have never seen the equal) to establish instant contact with everyone he meets. To take an example at random, a recent car journey with him through the wheat growing areas of New South Wales resulted in many new acquaintances, such as petrol station attendants (it is necessary to allow extra time for this!) If pre-evangelism means building bridges and establishing confidence then John has no rival. It is part Aussie ("G'day mate, howyoudoing?") but really just Chappo. A mixture of overflowing warmth, arresting wit and genuine interest in everybody and everything, breaks through the barriers and draws people out of their shells with astonishing rapidity. At first, when accompanying John, I was inclined, as an inhibited Englishman, to blush, but now I delight in the more outrageous sallies. One of our first adventures was in a small lift packed with bodies, where no-one spoke or looked at the others, or even dared to breathe down a neighbouring neck; John, whose share of the available space was considerable, announced in the stiff atmosphere "I'm thinking thin!", whereupon there was an immediate relaxation of tension, grins appeared, shyness evaporated, and truly I think we could have started a meeting then and there. Such happenings, I quickly learned, were commonplace.

Yes, John was made for the job—no communication problems here! The downright humour and repartee possessed by his father, and his mother's sweetness and concern for others, have doubtless made their contribution to the genes of this remarkable man. An expert in these things might even discern elements in his make-up that have come down to him from the legendary aunts, Nellie, one of the best early women cricketers, and Millie and Vera, the non-stop talkers. All these, and more, have combined to produce a larger than life character who daily leaves a trail of people, glad even if a little startled, that he passed their way that morning.

The evangelist whose ministry tells in the long-term must also have theological and biblical depth of understanding. We noted this in John on his very first visit to St Helen's when, some twenty years ago, he lectured on God, His sovereignty, holiness and purposes. He must also be firm enough in his own convictions not to be deflected by the latest fashionable currents of opinion in the churches. You can depend on John to deliver what he has been asked for; he is continually at the "work of an evangelist", and keeps us to the same priorities.

Yet, withal, the evangelist needs to be modest, recognising that he is but part of a team, where others have long planted and watered, and that in any event it is God who gives the increase. In this regard I see John's ministry as marvellously supportive to the churches. Here is no prima-donna demanding our admiration, but a true fellow-worker, advising, provoking to good thinking and endeavours, laughing us out of our follies and fears, and generous in positive encouragement.

Chappo was born to be a competitor, so that opponents on the tennis court can count on no quarter given, no easy points. In conversation too, the ball whistles back over the net, clarifying, correcting, and enlarging. C S Lewis was supposed to see even casual remarks as opportunity for debate and victory, and if there is something of this in John, it has served to make him an influential leader in church affairs, as well as a formidable force in Synod. What a politician he would have made! Certainly you would be relieved to have him on your side, as he moved in to expose faithlessness or compromise, and especially to sniff out injustice (a notable and attractive side to his character). Particularly I have learned to admire his integrity, so that personalities and friendships cannot deflect him from what he thinks to be the right course of action. And, inevitably, there is a cost in this.

The famous "stories" cannot be overlooked in any tribute. They are not like other people's! For one thing they appear to be unpremeditated, lying deep in some capacious memory file, yet emerging instinctively to make or match a point. Still new and unexpected ones come to light from time to time. But the old are better. These are the great favourites, often requested (I am a culprit here, but by no means the only one) and repeated. Really, someone must take in hand the recovery and recording of all this treasure (even if publication might be hazardous) for there is material here that is not only achingly funny, but often so piercingly to the point for present ministry, that others in future days should also learn from them. I fear, however, that unless told by the master, most of the magic will be gone.

What, then, is the secret of the joy, help, and blessing that this man has brought to so many? I have no better description of his ministry to suggest than the two elements in preaching put forward by Phillips Brooks in his famous Yale Lectures on Preaching of 1877, that is "Truth through Personality". Truth, to be sure, for since God called to Himself this boy in his schooldays, John has not wandered from the truth (as Brooks, like so many evangelicals of his generation, sadly did) but has diligently foraged in Scripture in order the better to equip himself. And this not in isolation, but in fellowship with a large company of contemporaries and friends who have enjoyed the powerful theological stimulus of unrivalled teaching at Moore College and the Sydney Missionary and Bible College for years past.

But Personality too, an individual element not to be ignored. God fashions instruments to carry His Name to the world. Tom is not Dick, nor is Dick Harry. Thus it happens that when God chooses and sends some singular and unusual character into His harvest field, unusual ministry will result, to the glory of the God who planned it all.

Meanwhile the story, so well told by Michael Orpwood, awaits you; when you reach the end, remember that it is not yet finished.

Dick Lucas
St Helen's Church
Bishopsgate
London

Contents

To Marg

Preface

Let me make no secret of my bias towards the man who is the subject of this book. Chappo is for me, as he is for many others, a very special friend.

For over twenty-five years, he has taught me more of the truth, and more compellingly, than anyone else. He is for me and my family, as he is for many others, an inspirational example. He is simply exceptional.

This book is not an exhaustive record of John's life and his extraordinary ministry as an evangelist, Bible teacher and encourager. It deals chronologically with John's first thirty or so years before examining, thematically, the major areas of his ministry—a ministry that, of course, continues.

This book also traces the history of the Anglican Department of Evangelism in the Diocese of Sydney and the work of the remarkable collection of evangelists who have been its servants. The Department was originally constituted as the Board of Diocesan Missions in 1927, less than three years before John was born. John came to the Department of Evangelism on 1 October 1968 and worked there continuously until his retirement on 31 July 1995.

While many of Chappo's stories and experiences are included here, it has not been possible to include them all. I feel in this something of the frustration of the author of John's Gospel, where in commenting on the One who has been the inspiration for John's life and work, he says "Jesus did many other things as well. If every one of them were written down, I suppose that even the whole world would not have room for the books that would be written" (John 21:25). If your favourite Chappo story is not here, I'm sorry. Hopefully, there will be sufficient to satisfy you.

Quotations attributed to John but not identified to a particular source come from my many conversations with him and from notes he has given me. Similarly, unidentified quotes from others come from personal conversation.

This book is a collegiate work. Its form makes that obvious. Many have, from their love for John, given help generously and enthusiastically. The contributions of almost seventy people named in the text have been included in one way or another. The contributions of others are not so obvious. I am greatly indebted to the generosity of Peter Smith in allowing me access to his research into the Diocese of Armidale and to Matthew Pickering for interviews he conducted with former Diocesan Missioners and their families. Numerous people with direct knowledge of the events I have described commented helpfully on various parts of the manuscript. Two women, both fine servants of the gospel, deserve particular mention. Janet Kearsley started me on my task and Evonne Paddison ensured that I completed it.

Chappo is a wonderful subject for an author. He is endlessly fascinating. His life is rich and full. I hope this book is worthy of him. I hope, too, that you will receive as much blessing and enjoyment from reading it as I have received both from my association with Chappo and from my writing about him.

Michael Orpwood
Balmain

John aged 15.

FROM BIRTH TO REBIRTH

The 1930s

The years from 1929-1939 were depression years in Australia. Unemployment rates began to rise from the middle of 1929 and were at their worst over the next four years. From 1929, the homeless grew as families were evicted onto the streets. Camps of tents and shanties grew up in and around the cities and major towns. The percentage of trade unionists unemployed in Australia peaked at 30% in the middle of 1932.[1] Among the countries of the western world, Australia's unemployment rates were surpassed only by those of Germany. 1930 was the year in which Mr Jack Lang, the Premier of New South Wales, refused the demands of Sir Otto Niemeyer of the Bank of England to slash the State's social welfare spending in order to finance its foreign debt. A State lottery was begun as a rescue scheme for the State's hospitals. In that most difficult of years, the most popular song was "On the Sunny Side of the Street".

1930 was also, by contrast, a year of great advance in the field of communication. In aviation, Kingsford Smith completed a round-the-world flight, Francis Chichester flew from London to Sydney in a Gipsy Moth and Amy Johnson became the first woman to fly solo from Britain to Australia, her flight taking nineteen days. Australian National Airlines commenced regular services between Sydney and Brisbane and between Sydney and Melbourne. In April, the radio-telephone system between Sydney and London began operation with a

1

conversation between the Australian Prime Minister, Mr James Scullin, and his British counterpart, Mr Ramsay MacDonald. In July, all State capitals were linked by trunkline telephone, except Perth which was linked to the rest of Australia, via Adelaide, in December.

On 19 August the two spans of the Sydney Harbour Bridge, then arching toward each other from the southern and northern shores, were joined.

John with his grandfather, James Varley.

1930 was the year in which the Australian cricket team, of which Don Bradman was a member, won back the Ashes in England and Phar Lap won the Melbourne Cup.

Towards the end of that year, on 2 December, and against the opposition of King George V, the first Australian-born Governor-General, Sir Isaac Isaacs, was appointed.

Within the Church of England in the Diocese of Sydney, the long episcopacy of Archbishop J C Wright was drawing to its close. From 1933, another long episcopacy, that of Howard Mowll, the missionary bishop from China, would begin its energetic and fruitful twenty-five-year life.

It was during the course of 1930, on 23 July in that year, that John Charles Chapman was born. It was a birth that passed without remark. Yet angels sang.

This man, his life and work, might never come to be recorded anywhere within the annals of the nation of Australia. Yet in a greater nation it would bring rejoicing to a greater king. The name of John Charles Chapman finds its record in the book of those to whom the almighty God has given freely of His rich and vibrant life, and by that same God's gift and through the faithful service of this man, the names of many others have been added to that book.

Dad and Mum

On 31 January 1916, Albury Crisp Chapman and Muriel Louise Varley were married at St Paul's, Kogarah. The groom was then twenty-six years of age and his bride twenty-four. After their marriage, they made their home in Rockdale. Eleven years later, with the help of a mortgage, they would be able to afford to build a house at Oatley.

Albury Chapman was the sixth child of Hume Jones Chapman and Eliza Day Crisp. He had been born at Germanton (later, because of nationalistic resentment of Germans generated by the First World War, renamed Holbrook) near Albury in New South Wales on 11 October 1889. His birth was preceded by the births of two brothers (one of whom had already died) and three sisters. Four children were to survive their early years, Millicent, Hume, Hastings and Albury. At the time of Albury's birth, his father was the post and telegraph master at Germanton. Albury had left school immediately after completing his primary education. He had been apprenticed as a fitter and turner. This training was followed by a time at sea as a marine engineer. He had helped manufacture munitions in England during the First World War. On his return to Australia, he commenced a period of service with the NSW Railways Department that continued until his retirement. He was engaged in construction work installing turbines in power stations. His work sometimes took him away from his home to places like Newcastle and Lithgow.

Albury Chapman, 1915.

Albury was a very outgoing man. He was strong in his convictions. There were some issues, in particular, on which he would argue forcefully and at length. He was a great humorist. He was inherently funny, often whimsical and witty. He laughed a lot and made others laugh with him. He was an active sportsman. He was the kind of man who enjoyed having a drink with his mates at the pub. In the evenings, he would often be pleasantly drunk.

Muriel Chapman had had a testing childhood, marked by personal grief and uncertainty. She had been born at Rookwood on 22 September 1891, the daughter of James Varley, a telegraph operator and later a postmaster, and Louise Caroline Gregory. Muriel was the second of three children, having an elder brother, Reg, and a younger sister, Vera. Muriel's mother had died when Muriel was nine. Her stepmother had died when she was eleven. Circumstances had forced her to live with her Aunt Nellie Donnan at Bexley. She was a highly intelligent woman, but poorly educated. Her schooling had been undertaken at eleven different schools and she, too, had not passed beyond primary level.

Muriel Chapman, 1916.

Muriel came from a sporting family that, on her mother's side, had produced the Gregorys of Australian cricket. She was a capable sportswoman herself, playing tennis and cricket. At cricket, she had represented New South Wales during 1910 in a team captained by her Aunt Nellie.

Muriel's aunt's family, the Donnans, were the administrators of the body that was the St George Cricket Club in the summer and the St George Baseball Club in the winter. It was at the Club that Muriel had met her husband who, through the year, played both sports. Albury was also a table tennis player and had represented the Railways Department in a team against their Victorian counterparts.

3

The unique Gregory family

The famous cricketing Gregory family contributed a great deal to the beginning of women's cricket in Sydney from 1886 to 1910. Nellie and Lily Gregory obviously played a lot of backyard cricket with their brothers—they were daughters of Edward James "Ned" Gregory, who played in the first Test match in 1877 and sisters of another Test player, Sydney "Syd" Edward Gregory. Without the benefit of school and club cricket before 1886 women had no other place to learn to play the game. Test player Harry Donnan, who married Nellie Gregory, added his support to the cricketing family by umpiring some of their games.

It is highly unlikely that any other State side, male or female, has ever before or since been represented by five members of one family. When NSW met Victoria in the first match of the 1910 series the NSW side included three Gregory sisters and two of their nieces. They were Mrs Nellie Donnan, Mrs Meagher and Mrs Clymer and the two nieces were Miss Varley–daughter of Mrs Varley, another sister of Syd Gregory—and Miss Donnan. By 1910 the Gregory sporting dynasty could boast that over twenty children had represented NSW in a variety of sports—cricket, football, sailing and athletics. Nellie Donnan became the first President of the NSWWCA, which was founded in 1927.

Wicket Women: Cricket & Women in Australia
Richard Cashman and Amanda Weaver.[2]

After nine years of marriage, their first son, James, was born on 23 April 1925. Five years later (three years after they had moved to Oatley), their second son, John Charles, was born. At the time of John's birth, Albury Chapman was forty years of age.

As was the case with almost everyone who had experienced it, the depression of the 1930s made a powerful impression on Albury Chapman. He had seen his neighbours in Oatley growing vegetables in their backyards and fishing in the Georges River in the daily struggle to stay alive. He and his wife were poor. He was obsessed with the need to avoid debt and with the financial imperative to pay off his mortgage. Yet the Chapmans were remarkably quick to help those in trouble. Their poverty never hindered their generosity.

Fred Davis was a neighbour who sold oysters. He didn't farm them. He bought them in the shell, opened them, bottled them and sold them. When his house burnt down, he, his wife and their daughter, Iris, and son,

St George Baseball Club, 1910.
Albury Chapman top right.

Fred, were immediately taken in by the Chapmans. Mr and Mrs Davis and their son went back soon afterwards to live in a tent on their property, but Iris continued to sleep at the Chapmans' home for many months. At no stage were the boys ever allowed to believe that their family was anything other than extremely lucky to have their neighbours living with them. If someone needed help, you helped them. That was what you did. There could be no question about it.

Albury Chapman owned a boat, "The Wattle". He would often head off to the boatshed on the Georges River at the bottom of the street with his neighbour, "Stoopy" Spears, another railway man like himself, to do some fishing. (Whenever Stoopy's name came up in conversation, Albury would tell his sons, in all solemnity, "Stoopy Spears? First man to cross the Blue Mountains in an open boat!" The younger son was so impressed with this

Stoopy Spears in the stern of "The Wattle".

piece of knowledge that he imparted it, with equal solemnity and with full conviction, to his school teacher.) A few doors down from the Chapmans was Mrs O'Connell, a widow who was a great friend of John's parents. Whenever Albury came home with some fish, one would be taken to Mrs O'Connell. The family would regularly take vegetables to her as well.

The depression had also brought Albury Chapman to the conclusion that gaining employment was of the greatest importance, but the employment could not be of any kind. Ultimate security lay only in a government job. He would impress this on his sons again and again and urge them to fulfil this wisdom.

Albury was staunchly Labor. The depression reinforced his strong prejudice for the Labor party. He knew that only Labor cared for the working class.

Rosa Street

In 1927, Albury and Muriel Chapman and their two-year-old son, James, moved to Oatley. They built a house at 41A Rosa Street (later renumbered 49). Despite its odd street number, it was the first house in its block, being surrounded on either side by natural bushland. The house was a brick cottage with a series of rooms opening off a common room that comprised an unnecessarily large entry foyer. The house no longer exists, having been replaced by home units. Rosa Street then was a street with a scattering of trim cottages inhabited mainly by artisans and their young families. The street ran along the spine of land shaped as a stubby finger by the winding Georges River, still tidal at that part, and its bays, Gungah Bay and Oatley Bay, before it merged with the bushland near the water's edge.

Typical of its era, No. 41A had none of the conveniences that are standard today. There was no refrigerator. The iceman, twice a week, delivered blocks of ice to be placed in the top of the wooden, tin-lined ice box. There was no washing

Jim and John, 1938.

machine. Washing was done mostly in a gas copper although Mrs Chapman used to scrub dungarees outside on one of the concrete paths. (Her husband seemed to have made the laying of new paths something of his life's work.) The two boys shared the back verandah. Muriel's father lived with them. Whenever John came home from school, he was always to be found peeling vegetables in the kitchen and always grandson and grandfather would recite the same litany:

"Where is Mum? What is there to eat?"

"She has run away with a soldier. But it doesn't matter. She was too tough to eat anyway."

The Chapman household was generally a happy one. Muriel Chapman, although not to the same extent as her husband, shared a strongly developed sense of humour. They laughed often as a family. Jokes were regularly told, but quickness in repartee was thought to be the highest form of humour. The strong sense of humour rubbed off on both the boys.

An introduction to oratory and repartee

As a child, I remember my father taking me to hear politicians campaigning from the backs of trucks in Oatley. It was the way they answered hecklers that he loved. If they were good, we would walk up to Mortdale to hear the same speakers again. My father saw the funny side to situations and his was a wry, dry humour—often hard when directed against people. I remember one Christmas when my Aunt Millie (my father's sister) visited us and I was unable to eat for laughing because of the banter between my father and my aunt.

John Chapman
on an early source of humour in his life.

When Jim was fifteen and John was nine, Jim was taken out of secondary school. Albury had discovered that Jim could secure one of those most important stations in life, a government job. The elder brother left the family home and started work in Canberra as a telegraph boy.

St Paul's, Oatley

Three doors down from the Chapmans', on the corner of Rosa Street and Neville Street, was St Paul's Church of England, Oatley. When Albury Chapman built his house, the church was the only other building in their block. St Paul's was like a little country church. It was made of weatherboards and had a galvanised iron roof. The original building was completed in December 1911 and served as both school and church. It has now been moved sideways and exists as "Arndu", the current St Paul's Pre-school Centre. St Paul's was one of seven churches in the Parish of Mortdale and Penshurst cum Oatley and Peakhurst. Its rector, since his appointment in 1929, was William John Siddens. He wore a stole when conducting services and took the eastward position. The congregation bowed their heads during the Apostles' Creed when they confessed their belief in Jesus Christ. Siddens gave all the appearances of being a middle church liberal.

Bricks of clay

John has told the story many, many times of how, before his conversion, he would go to church and sit there during the sermon totally dead to the preaching of God's Word. He found the sermon so uninteresting, he said, that he would sit and count the bricks in the wall behind the preacher, brick by brick, row upon row. He had done it so many times he knew exactly how many bricks there were.

When I discovered that St Paul's was a weatherboard building without a brick in sight, I was puzzled. Perhaps John's early churchgoing had occurred somewhere else?

When I raised this issue with him, John gave his characteristic chuckle. His eyes twinkled. Smiling a smile that mixed a suggestion of guilt with a large amount of childlike innocence, he said "Oh, it's just one of my stories".

Later, John added that the description of the material changed to reflect the construction of the place in which he was giving the illustration at the time— bricks, boards, stones, panels...

Michael Orpwood
on the revelations of writing biography.

There were wide differences of opinion between John's parents as to the place of the church in their lives. John's father never went, except to weddings and funerals. He was strongly anti-clerical. His opinion was that clergy were parasites on the community, that they wheedled money out of people who could ill-afford to part with it and, once they had got it, they did no good with it.

By contrast, Muriel Chapman was a woman of prayer who read her Bible. She went to St Paul's "for ever". She was a stalwart. Her major contribution to church life during the boys' childhood was through endlessly making jam for sale on the church's street stall. It was not until some time after she had begun attending St Paul's that she was brought to Christ, principally through the prayer and ministry of her nieces. Royle Hawkes, whose close friendship with John began in his early teenage years at Oatley, remembers Mrs Chapman (old Mrs Chappie, as he calls her) as "one of the softest, loveliest, kindest ladies that I ever met. She was one of those consistently kind people who can never quite work out why everyone else is being so kind to them."[3]

Both Jim and John went regularly to Sunday School. It met in the little hall behind the church. They were taught by some teenage girls who lived in the street.

In Sunday School, they used the material produced by the General Board of Religious Education in Melbourne. It concentrated on Anglican culture rather than on Scripture. They learnt the seasons of the church year and the appropriate colours for those seasons. They went on Sunday School excursions to visit the great Anglican churches in the city.

John also sang in the choir. His fine soprano voice was greatly appreciated by the congregation. He quite enjoyed the attention his singing brought him.

Some neighbours

A little further down Rosa Street towards Oatley Bay and on the opposite side, at No. 92, lived the Chiswells, Ernest and Florence, and their three boys, Peter, Barry and Ernie. Mr Chiswell and his brother were furniture makers. Mrs Chiswell was a keen supporter of the local Boy Scouts. John knew of them—the Chiswell boys played a lot of good tennis—but they were not particular friends. Young Peter Chiswell would often see Albury Chapman walking past their home on his way to the boatshed and his fishing. The Chiswells were not a church-going family.

At a later time and in another place, John and Peter Chiswell would form a remarkable alliance and a lifelong friendship.

Growth and discovery

John went to the local primary school at Oatley.

On the evening of Sunday, 3 September 1939, as John was nearing the end of fourth class at Oatley Primary School, the Australian Prime Minister, Mr R G Menzies, announced to the nation in a radio broadcast, "It is my melancholy duty to inform you officially that, in consequence of a persistence by Germany in her invasion of Poland, Great Britain has declared war upon her and that, as a result, Australia is also at war". The years from now until the middle of 1945 were to be years of war.

At the end of sixth class, John had not done well enough to get into a selective high school. His Aunt Vera had advised his parents that it was not possible to be properly educated if you didn't get into one of the better high schools and so John repeated sixth class at Mortdale. The family shared the common belief that a good education was necessary in order to get a good job, although good education did not necessarily entail a university education. Universities, Albury Chapman believed, ruined many good people by turning them into theoreticians.

From Mortdale, John went to Sutherland Intermediate High School for three years, from 1943-1945. His last two years of secondary education were completed at Sydney Technical High School (then known as Sydney Technical Boys' High School). Because John's parents had had no experience of secondary education, all decisions about courses were left to their son.

Sutherland was a small high school. John enjoyed his time there immensely. He felt like a big fish in a little pond although one of his teachers at that time, Win Dunkley, says that he was not the sort of person who stood out. Sutherland High was to have a powerful formative influence in John's life. Many of the things that would come to give him so much enjoyment later in life started there. Through school excursions, John was introduced to the world of music, opera and drama. At the same time, his cousin, Greg Bradford, also introduced him to classical music. Even though many of the performances he was taken to were, because of the Second World War, not up to international standard, they nevertheless opened a door of endless enjoyment for him.

Pie in the sky?

It was the night the Japanese subs entered Sydney Harbour (Monday, 1 June 1942). First of all, the air raid sirens went off. My mother, who did everything by the book, had cut out the double supplement in the Sydney Morning Herald that told you everything you had to do when the air raid came. So she meticulously got to work to do it. First of all, you had to fill up the bath and the tubs in case the mains were hit. Anything that could have water in it had water in it. Then you had to get the strongest table into the middle of the house. So my mother moved the kitchen table—which had an inch thick terrazzo top 6 feet long and 3 feet wide—she single-handedly dragged it into the hall (it took us days to manoeuvre it out again; to this day we don't know how she did it) while the rest of us stayed in bed.

Mother: "Get up Dad."

Dad: "Go and see if you can find Uncle Jack" (he was an air raid warden) "and see if it's a real one or if it's just another of those pretending ones."

Mother: "No Dad, it's a real one. I can hear guns going off."

Dad: "No it's not. Who'd be firing guns at us? It's not."

So, finally, my mother had done everything. She sat in glorious isolation under the table. And then she realised she didn't have her dentures. And she said:

"I haven't got my teeth. Dad, I haven't got my teeth."

And he said in a voice that could only just be heard:

"Toots, you needn't worry. If the Japs are going to drop anything, it won't be a hot pie!"

John Chapman
describing his father's sense of humour.

At Sutherland High, John sat next to a boy named Dick Tisher. Dick Tisher's friendship was a very important part of John's early Christian growth. Dick was converted during their second year. He evangelised John by talking to him very directly. He told him the gospel with no great finesse. He did just about all the things John has subsequently advised people not to do in sharing their faith with others. Dick's conversation was blunt. "Chappo," he said on one occasion, "you wouldn't know a Christian if you fell over one in the park". John was shocked by this summary judgment as he thought that, being a regular churchgoer, he was a Christian already.

Dick Tisher took John to where he could hear the gospel preached and explained. Win Dunkley remembers that an ISCF group was started at the school in her time and that Dick and John were both members of it. Dick Tisher was also a member of the Sutherland Congregational Church. In contrast to many other areas of New South Wales, the Congregational Church had, during the 1940s, a number of particularly strong congregations grouped in and around the St George area. The minister at Sutherland, Keith Matta, ran children's holiday camps. Dick Tisher took John to a holiday camp at Stanwell Tops, a cliff top area of bushland about half way between Sydney and Wollongong on the south coast. The boys slept in tents while the girls were in a building like a guest house. It had a large room in which they all ate. Mrs Matta did the cooking. Keith Matta gave the talks. John is sure he did not listen to what was said. When he returned home, he sensed he had been with good people, so he decided that he would be good. "And then," John says, "I discovered that I couldn't be good".

During those early high school years, John often went during school holidays to stay with his widowed aunt, Millie Mason, and his cousins, Nancy and Jack. John says:

> Jack grew "cut" flowers in gardens that they owned. My aunt worked as a clerk with the Railways Department at Central Railway—my uncle had died in 1927. I don't know when these people had come to Christ, but they had, and I remember they used to pray around the table after church.

> I had never before been with people who prayed prayers that weren't out of the Prayer Book and formal. I was shocked. It didn't seem right to speak to God like that.
>
> My cousin Nance married Ian Emmett who was in the Baptist Theological College and later pastor of the Baptist Church at Dundas (but not before they had both served as missionaries in India with the Australian Baptist Mission where they were married). I was introduced to this church. All this was going on at the same time that Dick Tisher was beavering away.
>
> While I don't remember the Masons or Ian ever talking to me directly, I do know that their witness, as much as anything, undermined my confidence in formal religion. (My other cousin Jean Firth was Nancy and Jack's elder sister.

Albury Chapman, 1950.

> She was already a missionary in Colombia, South America, with Worldwide Evangelism Crusade.)

At the end of the year, Dick Tisher went to Canterbury High School and John went to Sydney Technical High School. John recalls, "So I'm now in the situation where I am away from Dick. I'm fairly certain I'm not Christian and I don't really know what to do to become Christian. And I remember praying that I would stay alive until I could find out. I was genuinely frightened that I would go to Hell! I finally worked out that the only place where I had seen people becoming Christians was at these holiday camps. So the next year, 1946, in fourth year of high school, I went in the August-September holidays to get converted. (It was at the Salvation Army centre at the northern beachside suburb of Collaroy.) That's what I'd really gone for. I think it was probably to formalise what had already taken place."

The year of John's conversion was also the year in which Albury Chapman retired from work.

When John went to Sydney Technical High School, he suddenly became a small fish in a very large pond. He felt so insecure that he chose to do the subjects his friends did rather than the ones he would have preferred. The thought of being in a class without anyone he knew was simply beyond contemplation. Instead of doing humanities, he did all maths subjects. Consequently, on completing secondary school, John had a matriculation to do Mathematics but not to be an English/History teacher.

From Sydney Technical High, John went to Sydney Technical College to do a four-year Diploma in Manual Arts. The Diploma had just been introduced as a pilot course and was designed to give manual arts teachers graduate status within the New South Wales Department of Education. As well as the manual arts subjects (Woodwork and Metalwork in all their forms, some basic Ceramics and Pencil Sketching) it introduced him to Psychology, English Literature and History (both Ancient and Modern). In fact, it was like a liberal arts college course. This was another educational experience that John enjoyed immensely.

One of John's friends at Sydney Technical High School, Norman "Tubby" Lenton, was converted in the Easter of 1947. He lived at Como and went to the Como Congregational Church. John would often go with him there for the evening services. At Como, he was pastored by students of the Sydney Missionary and Bible College who introduced him to many of the Christian disciplines, such as daily prayer and daily Bible reading.

The world's worst speller

My spelling was so bad that, every morning, my mother would dictate to me the editorial from that day's Sydney Morning Herald. She would mark my work and when I came home from school it would be waiting for me showing all the corrections. After three years, my spelling had not improved one scrap but my general knowledge was enormous. In third year at Teachers' College when I handed in a Psych. essay, it came back with the comment, "Your spelling is no longer a problem. It's a failure."

John Chapman
giving an example of his ability to laugh at himself.

Changes in the Parish

In 1945, W J Siddens left the Oatley Parish to become the rector of St Thomas', North Sydney. He was succeeded by Gordon Motram who embraced the same churchmanship as Siddens. Shortly after Motram's appointment, on 1 April 1946, the Parish was split in two. It was a venture in diocesan politics. One part of the parish became the Provisional District of Mortdale and Oatley. The Provisional District contained St Paul's, Oatley (since replaced with a new building), St Peter's, Mortdale, (now the site of a Franklin's supermarket) and All Saints', Oatley West. Noel Paddison, an evangelical, was appointed curate-in-charge.

Paddison had acquired only limited parish experience before his appointment. He was an academically gifted man whose natural interest lay more in reading philosophy than biblical theology. On his arrival, he introduced changes. In celebrating the holy communion, he took the northward position. He did away with stoles and with burses and veils. Confronting him in making these changes was the strong conservatism of the three congregations, particularly the Mortdale congregation. Paddison faced a hard task. Some, in particular, gave stubborn opposition.

Before his appointment, Paddison had been acting as locum tenens at Christ Church, Gladesville. While there, he had met a young man, Douglas Abbott, who had completed war service with the RAN in the latter part of 1946 and was proposing to enter Moore College at the beginning of the 1948 academic year. Doug Abbott, after coming out of the navy, had become involved with Graham Delbridge in the work of the Church of England Youth Department, then an instrumentality of the Home Mission Society. Delbridge had been appointed by Archbishop Mowll as the inaugural Chaplain for Youth in the Diocese of Sydney in December 1942. Doug Abbott had conducted residential conferences (called "houseparties") for youth on behalf of the Youth Department as well as some parish houseparties at properties in the Blue Mountains and at the properties the Youth Department had acquired on the shores of Port Hacking in the Royal National Park. The Blue Mountains houseparties, held in various houses in Katoomba, Leura and Wentworth Falls, were run in conjunction with the annual Katoomba Convention. There were Bible studies in the mornings and the participants went to the Convention meetings at night.

Houseparties were a considerable innovation. Doug Abbott recalls:
Although we now accept mixed houseparties as a fact of life, when these first started in the second half of the 1940s, they were quite revolutionary. I can remember taking a houseparty for St Matthew's, Bondi, in 1947 and the rector quite understandably had many questions that he posed to Graham Delbridge along the lines of the segregation of sleeping facilities, whether the young people were covered for insurance and all these other things. The idea of young people going away for a weekend on a houseparty was quite revolutionary in Christian circles in those days.[4]

Paddison offered Doug Abbott a job as his catechist. Doug Abbott worked in the Provisional District throughout 1948 and 1949 and was given a high degree of responsibility. Through taking two or three services every Sunday, baptising, and speaking at men's teas and youth fellowship teas, he was also given unbounded opportunity.

The teenage teacher and preacher

At the time of his conversion, John was strongly attracted by the teaching and fellowship of the Congregational Church. He could see very little of any value in contemporary Anglicanism. He would have spent his time exclusively with the Congregationalists had it not been for the opposition of his parents, his father in particular. His father gave him permission to go wherever he wanted on Sunday night, but only if he had been to St Paul's on Sunday morning. His father felt that, if John had to be involved in the life of the church, at least he should do it at a place that practised orthodoxy.

John did not have a lot in common with the others of his age within the St Paul's congregation. There was no easy acceptance. They had not known an evangelical emphasis in their churchgoing and were rather worldly. Despite the differences, John quickly became a leader of a fellowship group at St Paul's and also began teaching Sunday School. A change had been made in the materials used for teaching. The new books were the Children's Special Service Mission Sunday School Teachers' Manuals, Books 1-4. John found them enormously helpful. "I learned more from them than anything."

Doug Abbott quickly discerned something of John's potential. He started to take a particular interest in the development of the lively teenager. He took John with him to services at Oatley West and Mortdale. He also introduced him to diocesan youth work, taking him to his first Youth Department houseparties. John assisted in various ways at these. Houseparties also enabled him to give vent to his increasingly outgoing nature. On an early occasion, at an old weatherboard cottage named "Drumart" at Wentworth Falls that Delbridge had booked during the Katoomba Convention, the group held a fancy dress night based on the characters in "Alice in Wonderland". Everyone dressed up. John, it seems, was the Duchess's baby who turns into a pig. In any event, he was dressed as a baby and stuffed into a pram. At the height of the hilarity, the rector of Wentworth Falls, Bert Smith, called in. Smith was a man of rather old-fashioned morality. He clearly believed that all kinds of debauchery were taking place and he equally clearly did not approve!

Other things were happening as well. John has written of them in these terms:
I remember going to a weekend conference some eighteen months after I was converted, and a girl there asked me if I was a Christian. I answered "Yes."
"Tell me" she said, "what I have to do to become a Christian?"
I didn't have the faintest idea where to begin.
As I write this now, I remember well the mixed emotions which swamped me. First, joy—because more than anything else I wanted to see people converted. Second, shame—because I didn't know what to say. Third, anger (with myself)—for allowing such a situation to arise. All these emotions muddled together produced the only possible answer: "I'll take you to someone who can tell you".
So I did that, and she was converted–but not by my words or witness.

That incident left an indelible imprint on my memory, and that day I vowed that such a situation would never happen again. In the future I would know exactly what to say.

So I set out to learn the gospel. Which I did.

Being now thoroughly equipped, I embarked on a flurry of evangelistic activity. The family received the full blast, and a small sermon was delivered at breakfast each day for months! I remember my exasperated father saying one morning, "You don't ever eat your breakfast at church do you? Why must I always have church at breakfast?"[5]

At some time during 1949, Doug Abbott persuaded Paddison to allow the eighteen-year old John to do some lay reading although there were others in the church who, from their love for the old ways, did not support the idea. With three church centres in the Provisional District to care for, there was a considerable load on Sundays. Paddison had a roster of lay readers and John was added to it.

The wisdom of youth

On more than one occasion when John first started preaching, he gave very fervent evangelistic-type addresses and then invited any member of the congregation who would like to discuss their personal problems with him to stay behind after the service. Now you can imagine that this went down like a lead balloon with some of the older members of the congregation who probably wouldn't have even discussed their personal problems with the rector let alone with a youth of less than twenty years of age. I spent some of my time trying to get him to become a little more circumspect in those matters and, over a period of time, he did.

Doug Abbott
describing John's early approach to preaching.

John enjoyed donning cassock and surplice. He began his public preaching with youthful confidence and exuberance, with the same enthusiasm he would bring to many later tasks. In public evangelism, John's proclamation of the gospel has always lacked subtlety. The truth has had to be made abundantly clear. This has spilled over into other areas. In his theology and Bible teaching, issues are often presented in black and white terms. This can be both confronting and stimulating, often stopping his

listeners in their tracks and requiring them to re-examine the fundamentals of their faith.

Over the next few years, John was a regular on the roster. From the outset, even though he was totally untrained, he was a captivating speaker. The great gift of oratory that would be shaped and honed into a formidable weapon in the Lord's service was evident even then. Increasingly, the majority of the congregations liked to hear him preach.

Boating, 1950. John at right in front row.

While John was an effective preacher, the members of the Oatley fellowship found themselves drawn to Christ as much by John's friendship as by his preaching. It had a profound effect on them. He seemed endlessly available to them. He would ride his bike, his hat flapping in the breeze, to the tennis courts at Oatley West where he played tennis with them. For hours, he played table tennis with them in the little back hall of the church. He took them out on the river in his father's boat. He took them on other outings. Royle Hawkes, for a period, was struggling in maths. He would go and sit with John in his room in Rosa Street and John would coach him there.

In personal evangelism, in contrast with public evangelism, John seemed not to confront people with the gospel in one-to-one relationships but rather, through genuine friendship, to draw them into the orbit of gospel preaching. Because of his recent experiences, his main method of evangelism was to get his friends to a Christian camp, particularly one run by the Youth Department.

Among evangelicals, the pre-eminence given to the supremacy of Holy Scripture—its inspiration, its place as the source of ultimate authority—may be so dominant as to cause the desire to know and to teach the Word of God to dwarf other qualities of Christian leadership. It is interesting that the lists of qualities of church leaders in the New Testament comprise numerous moral characteristics and functions that do not particularly emphasise formal teaching.[6] Teaching is an important and significant function. The elder or bishop, for example, must be "an apt teacher" (1 Timothy 3:2). But, more than that, he must also be a thoroughgoing example of godliness to all—to insiders and to outsiders. The leaders of the church are to be leaders by the wholeness of their example.

Sunday School

He was my Sunday School teacher when I finally did start going to church before confirmation. There was a group of about six of us who John used to teach. Oh, I must have been about fourteen at the time. We used to meet in the rector's pokey little vestry at St Paul's. And it was a real riot. Really, it was a bit like if you would turn on Christian radio at 5.15 and listen to "Yes What". That was a slightly toned-up version of what Sunday School classes were like. For although he was very, very good from the pulpit and in big-style teaching, he could never control us as a group of teenage boys. And so he'd sit us down and the whole of the lesson would be a series of interruptions—interruptions we had strategically planned. For example, the bloke who played the organ was in the class and he would break in at the appropriate moment and disrupt everything and then somebody who was rostered to do the collection would break in. I can't ever, ever remember any of the things that John taught us in Sunday School. I can't remember one lesson or one fact in a long period of Sunday School teaching although my mind is full of memories of things he taught us in sermons and in personal conversations over the years. So I would say that was not his gift—controlling young boys in a small class—although I think he probably got better at it as he went on in his teaching.

Royle Hawkes
recalling something of his early Christian education.

John's qualities of morality, example, individual care for people, his ready friendliness and openness, and his teaching and preaching, so evident in his Oatley days, were qualities he would demonstrate all through his Christian life. He was somehow able to keep them all in the most beguiling balance. His only weakness, it seems, was teaching Sunday School.

When John left the parish at the end of 1957 to go to Armidale, his absence left a gap in the lives of the Oatley folk that they all felt very keenly.

The Youth Department

By 1950, John was a member of the Evangelical Union at Teachers' College and was strongly involved in the work of the Youth Department. Graham Delbridge, as the head of the Department, "had gathered around him a fine band of voluntary workers".[7] By 1950, this band included Doreen Nathan (later a missionary with the Church Missionary Society in Madras, India), Jeffrey Roper (who became the Secretary of the CMS in Queensland), his wife Ursula, Allen Quee (CMS, Indonesia and later Secretary of CMS in South Australia), John Turner, Graeme Goldsworthy and Ray and Dorothy Wheeler.

The group used to meet for prayer in the Youth Department's offices in the CENEF Building (then adjoining the Free Presbyterian Church in Castlereagh Street between Bathurst and Park Streets). They met after work on Friday afternoons. They prayed about anything and everything imaginable.

Over each long weekend, at Easter and for ten days during the Christmas/New Year holidays, the Youth Department ran houseparties at its camp sites at Port Hacking. These were always evangelistic in their focus. Graham Delbridge and the other leaders, including John, spoke at them giving short talks like those of J C Ryle's *Expository Thoughts*. One or two of the leaders were placed in each room and were expected to speak individually to each person about their spiritual condition during the course of the weekend. John says, "I remember Easter was the best because we had four days to talk to people and not the terrible rush of having to do it over a day and a half". At these, John learned the importance of evangelism and some simple gospel talks. He gained practice in personal evangelism and follow-up.

He also began to catch a wider vision. "Graham was a wonderful evangelist who also inspired me to think that we could evangelise Australia if we really tried! Like Wesley of old, the world was Graham's parish."

These houseparties were a particular object of the group's prayer life. They would pray for people from their parishes whom they would be bringing to them and for people they had met and spoken to there. But their prayers also embraced a grander vision—a

Doug Abbott and John—Port Hacking, 1952.

vision beyond their immediate gaze.

It is intriguing how God answers prayer. The answer to small finite prayers is sometimes as small and finite as the prayers themselves. But the answer to larger and more ambitious prayers can often exceed those prayers. Sometimes it seems that God not only answers a prayer as it is prayed but that He continues to answer it moment by moment thereafter. A prayer may only seek to soften a person's indifference to the wonders of God's plan of salvation in Jesus, yet that prayer may be answered in the person's redemption, in the person's growth in wisdom and obedience and in the person's being made fruitful by God's Spirit to be a multiplier of gifts and ministries. A person's prayer, in the will of God, can continually be answered. It can grow like snow disturbed into a mountain slide. Without our knowing, others, too, may be at prayer for the same purpose. Prayer may be added to prayer, the apparently disparate prayers of God's people being somehow linked in His grace and gathering power. God is indeed "able to do immeasurably more than all we ask or imagine" (Ephesians 3:20). It can also be that God will use those whom He has moved to pray as agents in answer to their prayers. And so it was to be. Some of the prayers of that fine band of voluntary workers were about to be answered in a way that would be beyond their most imagined hopes, not only in the there and then but also in the here and now.

---

1   L J Louis and Ian Turner, *The Depression of the 1930s*, Cassell Australia, 1968, p 89.

2   Richard Cashman & Amanda Weaver, *Wicket Women: Cricket & Women in Australia*, NSW University Press, 1991, p 2.

3   Transcription from a tape recording provided to the author.

4   Transcription from a tape recording provided to the author.

5   John C Chapman, *Know and Tell the Gospel*, Hodder & Stoughton, 1981, pp 13–14.

6   See, for example, 1 Timothy 3:1–13.

7   Marcus L Loane, *Mark These Men*, Acorn Press Ltd, 1985, p 92.

John, 1965.

ARMIDALE

The first visits

Prior to Easter 1951, Graham Delbridge was asked by John Wagstaff, the vicar of Bingara in the Diocese of Armidale, if he could send someone to run a youth camp. Bingara, located on the Gwydir River to the west of Inverell, is a small unprepossessing country town, typical of a thousand of its kind in Australia. It is in a sheep-producing and wool-growing area.

Wagstaff's was a simple but significant request. It was an initiative prompted by a desire to strengthen and advance the ministry to youth in the Diocese. The diocesan Youth Director, Archdeacon R I H Stockdale, had urged the Synod the previous year to make that a high priority. "The whole future of the Church and the whole hope of the world's peace and prosperity lies in the hands of the Youth", he had written in his Youth Report.[1] The youth camp at Bingara was to be the first diocesan-wide youth camp ever held in the Diocese of Armidale.

Delbridge, in his typically unreflective but seemingly intuitive way, sent the twenty-year-old John Chapman and Allen Quee. Like so many things in the economy of God, a plan of the most infinite mercy began to unfold with the making of that decision. It was a plan of several strategies and with a range of personnel. Its elements and execution did not focus on John alone. Some of its participants were conscious of the parts they played while others were oblivious. Some walked in step with God and some did not. Yet none involved could ever

19

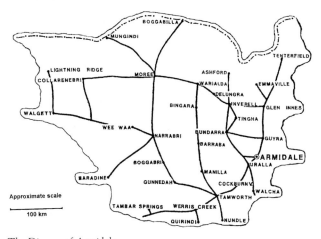

The Diocese of Armidale.

have predicted the full nature and extent of the object God had purposed and would bring to pass. Bold prayer was being met with bolder grace.

The Diocese of Armidale occupies a roughly circular region in northern New South Wales with an average distance of about 325 kilometres between its opposite points. At its extremities are Boggabilla on the Queensland border in the north, Armidale in the east, Quirindi at the edge of the Great Dividing Range in the south and Walgett near the junction of the Namoi and Barwon Rivers in the west. In 1951, it was a typical middle church Australian diocese. A number of its parishes were mediocre and most were low-key but nevertheless important in the life of their rural communities. The bulk of the clergy were ritualists, some fiercely so. There were some old Tractarians. There were some who followed Anglo-Catholic practice. Church services were totally formal and liturgical in style. Very few of the clergy were competent teachers of the Bible. Church membership was largely nominal.

The bishop, since 1929, was John Stoward Moyes. John S Moyes was a proud man who thought his judgments sound and would never admit to error. Despite having evangelical roots, he had developed into a middle churchman with a deep appreciation of church ritual. He had been the president of the Student Christian

Bishop John S Moyes.

Movement in Adelaide soon after the evangelicals in Cambridge, England, had split from it over the doctrine of substitutionary atonement. He was disdainful of the Evangelical Union. He had been one of the twelve candidates nominated in the election that resulted in Howard Mowll becoming Archbishop of Sydney but was eliminated in the first round of voting.

Moyes was keen to see his diocese grow. He was anxious to see it improve. He wanted it to be more broadly Anglican. In this, he faced a number of problems.

Moyes found it hard to attract well-trained clergy to come and work. The calibre of some was not particularly high. This was not peculiar to the Diocese of Armidale. It was a difficulty all country dioceses faced. Moyes was forced to take almost anyone who was willing to travel north. Mowll in Sydney had introduced an ordination policy for his diocese that required candidates to complete a Licentiate of Theology (ThL) if they were to be considered for service in a Sydney parish. Some Moore College students who had not completed their ThLs were accepted by country dioceses such as Armidale. Others, trained elsewhere, who would have preferred but were unable to obtain an appointment in the Diocese of Newcastle, also went to Armidale.

Prior to 1955, St John's College, Morpeth, was owned by all the New South Wales Dioceses except Sydney. Moyes, whether or not he had any particular views on the matter, was under some obligation to use it as a training college for Armidale candidates and to appoint its graduates to vacancies within his diocese. It is more than likely that Moyes did have particular views about the quality of the St John's alumni. A number of incidents concerning them would have caused him considerable distress. On 21 February 1955, at a special session of the Synod of the Diocese of Newcastle, it was decided that Newcastle should buy out the interests of the other Dioceses in the College.[2] Its link with Armidale was broken. This gave Moyes greater freedom to invite graduates of other Australian colleges. He may well have concluded that whatever reservations he had about the appointment of Moore College graduates, they were preferable to the problems caused by the graduates of St John's.

In his eagerness to attract clergy, Moyes at times ordained more men than he had vacancies. He would then bring pressure on his vicars to accept the new appointees as their curates. Moyes' efforts were sometimes met with reluctance. Money for ministry was usually hard to come by in the country Diocese. The problem of financial support was such that one parish organised an annual race day as its principal means of fundraising.

The late 1940s and early 1950s saw, throughout Australian dioceses, a strengthening focus on ministry to youth. Moyes had appointed Stockdale as Youth Director to give particular attention to the development of this area of work. In June 1949, Stockdale had attended a six-day Commonwealth Anglican Youth Leaders' Conference at Point Lonsdale in Victoria. Stockdale appreciated the daunting task of establishing effective youth work in each of the thirty-one parishes in the Diocese. There were great difficulties in regularly bringing people from within the far-flung extremities of a parish into a group and maintaining a sufficient level of energy to ensure the vitality of the group's life. Stockdale lamented the lack of a central youth organisation with either a Youth Commissioner or a Director of Youth in charge. There was no one to give ongoing direction and "new ideas and fresh enthusiasm". But he was not without optimism.

> There are hopeful signs... in this Diocese of a fresh beginning in several parishes. With a former Youth Commissioner, now vicar of Bingara, ready to give the Diocese the benefit of his experience, there should be big things ahead.
>
> "Let us arise and build."[3]

CHAPTER TWO

Following Stockdale's 1950 Synod report, the Religious Instruction Council of the Diocese appointed Stockdale, Bob Kirby and John Wagstaff as a Youth Council to organise diocesan youth work. The Council made a survey of current activities. It showed that about half the parishes in the Diocese had youth fellowship groups of one kind or another meeting weekly or fortnightly. Two youth rallies were held, one at Bingara and the other at Gunnedah.

The trip by John and Allen Quee to the inaugural diocesan youth camp at Bingara was an unforgettable experience. They caught the Daylight Express from Sydney to Tamworth. At Tamworth, they were picked up in the Bingara taxi that had travelled a distance of 150 kilometres from Bingara to meet them and they were driven the 150 kilometres of the return journey. It was by far the longest taxi trip John had ever undertaken. When they arrived at the vicarage in Bingara, it was unoccupied. There was no-one to pay the fare. The taxi driver was not at all concerned. He casually let himself into the house and made a call on its phone to the local exchange. Country telephone operators were invariably the best informed on local affairs and consequently the best source of local knowledge. After chatting for a minute, he put the phone down and said, "She thinks he's at Derra".

Wagstaff's preparation for the youth mission had been quite ingenious. Earlier this century, Australia, it was said, rode on the sheep's back. The major primary industry was the production of wool. Sheep were run across large areas of New South Wales. Their wool grew through the autumn and winter and was sheared during the spring and early summer. Each sheep farmer had on his property a shearing shed and shearers' quarters. At shearing time, teams of shearers travelled from property to property and lodged in the shearers' quarters. The sheep were rounded up and brought into the yards alongside the shed where there were usually several large gum trees for shade. Shearing sheds are rough places, roughly built for rough work. The timbers are often crudely hewn and the corrugated iron roof and walls fixed directly to them. The walls are unlined. These sheds are scenes of intense activity for a few days but lie idle for the rest of the year. They are places for work rather than for words.

About 60-65 young people from Bingara and surrounding towns, such as Armidale, Gunnedah, Tamworth and Barraba, had been gathered for the weekend. They represented just five of the parishes in the Diocese. With the simple practicality that typifies much of country life, in the way of making-do, they camped on a property out of Bingara called "Derra Derra". John and Allen Quee were in the shearing shed with the boys while the girls occupied the shearers' quarters. The floor of a shearing shed is elevated and the floorboards are laid with gaps between them to allow sheep dung and other refuse to be easily swept away. John complained of getting "striped pneumonia". It was Spartan accommodation to say the least.

John and Allen Quee ran the programme between them. They naturally followed the Youth Department pattern. It was John's first experience of so many unconverted people. Either out in the open air or there in the shed, between the baler and its press, the classing tables and the shearers' stands, these two young men preached the gospel of the Lord Jesus Christ to the flock.

The organisers were so pleased with the success of this venture that, later that year, John and Allen Quee were invited back for the King's Birthday long weekend in June. This time they went to a large property near Gunnedah called "Frogmore Park". The weekend was attended by 150 young people and some of the younger clergy from the Diocese. "It was a really big deal," as John describes it. "The bishop and the dean and several of the senior clergy were brought down to see this 'great sight'. I was shaken by the lack of experience of the younger clergy and some didn't even seem to understand the gospel." Stockdale wrote in his 1952 Youth Report to Synod:

> The camp proved of immense value, as its influence spread to almost every corner of the Diocese. Following this, the Gunnedah members began to hold fortnightly "squash" meetings as well as their regular weekly meetings. At these meetings such things were discussed as the Church, the Creeds, the Bible, Prayer, the Sacraments, the Christian Life, and so on.[4]

He also reported that Miss Effie Sourry had been appointed Youth Commissioner for the Diocese. "Miss Sourry has gone to St Christopher's College in Melbourne to receive twelve months' special training for her great task."[5]

Teaching manual arts

By the end of 1951, John had finished his Diploma in Manual Arts and was ready to teach. As a means of staffing the smaller and often remote country schools that are spread throughout rural New South Wales, it was the practice at that time for all young teachers, immediately after graduation, to be appointed for their first few years to country service. Because of John's recent experiences in the Armidale Diocese, and having come to know some of its people, he applied for service there.

In 1952, John began teaching at Manilla (forty-five kilometres north-west of Tamworth) for three days of the week and at Tamworth High School for the other two days. The next year, he taught at Tamworth for three days and Werris Creek (fifty-five kilometres to the south-west) for two days. The following two years, 1954 and 1955, were at Gunnedah (seventy-five kilometres to the west of Tamworth). For most of that time, John taught Woodwork and some Technical Drawing.

At Manilla, John led the local church fellowship. Another teacher from Sydney, Keith Wilson, a parishioner of St Paul's, Chatswood, had been appointed to Tamworth High. John and Keith continued to run youth camps for the Armidale Diocese.

In 1952, John began a ThL by correspondence through the General Board of Religious Education. Correspondence students were issued with a reading list, but no notes, and were presented for examination through the Australian College of Theology.

In 1954 and 1955 when John was at Gunnedah, his vicar was Archdeacon Stockdale. "Stockie" and his wife, Catriona, affectionately embraced John as if he were one of their own children. He was a regular guest at their dinner table. Mrs

Stockdale, who suffered from curvature of the spine, was a remarkable woman. She was a graduate and a headmistress-elect when she decided to give up her career to marry her husband. She was a great support to him and was dearly loved in return. She was a wonderfully intelligent woman who easily matched and stimulated John's intellect.

The blessings of the gospel

I first met John in 1954 at a Youth Camp at Gunnedah to which I had gone as a young teacher in the Parish of Warialda. Although I had heard the Christian gospel, I certainly lacked any assurance of salvation until one of those talks given by John Chapman made me rethink my position. Back in my room in the homestead where I was living I re-read Paul's words in 2 Timothy 4 with all its certitude of eternal life with God, won, not because of Paul's work for the gospel, great as it was, but because of the grace of God. This discovery through John's ministry opened to me the blessings of the gospel.

Ross McDonald

who worked in the Armidale Diocese as a layman from 1954-56 and as a clergyman from 1960-62.

1955 also marked the beginning of a close, endearing and significant friendship for two young Christian men that would continue for the rest of their lives.

Peter Chiswell, John's neighbour from Rosa Street, had also attended Sydney Technical High School, being in the early years of high school when John arrived there as a senior student in 1946 to complete his secondary education. Peter had become a parishioner at St Paul's, Oatley, and had been converted there in 1952. After completing his schooling, he studied for his Bachelor of Civil Engineering degree at the University of New South Wales. As an undergraduate, he worked at Bendemeer (on the New England Highway about forty kilometres to the northwest of Tamworth) during the university holidays and stayed with John over several weekends at Tamworth. After graduation, Peter Chiswell was appointed, in 1955, to the shire council at Bulahdelah. The two young men from Oatley visited each other on several occasions during that year. Among other things, they found they shared a common love of tennis. What, until then, had been simply an acquaintance became a friendship.

It was natural, when John and Peter Chiswell met, to compare churchgoing in Armidale with churchgoing as they had experienced it in Sydney. It was clear to them that there was a lack of Christians among the members of the Anglican church in the Armidale Diocese and that this was because those who attended were largely untaught. The Bible was not being clearly explained. There was a great deal of fuzziness in sermons. They longed that good Bible teaching would take place in every parish.

During the Christmas/New Year holidays each year, John returned to Sydney. Ever the activist, these times were far from being holidays. He continued to be involved in Youth Department houseparties and regularly attended the annual Katoomba Christian Convention. He made an impact wherever he went.

Education in humour

While I was teaching at Tamworth and Gunnedah, my Aunt Millie used to send me cuttings from the paper that had tickled her. They were never folded but stuffed into a manilla envelope until it was cylindrical—then she would seal it and send it to me. The blokes in the staff room would say, "There's another letter from your aunt. Open it and pass them around." She never wrote anything, just collected cartoons and funny articles. She loved misprints and wrong spellings. I remember one from the Illawarra Mercury described a wedding reception as being "hell in the parish hall" instead of "held in the parish hall". If ever a bishop appeared in a cope and mitre, she would cut it out and write a caption "ONE OF THE BOYS". I remember she once sent a cutting from an In Memoriam column which read:

The last trump sounded
The angel beckoned "Come"
The pearly gates flew open—
And in walked Mum.

to which Millie wrote, "You could sing it to (the hymn tune) Aurelia if you wanted to".

John Chapman
recalling another family influence in the staff room.

In the five years since the first evangelistic mission at "Derra Derra" station, a vision had been steadily developing in John's mind for the Armidale Diocese. He had seen enough to know that most of the clergy were not informed in areas that he saw to be important. There was a clear role for him but there was also much more than one person could do. Everywhere he went, he spoke to others about the needs of this part of the country. He wanted others to see and to feel it as he felt it. He wanted them to capture the vision too.

Return to Oatley

By 1956, John was back in Sydney, living again with his parents at Oatley, and teaching at East Hills Boys' High. In the year before his return, Reg Hanlon had been appointed curate-in-charge of St Paul's, Oatley. On John's return, he promptly appointed him as his warden.

This was an extraordinarily busy year for the twenty-five-year-old teacher. At school, he ran the Inter-School Christian Fellowship attended by 80–100 students. At St Paul's, he preached regularly and also led a weekly Bible study. He spoke at a monthly meeting of fellowships from Oatley and the neighbouring provisional parish of Peakhurst held in the home of the choirmaster from Holy Trinity, Trevor Phipps and his wife and daughters—"the monthly squash" as meetings of this kind were commonly called. Its members included Warren Gotley, who would later serve the Diocese of Sydney with such distinction as its Secretary, Jennifer Greaves who would become his wife, and some who would later resume their acquaintance with John in Tamworth, such as Grahame Scarratt (who subsequently married Patty Phipps) and

Don Robertson. John and Reg Hanlon preached to peak-hour commuters on Oatley railway station. John spoke at Youth Department houseparties. He was everywhere. And everywhere he was clearly noticeable, always at centre stage, and always dynamic, vibrant and inspiring. His focus was the gospel, always the gospel. His speech was clear and direct. His manner was joyful. His style lacked pretension. Everything was liberally laced with humour. His enthusiasm was infectious.

Old friends

It is true that Pam and I have known John for a very long time. My first encounter with John was when I was a fellowship member at Holy Trinity, Dulwich Hill. He came to speak at a youth fellowship gathering at the branch church, St Aidan's, which was down near Dulwich Hill station. I can remember that he spoke on Psalm 1. He turned his chair around so the back faced the assembled company, sat on it with his elbows on the top of the chair and said, "You stand up to preach and sit down to teach. I am going to teach this evening." This was a startling introduction and really gained our attention. I have never forgotten the experience and the power of the personality that was reflected on that first encounter.

We knew John's influence in the days when he was associated with Peter Chiswell and Reg Hanlon at Oatley and we shared his year in College with him. Pam recalls the evenings at St Bede's, Beverly Hills, when John came in after church on Sunday nights and spent time with us. Young people from the fellowship would come and some of John's friends from further afield would gather. The lounge room was small and people sat on the floor with their backs against the wall. The legacy in the lounge room was a row of greasy hair oil marks on the wallpaper. The evenings were hilarious and edifying as John shared in his inimitable fashion about his work in Armidale. It was great fun, but focused, as we shared about the work of Christ in that atmosphere. I am sure that John touched the lives of many people in these informal encounters.

Harry Goodhew
Archbishop of Sydney.

Pam Coughlan (later Goodhew), winner of Archbishop Mowll's fishing trophy with her catch at Rathane, 1952.

Standing: Mervyn Huggett, John (King Neptune), Doug Abbott. Seated: Harry Goodhew—Rathane, 1952.

Throughout this time, John somehow continued his ThL studies.

John's life had clearly become too hectic. "It became apparent to me," he says, "that, if I wasn't to go potty, I had to make a decision either to teach school properly or to do ministry. If I could have done both, I would have, but I just couldn't pull it off. I had to make a choice. It was not a difficult one to make. The relative importance of preaching and Bible teaching have effects which reach into eternity. I am sure that teaching children to make letter racks and sugar scoops does not." John had by now become totally fixed with the vision for the Armidale Diocese. He wanted to commit himself to the service of its people, to see sound Bible teaching established in every place. If anything worthwhile was to be achieved, a long-term commitment was needed. He thought it would occupy the whole of his working life. He wrote to Bishop Moyes and asked if the bishop would be prepared to pay for his tuition at Moore College as an Armidale candidate. He had completed seven out of the ten subjects necessary to obtain his ThL and estimated that he would need two years of further study before graduation. All his study to that time had consisted of set reading and he still felt basically ignorant theologically. He was keen to attend lectures.

Moyes' reply came by return mail. Without interview, without having to present himself to any examining chaplains, without any further contact, Moyes had said yes. Moyes had also agreed to two years of study.

When John announced his decision to seek ordination to his parents, his father thought John had gone mad. He voiced his strong objection again and again. There were many arguments.

Why in an argument is it easier to say something hard, cruel and biting than to say something calming and conciliatory? Negative reactions and attitudes just seem to come naturally to me, and I suspect I am not unique! How often I said, "I will not fight with my father again". Those encounters were so unpleasant. I hated them and I am sure he hated them too.[6]

Peter Chiswell had also, and of his own conviction, become a captive of the Armidale vision—a vision of each parish staffed by a competent Bible teacher (which in his and John's minds meant an evangelical) and with an evangelical bishop. Both he and John were strongly encouraged that it was a vision they shared totally. Peter Chiswell also thought of it as a lifetime's commitment. It needed to be if anything truly worthwhile was to be achieved. He applied to Moyes and he, too, was accepted as an Armidale candidate for study at Moore College.

Other awakenings in Armidale

Independently of John's ministry, the Spirit of God was moving in other ways in the Armidale Diocese. Ross McDonald, a young teacher from Warialda who had met John at a youth camp at Gunnedah in 1954 records:

The Parish of Warialda had its own evangelical awakening. The rector during my time there was one John Louis Grant Sullivan. My school was about eighteen miles north west of the little but quite historic town of Warialda on a very large property called "Gunyerwarildi". I had been a faithful Anglican since my boyhood in Goulburn, in whose Cathedral I had been a server, so I volunteered my services to Sullivan to assist in whatever way I could. I taught Sunday School in Warialda and I also used to drive to Gravesend to take Sunday School. Sullivan obtained the bishop's licence for me to preach and I gave my first rather shaky sermons at Gravesend.

Sullivan himself was a strange character. At one time he was a member of the Cowley Fathers, wandering the parish in monastic garb and at a later time acting as an exponent of evangelicalism, as he understood it. It was during this latter phase he decided to invite Geoff Bingham, then at the peak of his very influential ministry at Holy Trinity, Millers Point. Bingham's call for holiness of life had considerable influence on me and on other parishioners. Among those converted was Daryl Robinson, a general store owner from Gravesend. He was to enter Moore College with me in 1957 and to work in the Diocese of Armidale for many years. Sullivan hadn't much idea of what he had unleashed on the parish nor much idea of how to follow up this work of the gospel, so he invited David Hewetson to take a further series of meetings. These were similarly highly effective. As a result, I decided to explore the call of God to enter the ministry and approached Bishop Moyes to seek his support. He gave me a brief interview and agreed to see me through Moore College at the expense of the Diocese for three years.[7]

Sullivan had a stormy relationship with his bishop. When it was discovered that Sullivan had taken funds from an account established by his predecessor to replace the small wooden church of St Simon and St Jude with a more worthy place of worship, Moyes demanded and obtained Sullivan's resignation.

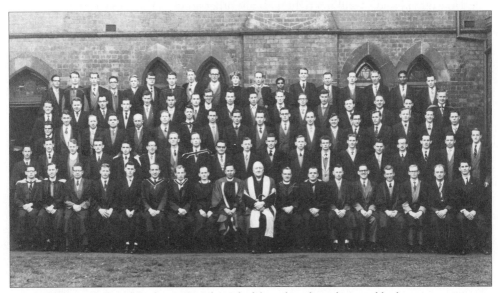

Moore College students and faculty, 1957. John is third from the right in the second back row.

Moore College

John, Peter Chiswell, Ross McDonald and Daryl Robinson entered Moore College in 1957. Marcus Loane was its principal and Broughton Knox its vice-principal. Its staff included Donald Robinson, Alan Cole and Bruce Smith. John studied one subject that year, Greek I.

John was as iconoclastic at college as he had been everywhere else. He had the large downstairs room at the common room end of the City Road wing. The 5.00 am tram seemed to come through his window every morning.

The theological student

One Saturday afternoon, John's room was like the Goon Show gone wrong with noise abounding and sundry outside equipment scattered all over it. The late Ian Hulme-Moir (a Med. student) was vainly trying to study in another room. In desperation, he filled a bucket with water and headed towards the door. He threw the bucket of water into the room as the sartorial Ken Baker opened it to leave. Ken's freshly cleaned and pressed trousers copped most, but not all, of the contents.

Peter Chiswell
commenting on John's approach to studying theology.

John's room was where the students gathered. It was a great place to talk. The talk went on and on into the early hours of the morning until everyone was whacked. It was also a great place to laugh, to laugh so much you would cry. It was a positive and stimulating place. It was a place from which people went fired-up for the gospel. It was yet another place, a particularly strategic place, for sharing the vision of Armidale.

Ray Smith and his wife, then Shirley Gilmore, had first met John at a Youth Department houseparty at Leura in January 1955. Ray had begun college a year earlier than John. On the completion of his studies, he had been thinking of service with the Bush Church Aid Society. He was persuaded as he listened to John to seek acceptance as an Armidale candidate.

One incident that John's contemporaries vividly remember occurred, of all places, on the Moore College roof. The students of the adjoining Women's College of Sydney University were in the practice of singing Christmas carols on the lawns of their college each year. Their music-making created such excitement among the audience that its members would douse the women students with water. But not the men of Moore College. Their Principal had forbidden them to do so. Instead, Moore College had its neighbours in during the evening for cake. John and Graeme Goldsworthy decided to enhance the event, John as solo vocalist and Graeme as his accompanist on trumpet. John was a competent singer. During his last two years at Sydney Technical College he had taken singing lessons at the New South Wales Conservatorium of Music. For the occasion, Graeme had put water down the bell of his instrument so that when he blew a note, it sounded like someone gargling. The two performers climbed onto the parapet over the door to the memorial wing

The angel.

while their guests and the other students assembled in the quadrangle below. John lay on the floor of the parapet, bare legged under a surplice. He had taken the guise of an angel. Two pillow cases had been attached to the back of his surplice to resemble wings and these were held up by other students on the roof. At the appropriate moment, he flew up out of the parapet. As Graeme Goldsworthy played his trumpet, John, with a spotlight trained on him and starkly white against the darkness, sang Good King Wenceslas. When he sang the line "Brightly shone the moon that night," a cardboard moon was supposed to appear. The operator missed his cue. "Moon!" John bellowed, and it rose sublimely. For an encore, the duo performed Nymphs and Shepherds. It was a spectacle to behold. That night, it stopped the traffic in Carillon Avenue.

The Enrolling Class of 1957

Leonard Abbott	Russell Fowler	Hugh Oatway
John Adams	Kaipuraidom George	Peter (Richard) Payn
John Beath-Filby	William Gregory	Duncan Stanley Richardson
Peter Carman	Graham Harrison	Daryl Robinson
Ivan Carter	Noel Hart	Bruce Sinclair
John Chapman	David Johnstone	Walter Stanley Skillicorn
Peter Chiswell	John Jones	Geoffrey Taylor
Ronald Coleman	Peter Kemp	Abraham Thomas
Grahame Defty	Richard (Tony) Lamb	Colin Tunbridge
Frederick Edwards	Maurice Lee	Ian Tweedell
Ralph Feldman	Ross McDonald	Edward Watkins
Robert Friend	Kenneth McIntyre	Donald Wilson
John Fowler	Keith McKenzie	

In June 1957, Dudley Foord had accepted an invitation from Frank Elliott, curate in the Parish of Merewether in the Diocese of Newcastle, to speak at a youth weekend. Dudley was forced to withdraw and asked John to go in his place. Frank Elliott's wife, Iris, was deputed to meet John at Hamilton railway station. She waited until all but one person had left the platform, "a chubby, baby-faced young man". During the course of the weekend, John told them, with his usual infectious enthusiasm, of his plans to go to Armidale. Later that year, Bishop de Witt Batty telephoned Elliott to say that he was soon to retire "and could not take the responsibility of handing on a 'militant Protestant' to his successor".[8] Frank Elliott was both flattered by the description and greatly relieved. He had found working in the Newcastle Diocese very oppressive. De Witt Batty said he would arrange for Elliott to go to Sydney or Armidale. Frank Elliott, keen to preach the gospel, his original motivation in seeking the Merewether appointment, chose Armidale.

Ordination

At the end of 1957, Bishop Moyes was faced with a problem concerning the parish of Moree. People from the town, including some of its leaders, had made various representations to the bishop. Moyes felt that, in order to at least deal with local dissatisfaction, it would be appropriate to make a change. He asked Archdeacon Stockdale, then at Gunnedah, if he would become the new vicar of Moree. It was a hard request. Stockdale was then in his mid-fifties. He and his disabled wife were comfortably settled at Gunnedah. Stockdale told his Bishop that he would not go unless he could have the assistance of a younger man. He nominated John Chapman as his curate. Moyes agreed.

Ordinations may be conducted on a Sunday or a saint's day. Moyes had long established the practice of ordaining men on the Day of St Thomas the Apostle, 21 December, being the first saint's day after the college year ends. It was a policy based in practical expedience. Ordinands had just completed their studies and vicars needed curates to help with the Christmas communions and to look after their parishes while they enjoyed their summer holidays. Moyes promptly terminated John's career as a theological student and, in order to keep his part of the bargain with Stockdale, ordained John in St Peter's Cathedral, Armidale, on 21 December 1957. Moyes appointed him as Stockdale's curate. John's presence undoubtedly enabled Mrs Stockdale to survive the difficult relocation to Moree.

He is there and he is not silent

John was one of the eight of us who gathered at Bishopscourt for the ordination retreat of December 1957. Although the retreat was supposed to be a silent one, it wasn't long before Chappo broke out and we had a hilarious time. Mrs Moyes said that it was the noisiest silent retreat that she had ever known about. She and the bishop ate in a small alcove off the main dining room and she would dearly have liked to have joined the fun.

Frank Elliott
remembering a great talker.

Moyes ordained seven men that St Thomas' Day. All were from Sydney. Ordained as deacons were John Chapman, Fred Edwards and Alex Richards. Ordained as priests were Matthew Burrows, Frank Elliott, Bruce Holland and Murray Richter. Elliott was appointed vicar of Nundle and Richter vicar of Baradine. Trevor Griffiths had earlier been appointed to Mungindi which meant that, at the end of 1957, there were three parishes in the Diocese with an evangelical minister.

In 1958 and 1959, John was assistant curate at Moree.

John with Archdeacon Ian Stockdale, 1958.

Moree is situated on the Great Western Plains of New South Wales, an area of vast flatness where "the horizon is one inch off the ground". John has written:

"Those western plains were so flat that ninety per cent of the scenery before me seemed to be sky. I used to wait eagerly for evening to come. The sunsets were so brilliant, and night after night the whole sky lit up in blazing colour."[9]

The radio station occupied the highest point in Moree. When the Gwydir River came over its banks, as it would often do during the rainy season in late summer, that was the only point that never flooded. The Moree parish comprised an area measuring about 150 kilometres by 100 kilometres. Consequently, Stockdale and his curate had a lot of ground to cover. On Sundays, neither of them would drive less than 150 kilometres taking services with groups of eleven or twelve people in a variety of tiny buildings "like overgrown dog kennels". By the end of the day they were usually weary and evening services could be something of a struggle. But, as it would later do for many others, John's warm friendship, his enthusiasm and his dynamic ministry revitalised Stockdale's work.

First communion

John dined out for some time on the story of how he celebrated his first communion at Christmas at Moree. It was the third service and he had been warned to expect a big crowd. He preached a fire and brimstone sermon on the risks of partaking unworthily, then consecrated an ample quantity of wine, only to find that far too few were coming to take communion. Under the watchful eye of his new congregation he felt obliged to consume every drop of port himself. At the door his hand was so unsteady he decided the best thing to do was simply to hold it out straight and allow the parishioners to shake it themselves.

John and Dorothy Wheeler
who frequently had John to dinner.

During those two years, John completed the last two subjects required for his ThL, Greek I and II. Despite his unorthodox theological education, or what had passed for it, and despite all the distractions, he had done sufficiently well to be awarded second class honours on graduation.

In December 1958, Moyes ordained seven deacons and three priests, including six from Moore College. John continued at Moree, Peter Chiswell was appointed to Quirindi, Ray Smith to Barraba, Doug Parker to West Tamworth, John Rostron to Glen Innes and Brian Harker to Gunnedah to join Stockdale's replacement, Robert Kirby.

The 1959 Billy Graham Crusade

When news was received in the Diocese of Armidale that the American evangelist, Billy Graham, was to visit Australia in 1959, the local ministers' fraternal was keen to bring the crusade broadcasts to Armidale. The Anglican evangelicals moved in Synod that Billy Graham's addresses be broadcast in St Peter's Cathedral by means of a landline. Canon Kirby and other senior clergy were very strongly opposed to the proposal. Moyes spoke in the debate. He believed his diocese should be involved in the crusade. He quoted Paul in Philippians 1:

Ordination, December, 1958.
From left to right: Bruce Lancaster, Colin Wellard, Ray Smith, Peter Chiswell, Bishop Moyes, Doug Parker, John Beer, Brian Harker, John, John Rostron, Alex Richards.

> Some indeed preach Christ from envy and rivalry, but others from good will. The latter do it out of love, knowing that I am put here for the defence of the gospel; the former proclaim Christ out of partisanship, not sincerely but thinking to afflict me in my imprisonment. What then? Only that, in every way, whether in pretence or truth, Christ is proclaimed; and in that I rejoice.

The motion was carried.

The 1959 Crusade was one of the most remarkable events in the history of Australian evangelism. In Sydney, for example, on 10 May 1959, 150,000 people attended adjoining venues to hear Billy Graham speak—70,000 at the Sydney Cricket Ground and 80,000 at the Showground. A total audience of more than one million people out of the Australian population of ten million people heard him speak during the course of his visit. The majority listened to direct broadcasts.

In the course of doing the counsellor training to assist those who might commit their lives to Christ through hearing the crusade broadcasts, Archdeacon Stockdale came into a significantly deeper relationship with Jesus.

Youth Director

John's ability with youth had endeared him to John S Moyes. From Moree, Moyes appointed John to be the Youth Director for the Diocese. His place at Moree was taken by Ray and Shirley Smith. John was now strategically based in the Diocesan Registry in Armidale. It would be his base for the next nine years.

Bishop Moyes and John at Ray and Shirley Smith's wedding.

The form of church life at St Peter's Cathedral in Armidale in 1960 was of an age now past. It resembled ecclesiastical practice of the somewhat eccentric kind that has often been fondly, and sometimes not so fondly, satirised.

Each day, except Saturday, the bishop, a proud and sometimes imperious man wearing bishop's gaiters and a frock-coat, would arrive in his Ford Fairlane with a St George flag fluttering from a miniature mast on the bonnet to be joined by the Cathedral staff for 7.00 am Morning Prayer and Holy Communion. Even on the bleakest winter mornings, he would inquire of his underlings whether they had had their cold showers—a practice he said he always followed. The dean, Matthew Kenneth Jones, and the bishop had quarrelled and were not on speaking terms. They communicated by letter and rarely lost an opportunity to irritate each other. Dean Jones retired in mid-1960, his place being taken by Evan Wetherall of South Brisbane. [10]

Ross McDonald and John leading the flock. St Peter's Youth Group Camp, 1960.

John at work.

Moyes saw great leadership potential in the thirty-year-old John Chapman. He saw him as a future bishop. He suggested he should do post-graduate studies. More importantly from Moyes' perspective, he wanted John to be more rounded, more Anglican. He wanted John to have the same approach to the sacraments as he had. Moyes thought he could influence John and sought to make him his protege. Moyes had tried to do the same thing with another charismatic leader, a high churchman, Keith Brasington. John, for his part, while having great affection for the older man, resisted these influences. He questioned the bishop and, in doing so, tried to sow the seeds of his ideas.

After the evening services in the Cathedral, John often gathered up the student members of the congregation and took them back to the little weatherboard house at 126 O'Dell Street near the hospital he shared with other young Cathedral staff like Ross McDonald and Colin Wellard. They drank coffee there and talked about the Christian life. John would go over the sermon or substitute a more biblical one in its place and the students would be taught and encouraged.

As Youth Director, John was provided with a car as his work took him to all parts of the Diocese. The car was a Holden panel van, the cheapest reliable transport the Diocese could afford. His duties would often cause him to be away for weeks on end, travelling from parish to parish.

The Uralla railway gates

One night I was belting home from church on the New England Highway in the panel van. I think I could have been doing 100 km—more maybe—I was so glad we had finished early. Just north of Uralla, the railway line crosses the road. There were some hand-operated gates there but I don't think I had ever seen them closed in the whole of my life. There was a bloke on the other side of the line with his lights on high beam. He'd been stopped by the gates. I'd seen him a long way off and had put my lights on low beam. And the closer I got to his lights, the less I could see.

And then, suddenly, my lights on low beam hit the plate on the gate and the red oil lamp. I threw out all the anchors and I s'pose I was doing about seventy km when I hit the gate. Two things happened. It lifted the gate off its hinges—you know those great big railway gates—and it wrapped itself round the car. I couldn't open the door!

The gate keeper—little guy with a hurricane lantern—rushed up and kept saying to me, "What do you mean by driving your car like a bat out of hell?" I said, "Watch your language! And push this car off the line!" And then he caught sight of my dog collar. "Father," he said. "I'm very sorry," he said. And I said, "Just get me off the line!" Which he did just before the Glen Innes Mail came roaring through.

They prized the gate off the car. I asked him what I could do to help him with it. "Just chuck it down the bank there," he said. And when I looked down the bottom of the slope, there was a whole pile of mangled gates!

Then a policeman came. And the policeman said to the little guy with the lantern, "Where were you when he hit it?" And he said, "I was behind it waving my lantern trying to get him to see it". And he said, "I've spoken to you before about that," he said. "Get off the road and let 'em kill themselves. You'll kill yourself one day."

John Chapman
recounting one of the many versions of this famous story.

On his travels, John commonly held meetings for youth leaders, Sunday School teachers and scripture teachers. At each meeting he included a component that was directly evangelistic in nature as his assessment was that many of those he taught were unconverted. Much of John's weekend work in the parishes was also strongly evangelistic. It was in doing this work that John continued to develop the evangelistic skills he had begun to acquire in his Youth Department days. In everything, John was overwhelmingly motivated to have people commit themselves to Jesus as Saviour and Lord and to ensure that, somehow, they regularly heard the Bible

Peeling spuds.

35

well expounded. As ever, he was endlessly alive, vibrant and exuberant. He seemed naturally to appropriate the fullness of life. His friendship was real and all embracing. His enthusiasm for evangelism was compelling. He was the best company.

Laughing fit to bust

About 1960 we had a parish mission. Reg Hanlon was our chief speaker with John as assistant. Reg spoke in the parish church each evening while John, accompanied by my wife, Iris, went 20 miles down the road to a place called Dungowan. Iris laughed so much on the way there and back that she had to see the doctor who said that she was bordering on getting a hernia. Reg and Shirley Hanlon had a caravan in our back yard and insisted on living out there. But after the first day they just had to come in and have breakfast with us as they could not stand the strain of missing out on all the fun we were having.

Frank Elliott
recalling a parish mission in Nundle.

John would often go with Bishop Moyes when Moyes conducted parish missions. In the afternoons during the week John would hold a children's mission. John says:

I remember soon after I was ordained, I saw Owen Shelley running a children's mission and I realised that I could do most of the things he was doing (not as well, I fear) so I started running children's missions which I did for many years.

"John had a real gift for children's ministry and always commanded an audience that was all eyes and ears for him."[11] In the evenings of the mission, he would energetically lead the singing before the bishop spoke.[12] John says, "Every once in a while, the bishop would let me answer questions from a question box but, when he heard my answers, he would take over again until he forgot what I was like".

Armidale is a centre of education. It has numerous schools and colleges and the campus of the University of New England is there. The Australian Fellowship of Evangelical Students had been established in Armidale for some years and a strong Graduates' Fellowship of the AFES had also grown. Its members included John and Dorothy Wheeler, Dick Tisher, Vic and Stephanie Bisset, Grant Harman, Peter Peters and Ross McDonald. The Wheelers considered that one of the primary tasks of the Graduates' Fellowship was to help undergraduate students. In 1959, they offered their lounge room as a venue for Sunday afternoon meetings of the Evangelical Union and the EU continued to meet there until the Wheelers went overseas in 1964. John was one of the few local clergy who could subscribe to the AFES's doctrinal basis. Consequently, he was regularly invited to speak at the Sunday afternoon meetings. John prepared thoroughly for these talks. On one occasion, he read Leon Morris' *Apostolic Preaching of the Cross* in preparation for a talk on justification and, in the course of his preparation, discovered what justification really was. John also found the meetings of the Graduates' Fellowship to be highly stimulating. He learned a great deal through them and was introduced by them to numerous Inter-Varsity Press publications.

Story-teller and performer

John is a very active guy—notably slimmer in those days—and was always doing something or talking to someone. Young people and children really liked him and responded to his love for Christ. He developed quite a fan following! Dorothy recalls students in our house listening intently to him and then suddenly bursting out into peals of laughter at a story or humorous aside. Generally after the "serious" business was over he would start telling stories and draw on his considerable talents as an actor. We well remember him taking off a cleric, famous for his family's connections with the theatre, and who had recently preached in the Cathedral. Before he had finished, John had used the whole area of our lounge room carpet. If the performance was anything like reality, we could well believe the alleged comment of the Cathedral sexton on the visitor that " 'is parish council 'ad better take out insurance against 'im falling out of the pulpit".

John and Dorothy Wheeler,
describing a typical EU meeting of the era in their lounge room.

Throughout this period, John made frequent visits to Moore College and to the Christian Unions at the Teachers' Colleges to try to persuade others to come to Armidale. He maintained his friendship with his fellow students from his brief Moore College days. He also regularly sent letters back to his friends in Sydney. It kept the Armidale cause before them and ensured that his work would have their prayer support. Several of his correspondents fellowshipped with him as they attended missions he conducted.

Neville Collins, who served in several parishes in the Diocese of Armidale, recalls:

Before I went to Moore College I used to spend some of my holidays working at Camp Howard with children and youth. I think it was here that I met John for the first time. Night after night, John would share his famous Aunt Millie stories. I'm sure there must have been some poetic licence but John had the capacity to make ordinary things seem very funny. I learned to live with less sleep than usual. During my second year at Moore College, while a candidate for Sydney Diocese, I visited Tamworth and began thinking about ministry in the country. The next year, my fiancée began teacher training at Armidale Teachers' College and this again renewed my connection with John and reinforced my desire for country ministry. John encouraged this and somehow the money was found to reimburse the Diocese of Sydney for my theological training. John was a very significant influence on the young Christians at university and Teachers' College. I was ordained in Armidale in 1961 by

Bishop J S Moyes and sent as the second assistant to the parish of Moree working with Archdeacon Stockdale and Ross McDonald. Moree was one of the parishes in the Diocese that would allow evangelicals a place for ministry and John had been one of the previous curates there. In those days everybody was measured in terms of John Chapman! He had a great rapport with many country people which was enriched by his time as a school teacher in country NSW prior to his ordination. In many ways I thank John for his encouragement and interest that enabled me to minister in the Diocese for over twenty-five years; that important part of my life may never have happened without John's involvement.[13]

John's work and its mobility had a secondary effect. It enabled him to act as the unofficial organising secretary of the evangelicals. His support and maintenance of the network was invaluable. He provided initiative and direction. He kept the priorities of preaching the gospel, teaching the Bible and prayer before them. In talking with the vicarage families, often until the early hours, he gave them great encouragement to press on despite their not being in the mainstream of diocesan life. For the meetings of Synod in 1958 and 1959, the evangelicals met in the hotel room of one of them to discuss their approach to the issues of the day. John gave them leadership. He was always well-organised and well-prepared, a man of detail and careful planning. From 1960, after John's appointment as Youth Director, Synod gatherings of the evangelicals invariably met in John's residence. Despite the seriousness of their purpose, the meetings were always great fun.

John gathered sufficient support to be elected to the Diocesan Council. It met once a quarter and dealt with diocesan affairs between meetings of the Synod. In his first year, he was its only evangelical member. That year, all his motions lapsed for want of a seconder. It was a difficult time. But John was not one for giving up. The following year, both he and Peter Chiswell were elected.

Amazing grace—the transformation of a diocese

Bishop Moyes was eighty when he retired in 1964. His successor would be appointed following the convening of an electoral Synod for the purpose. Under the ordinance that governed the election, nominations were first made, there being no restriction as to the number of nominees. All the members of Synod then voted together as one house for the persons nominated. The two nominees receiving the highest number of votes proceeded to the next ballot. The other nominees were eliminated. Voting was then conducted separately in the House of Clergy and the House of Laity with the requirement that, to be successful, a candidate had to obtain a majority in both Houses. If that round of voting was unsuccessful, a further vote by Houses was taken. If the second round of voting was also unsuccessful, the Synod had to adjourn for at least twenty-four hours and then a third ballot by Houses was held. If that ballot was unsuccessful, the process was at an end and another meeting of the Synod needed to be convened.

It was apparent that there would be two leading candidates. They were Dr John Munro, the rector of Dee Why in the Diocese of Sydney (and later Head of the Australian Broadcasting Commission's Religious Affairs Department), and John O Rymer, the chaplain at the University of New England in Armidale. Neither was an evangelical. Clive Kerle, an assistant bishop in the Diocese of Sydney, had been asked if he would agree to his nomination, but declined.

Peter Chiswell travelled to Sydney to talk to Munro in order to ascertain his views. He found that Munro was not favourably disposed to evangelicals. As well, Peter Chiswell had reservations about elements in Munro's personality if he were to be the bishop. Peter was led to believe that, if elected, Munro could not be expected to appoint any Moore College graduates. Rymer was a middle church moderate. In his case, however, it was thought he would give everyone, evangelicals and others, due consideration. To fulfil the vision John and the other young evangelicals had for Armidale, one strategy was to recruit to the Diocese anyone who loved the Word of God. John had been urging his Sydney friends and acquaintances—theological students, clergy, Christian school teachers, anyone—to make the move north. It was an important part of their planning that when the See fell vacant, they should look for a man who would allow competent Bible teachers of the kind Moore College was producing to come to the Diocese.

The evangelical vote comprised about one-third of the votes in Synod. John, Peter Chiswell and Ray Smith divided up the Diocese between them and visited each evangelical clergyman to ensure that the evangelical vote would not be split. Because of their lack of voting strength, they could not hope that an evangelical would be elected. It was never contemplated. But that did not mean that they should not be as well prepared and as well organised as they could be. To the contrary.

The electoral Synod began its proceedings in the Cathedral Hall alongside St Peter's Cathedral in Armidale on 11 August 1964. In the course of the debate, John spoke in favour of Rymer and Peter Chiswell spoke against Munro. When it was discovered that Peter Chiswell had spoken to Munro, there was uproar.

There was a sharp clash of piety over the propriety of Peter Chiswell's actions. John describes the difference in approach taken by the evangelicals and their opponents in this way:

> They thought that you did nothing by way of preparation and that, if you did nothing, the Holy Spirit somehow popped into your mind the right thing to do—and that you did things to get rid of everything else so the Spirit could do that. Whereas I thought that you put everything into your mind that you could and weighed it up carefully—and the Spirit would guide you by that method. So, what I thought was a godly and pious thing to do, they thought was ungodly. And I thought what they were doing was too stupid for words. So, Bob Kirby I remember saying to me at one stage (we had this sort of clergy meeting) and he said:
> "I just want to say that it's come to my notice that some people have held a clandestine meeting and plotted what they will do in the Synod".
> I said:
> "There's nothing clandestine about it. I had a few of my friends in. I've been discussing who ought to be the Bishop of Armidale with everybody

and anybody ever since we knew it was going to be vacant. As a matter of fact, Bob, I've spoken to you about it. But I did have friends in the other night—and, since this is Australia and not Russia, I intend to continue to do that and I'll talk to anybody in my own home."

And I said:

"Did we talk about this election? We did! Did we plan how we would try to get the man who was the best man? We did!"

And then he threw up his hands and said:

"Well, how is it possible that we will know the Spirit's guiding now?"

It was the first inkling I had that what I thought was godly he thought, in fact, was ungodly. I thought not to prepare and not to try and talk everything through was just wrong. I still think it's wrong! But I realised in this moment, that what they thought was happening was that somehow or other you could actually change the will of God, that in this situation you'd actually end up by thwarting the will of God. And I'm positive they thought that's what happened—because of the way we'd behaved.

It soon appeared that the laity were strongly opposed to Rymer. Both John and Peter Chiswell were personally shocked by the opposition of some of the laity to him, particularly that of the Armidale delegates. From among the laity, Munro had a clear majority. The senior clergy were also Munro men and lobbied very hard for him although their heavy-handed approach alienated some of the younger clergy. In the House of Clergy, the moderates sided with the evangelicals and the vote was deadlocked at twenty-five votes each.

One of those who had voted for Rymer was a young clergyman, Dick Kernebone. Dick Kernebone, through Moore College, had completed a London BD in the middle of the year. Moyes, for some unexplained reason, had ordained Kernebone to the diaconate on 29 June, less than two months before the election, breaking, for the first time, his practice of ordaining deacons and priests on St Thomas' Day. What was more remarkable was that, on the day of his ordination, Moyes had also licensed Kernebone to be assistant at St John's, Tamworth, despite the fact that Moyes had no work whatever to offer him. Kernebone had found work as a surveyor until a curacy became available. The electoral ordinance was such that everyone who had the bishop's licence was a member of the House of Clergy and entitled to vote. It did not matter whether a man was in active ministry or had retired or, as in Dick Kernebone's case, had never even begun.

In a speech made in a committee of the clergy concerning the deadlock, John said that he wanted a bishop who would give him a fair go as he felt that there were some people who did not want him in the Diocese. At this, there was further uproar. John was accused of creating the deadlock.

The senior clergy continued lobbying hard for Munro. After two ballots between Munro and Rymer had failed to produce the requisite majority in both Houses, the Synod adjourned for a day to allow for prayer and reflection before the final vote was taken.

On that final day, as John was walking into the Cathedral Hall, one of the clergy, J H Mills, who until then had supported Rymer, told John that he was going to change his vote and vote for Munro. John relayed this message to Peter Chiswell. "I think the cause is lost, mate," he said. "Old Mr Mills is going to change his vote." After the Synod had assembled and before the ballot was taken, the dean, Evan Wetherall, moved, without notice, for the House of Clergy to meet separately. This they did. Wetherall then urged his brethren to abort the Synod by voting informally. He argued that the numbers were too close. A new bishop, he said, would be placed in an impossibly difficult situation knowing that he did not command the confidence of half his clergy. This suggestion was strenuously opposed by many but was supported by all of Rymer's men. In the event, neither candidate was able to win a majority of the votes in both Houses. The Synod was dissolved. A new date was set for it to reconvene one month later.

Before the next meeting of Synod, Archdeacons Stockdale and Daunton-Fear began looking for a new candidate who might effect a compromise. The name that came most strongly to their minds was that of Bishop Clive Kerle. Kerle had visited widely in the Diocese when he was the General Secretary for New South Wales of the Church Missionary Society. He had come to be regarded fondly in many places throughout Armidale because of this work. The general perception was that he was warm and friendly in his manner and had a great heart for the gospel. Stockdale had also had Kerle run a parish mission for him a few years earlier and through these associations had developed a particular regard for the man. By the time the Synod met, Kerle had agreed to his name being included as a nominee. The other major nominee was Archdeacon Dann from Melbourne.

The non-evangelicals opposed Kerle's nomination vehemently. Some terrible accusations were hurled around although many of them were directed more to Kerle's supporters than to their candidate. Their underlying question was—Is Kerle going to conform to the normal, established pattern of the Diocese or is he going to change everything? Stockdale had replied that "Kerle is a fine Christian gentleman and he will do whatever is Christian". One particular concern was that Kerle would not wear a cope. The debate was acrimonious and exhausting. On this occasion, neither John nor Peter Chiswell made a speech. Two ballots were held. Most of the clergy were supporting Kerle but the laity were not. The turning point came late in one evening when Gordon Hutchinson, a real estate agent from Armidale, addressed the Synod. In a tone of some bewilderment, he spoke to the following effect:

> I can't work out what the problem is. We all agree that Kerle is a good man.
> He is a man of integrity and graciousness. If wearing a cope is the only thing
> that is stopping us from voting for Kerle, what is the problem? If you
> understand the point about what he will and what he won't wear and if that
> is important to you, well you ought to keep voting the way you are. For
> myself, I don't even know what a cope is. And if you're like me and you
> don't understand what they're talking about, it just doesn't seem a good
> enough reason to be against him. So, let's get the voting over so we can all
> go home.

Hutchinson's speech broke the deadlock. When the final vote was taken on 22 September 1964, there was a majority for Kerle in both Houses although the extent of the majority was never announced.

It was the Armidale custom for the bishop, on his enthronement, to wear a cope. Clive Kerle did not do so. The whole of the Cathedral Chapter made their protest by wearing copes. It was the first time in thirty years they had worn them. The high feelings of that day were to herald years of bitter struggle. But the turning point had been reached and it had been reached within a span of time so brief that no-one had dared to imagine it possible. Humanly, it had not been.

John was to spend almost exactly four more years in the country diocese. They were busy years. They showed a changing emphasis in the thrust of his work. While he had begun in 1960 as Youth Director, from 1965 onwards the reports of the Board of Christian Education reflected a growing interest in and involvement with Christian education for adults. John continued to conduct youth camps and Sunday School and scripture teachers' courses but in 1966 the Youth Director became the Director of Christian Education. In the following year, a suggestion was made that, because the Director was spending more time on adult Christian education and less with young people, the appointment of another person for youth and children's work should be considered. Peter Chiswell says "this period marked the development of John as an evangelist. Youth work was always largely evangelistic. Now, the interest in adult education caused John to become more widely committed to evangelism amongst adults. Without doubt, Bishop Clive Kerle's constant encouragement of the clergy in general to be evangelistic helped also."[14]

As part of John's concern during this period to evangelise adults, he developed his home meetings strategy, later to be known as "dialogue evangelism".[15]

When, in September 1968, John left the Diocese, his friends were naturally saddened. Yet they all recognised he had served the Diocese and its people grandly for almost nine years in the fields of Christian education and evangelism. In a tribute in the diocesan newsletter at the time, Archdeacon Stockdale wrote:

Ray Smith, Peter Chiswell and John.

"A gifted speaker with a burning zeal and quenchless enthusiasm for the Christian cause, John will be greatly missed by a large circle of friends and admirers throughout this Diocese. Much regret has been voiced at his departure, and best wishes are extended to him for a bright and rewarding future."[16]

1   The Ven. R I H Stockdale, *Youth Organisations and Prospects for the Future*, 1950 Youth Report to the Diocese of Armidale.

2   A P Elkin, *The Diocese of Newcastle*, Australasian Medical Publishing Company, 1955, p 593.

3   Stockdale's 1950 Youth Report.

4   Stockdale's 1952 Youth Report.

5   Stockdale's 1952 Youth Report.

6   John C Chapman, *A Fresh Start*, Hodder & Stoughton, 1983, p 23.

7   Letter from Ross F McDonald to the author dated 12 December 1994.

8   Letter from Frank Elliott to the author dated 1 August 1994.

9   Chapman, *A Fresh Start*, p 24.

10 Letter from Ross F McDonald to the author dated 12 December 1994.

11 Letter from John and Dorothy Wheeler to the author dated 20 December 1994.

12 John was a capable and confident singer. On four or five occasions over a couple of years, he sang on a radio programme, "The Regional Artists' Programme", that was broadcast from Tamworth. He sang some English art songs (including works by Roger Quilter) and songs by Tchaikovsky and Schubert. For three years he sang the bass solos in Handel's "Messiah" in St Peter's Cathedral in Armidale.

13 Letter from Neville Collins to the author dated 14 September 1994.

14 Letter from Peter Chiswell to Evonne Paddison dated 11 June 1995.

15 Dialogue evangelism is the subject of Chapter 5.

16 *The Link*, September 1968.

The Chorister, 1946.

THE CINDERELLA OF THE DIOCESE 1927-1955

Confluence

Almost co-inciding with John Chapman's birth was the birth of an organisation within the Anglican Church in the Diocese of Sydney that would become the base from which John's work would be conducted for a golden period of twenty-five years. After the completion of their formative development, the confluence in 1968 of John Chapman and the Department of Evangelism (formerly the Board of Diocesan Missions) began an era in which evangelism at last began to receive recognition of the kind that might be thought appropriate in a diocese that prided itself on its evangelical character. During the preceding forty years it was something of a miracle that the organisation had survived its haphazard beginnings and its chronic lack of finance. It endured only because of the stirling foundation laid by an unusual collection of evangelists. They were determinedly single-minded about soul winning. They were undaunted enthusiasts, prayerful, passionate, vigorous, resourceful and hardworking. They were not deterred by an appalling lack of funds and facilities. Their style was anything but dull. Many had a grand vision. They saw a harvest field of such magnitude that they might have hesitated at the task. Instead, they rejoiced at the limitless opportunity and in the certain hope that the Lord would gather to Himself an overflowing cornucopia.

John Chapman and the Department of Evangelism, two children of Australia's depression years, would grow to be synonymous in the endeavour to advance the gospel—"the power of God for the salvation of everyone who believes" (Romans 1:16).

A fitful start

The Department of Evangelism had its origin in the occasional appointment of Diocesan Missioners.

The first person appointed to an office of that title was Dr Everard Digges La Touche. In 1914, at the age of thirty-one, he was both the Diocesan Missioner and lecturer at Moore College in Dogmatic Theology. His appointment was supported by funds from the St Philip's Glebe. He has been described as "a quixotic Irishman with a sharp intellectual mind, an uncompromising Protestant outlook and a hair-trigger temper".[1] As Diocesan Missioner he had an itinerant ministry, speaking at special services. He was an aggressively fervent evangelist. With the outbreak of the First World War, his overwhelming desire was to fight for the Empire which he equated with the cause of Christ. His persistence, which included an operation to remove the varicose veins that had earlier led to his rejection on medical grounds, eventually enabled him to be accepted for military service in December 1914. He was mortally wounded within twelve hours of landing at Gallipoli in August 1915.

Fourteen years passed before the appointment of the next Diocesan Missioner. The appointment resulted from an initiative of Canon Langford Smith.

Sydney Edgar Langford Smith "was one of the most influential clergy in the Diocese when at the height of his ministry".[2] An outstanding evangelical churchman, he had become a member of the Standing Committee of Synod on his appointment to the parish of Summer Hill in 1916 and, three years later, became a member of the Cathedral Chapter. "But it was in Synod that he found his greatest forum, and he grew in stature during the twenties and thirties as one of its leading figures."[3] At the meeting of the Sydney Diocesan Synod in October 1927, Canon Langford Smith moved and Canon Langley seconded a motion:

> That in view of the paramount need of more aggressive evangelistic work
> in the Diocese, it is desirable that steps be taken to appoint Diocesan
> Missioners who shall be free from parochial duties.

The motion was carried. Langford Smith then introduced two ordinances. On 13 October 1927, they were passed.

The Diocesan Missions Ordinance of 1927 established a Board, to be known as the Board of Diocesan Missions. Its membership comprised the Archbishop ex officio, six persons elected by the Synod and three persons appointed by the Archbishop. Its functions were to recommend one or more persons to the Archbishop for appointment as Diocesan Missioner and, with the concurrence of the Archbishop, to fix their tenure of office and their duties. The Diocesan Missioners Stipend Ordinance of 1927 authorised the raising of a loan secured by mortgage over part of the St Philip's Glebe to pay their stipends.

While the ordinances did not specify what the functions of Diocesan Missioners were to be and "diocesan missions" was nowhere defined, the name of the organisation nevertheless reflected the hopes of its founding fathers. The Board's officers were to be evangelists-at-large in the Diocese who would conduct parish missions. Diocesan Missioners were, as Langford Smith's motion had proposed, to be released from parochial responsibilities. Their particular functions were to be arrived at in consultation with the Archbishop. The ordinances gave their more detailed attention to the role of the governing body.

The creation of the BDM was not accompanied by any financial commitment on the part of the Synod. No funds were budgeted for the new body. No provision of a house was made. Although endorsing the idea of missions within the Diocese, the Synod was unwilling or unable to pay for them.

The founding members of the BDM were the Archbishop, as president, the six Synod-elected members, Bishop D'Arcy Irvine (who was appointed chairman), Canon Langford Smith, Canon Langley, Canon H S Begbie, Mr P R Allen (hon. treasurer) and Mr H W F Rogers (hon. secretary), and the Archbishop's three appointees, Archdeacon Martin, Canon E Howard Lea and Mr H B Cowper. The BDM began its operations in June 1928 when the first meeting was held to consider the appointment of a Diocesan Missioner.

On 1 February 1929, nine months after the founding ordinances were passed, George Edward Alison Weeks commenced office as the Board's first appointee. He was then sixty years of age.

Weeks, MA (Cambridge), BD (Durham) and LLD (Trinity College, Dublin) was a true scholar with considerable academic achievements. He had had a wide variety of appointments. He had served in parishes in England and South Africa, he had been a naval chaplain and the headmaster of Hilton College, Natal. At the beginning of 1923, after having spent six years as Dean of Christ Church Cathedral, Nelson, New Zealand, Weeks was appointed headmaster of Trinity Grammar School, then located at The Towers, Dulwich Hill.

Trinity Grammar had just completed the first ten years of its life. At that stage it was a parish school, lacking adequate buildings and grounds, undercapitalised, under-equipped and poorly staffed. It was considered that Weeks' appointment "appealed to

George Weeks.

both traditional loyalty to the Old Country with all its attendant dignity and tradition, and to the liberal/academic evangelicalism which was the mood of the Diocese at the time".[4] The acquisition of such a scholar was no doubt calculated to enhance the School's academic standing and to improve its financial stability.

During Weeks' headmastership from 1923 to 1928, the School underwent its greatest upheavals. In those six tumultuous years, Trinity Grammar operated with grossly inadequate facilities in financial stringency from three successive campuses. In 1926, it moved from The Towers at Dulwich Hill via substandard temporary accommodation in the Dulwich Hill parish hall—partitioned into classrooms with hessian curtains—to its present site at Summer Hill. At the time, that site was also poorly suited to the School's immediate needs.

The founder of the School and its driving force was George Alexander Chambers, the rector of Holy Trinity, Dulwich Hill. Towards the end of 1927 he faced his greatest challenge to secure the School's future. He had returned to Sydney in December of that year following his consecration at Canterbury as the first bishop of the Diocese of Central Tanganyika in East Africa. He was obliged to leave Australia by October 1928 to take up his appointment. He had determined, three years earlier, that the School's survival depended on its becoming a diocesan school. He had now just a few months in which to act and he had much to do. He needed to find benefactors to reduce the School's debt, then standing at £35,000. He needed to change the nature and composition of the School council to facilitate its transition from a parochial school to a school established by an ordinance of the Synod. He needed to replace Weeks with a proven headmaster who was a true son of Sydney and who would command far greater support in Synod than Weeks could expect to receive. He prayed hard and worked hard. "His activity was awesome and irresistible."[5] He was to achieve his goals in every area. At the Synod of 1928, the debt-ridden Trinity Grammar became a diocesan school.

So far as the headmaster was concerned, Chambers had no ground to dismiss Weeks. Weeks was clearly capable. He was not unpopular. In extremely difficult circumstances, he had acquitted himself commendably. Chambers' only option was to make Weeks' headmastership untenable. At the beginning of 1928, Dr and Mrs Weeks' combined emolument was £600. On 1 March, the School council resolved "Owing to the present financial stringency of the School that the present allowance of £100 per annum to Mrs Weeks be discontinued and that the Headmaster be asked to contribute £100 for Board and attendance whilst he is in residence".[6]

Initially, this tactic of forcing a substantial reduction in the remuneration of the headmaster and his wife seems to have failed. With time running out, it may have been that Chambers was forced to appeal directly to Weeks to stand aside so that the future of the School to which both men were thoroughly committed might be secured, to sacrifice "the position he now preferred to any other".[7] In any event, Weeks, on 21 July 1928, tendered the resignation that had been drafted for him by the School council. He was to leave at the end of the year. In that same month, Chambers arranged Weeks' appointment as Diocesan Missioner as well as the appointment of the popular W G Hilliard, a former headmaster of the School, as Weeks' successor.[8]

And so it was, in the providence of God, that the BDM's first worker was found. In a manner unpredictable and without the public acclamation of the church, the first breath of life had been breathed into the diocesan fledgling.

Financial security hardly accompanied Weeks' new job. His stipend was met only after several clergy had given a written undertaking to ensure his financial support.

All parishes were informed of the appointment, and requests for the services of the Missioner were invited. The response was so general that, even after making arrangements for a full programme for the present year (1929), it was found that some requests would have to be deferred for consideration and arrangement at a later date.

In some parishes the services were of the nature of a parochial mission. In others, the service took the form of quiet days for the clergy of the rural deanery; special addresses to communicants and also to confirmees; and in one parish a special "Young Life" campaign was undertaken.

From all quarters most gratifying reports have been received, testifying to the work accomplished; the fresh spiritual vitality infused into the congregations, and the definite decisions made for the Lord Jesus Christ.[9]

George Weeks was "a commanding figure in the pulpit, an eloquent preacher and splendid lecturer".[10] He conducted missions at Gladesville, Port Kembla, Lidcombe, Waverley, Leura, Cooks River, Earlwood, East Sydney, Enmore and Roseville. It was at a mission taken at St Matthew's, Manly, that W A Watts, later to serve as rector in parishes including Sutherland, Cooks River and Lidcombe, was converted.

"The itinerant nature of the preaching did not suit him."[11] Weeks suffered the misfortune of a broken leg and, after he had spent only six months in office, his mother in England fell seriously ill. He resigned on 30 July 1929 and returned to that country to take up the position of rector of the Parish of Fenny Compton, a parish in the gift of Corpus Christi College, Cambridge. He died in England on 24 August 1941 at the age of seventy-three.

Finding a replacement Diocesan Missioner proved to be a difficult task. The Board was unable to find anyone who was free to accept a permanent appointment. In 1930, it experimented with the appointment of suitable parish clergy for short periods. In this capacity, Archdeacon H S Begbie, a founding member of the Board, was appointed on 1 October 1930 for three months.[12] The reason for his appointment was obvious. "He was a born evangelist, and soul winning was his greatest delight."[13] He conducted a series of missions at Eastwood, Beecroft, Gladesville, Summer Hill, Pyrmont, Wallerawang and Sutherland. He was well received. His brief ministry was fruitful. However, the scheme of temporary appointments proved impractical and after a short period it lapsed.

1930 also saw the election of D J Knox, then the rector of St Paul's, Chatswood, to the BDM.

The first flowering

Archdeacon H S Begbie organised a Young People's Welcome in the Sydney Town Hall for Archbishop Mowll shortly after Mowll's enthronement as Archbishop on 13 March 1934. It was an enthusiastic meeting and the Town Hall was packed to capacity. Alan Begbie, Archdeacon Begbie's ordained son, was one who presented an address of welcome to the Archbishop on that memorable occasion. Later in that same month, Mowll appointed the younger Begbie Diocesan Missioner, designating him more specifically as "Missioner to Young People". A heightened awareness of a need for work among younger people had arisen and fellowship groups for young people had begun in several places in the Diocese. Begbie's work was instrumental in assisting the spread of this movement so widely.

Alan Begbie.

Alan Begbie was commissioned by the Archbishop in a service conducted in St Andrew's Cathedral on the evening of 5 April 1934. He had just turned twenty-six years of age. The first of a series of more purposeful appointments to an organisation that until this time had existed as a child of delayed growth had now been made although, after Begbie's blaze of activity, another nine years would pass before a successor would be found. Mowll's main goal "to stimulate his diocese into a visible evangelistic witness"[14] as well as his strong focus on youth were both reflected in the appointment.

After ordination in 1931, Alan Begbie had been licensed as curate to D J Knox at Chatswood. David Knox was then a member of the BDM. He was tremendously keen to promote evangelism within the Diocese and was no doubt instrumental in bringing Begbie to Mowll's attention. Knox was succeeded as rector by R B Robinson in early 1933. Knox and Robinson had led a drive to raise enough money to pay Begbie's stipend as Diocesan Missioner. As had been the case with Dr Weeks, several clergy and some laity had personally undertaken to meet the amount.

Alan Begbie gospelling at Kiama beach mission, 1938.

David Knox was a determined and persistent advocate of the need for evangelism and Christian education in the Diocese.

Perhaps no one man did more to revive the Diocesan Board of Missions in 1934 than he did. It had been moribund for a number of years, and the shortage of men and funds in the Depression made it seem little more than a pipe dream. But he found the evangelist; he raised the money; and he set the work in motion.[15]

Over the next fifteen years he would continue to be one of its most persistent advocates in the major forums and councils of the Church and one of its staunchest supporters.

Alan Begbie's stipend was £250 per annum. Out of that, he had to provide for his own accommodation and run his own car, a single-seater Austin 7. A little later, through the generosity of a benefactor, he was given a larger model Austin. In January 1934, Begbie had become engaged to Effie Finigan. It would not be until two years later that they could afford to be married. When, during Begbie's term, a suggestion was made that his stipend should be increased by £25 per annum it was rejected by Knox. He argued that the amount of £250 was the same as he had received at the time of his marriage and he could therefore see no reason why it should be increased.

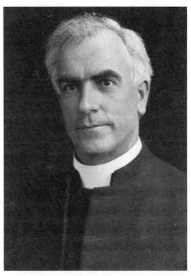

David James Knox.

On 5 September 1934, the BDM received its first diocesan financial support. It received a grant of £24.8.11 from the Standing Committee of Synod. This was no portent of a golden age. It would be more than twenty years before these purse strings would be loosened again.

There was a constant demand for missions from all parts of the Diocese, metropolitan and country, during Begbie's three years as Diocesan Missioner. Wholehearted and energetic, he conducted more than sixty missions in that period.

The typical mission ran from Sunday to Sunday. A children's meeting was held after school each afternoon at 4.00 pm. Begbie had been a member of the first beach mission team in Australia. His work with children had been sharpened by that training. The children's meetings were lively, with singing and a simple story from the Scriptures well-illustrated with visual and other teaching aids. An adults' meeting, directed more towards young adults but attended by adults of all ages, was held each evening. "He was a natural extrovert, always outgoing in his friendliness, easy and accessible in personal relations... He had a dash and flair that made his ministry very attractive for young people."[16]

The Missioner used the time during school holidays to visit other parishes, some of which would be the venue for a forthcoming mission, taking Sunday services and being introduced to the congregation.

Following a mission at Lindfield, Begbie received a letter from Mrs Delbridge, the mother of the man who would later become Bishop Delbridge, "giving thanks to God for much renewed blessing in her own life and for the challenge to the ministry of her young son Graham".[17] Jeffray Mills, who was later to be ordained and to serve as rector in parishes including St Mary's, Earlwood, Lithgow, Chatswood and Campsie, was converted at one of Begbie's meetings.

The pied ukulele piper

Alan had a very natural, buoyant enthusiasm—specially enthusiasm for sharing the gospel. He was magic with children, as indeed his father had been before him. He really loved them. He loved sport and because of his wide interests he could relate to and share with genuine pleasure in the interests of the young. He played a little ukulele. He had a lovely gift with music which was a great help, particularly with the children's meetings although it helped in others too. He had a strong voice, a good singing voice which fortunately had been well-trained so that it was able to stand up to the rigours of so many meetings without giving way. That was marvellous. He played his ukulele at a time when people didn't dream of doing things like playing guitars in church or anything like that so it was quite an unusual sort of thing to happen.

Effie Begbie
Alan Begbie's widow.

Alan Begbie ceased to be the Diocesan Missioner at the beginning of 1937. This was in accordance with the undertaking he had given to serve a three-year term of office. The demand for missions had not slackened and he had worked at an unrelenting pace. He felt he could not continue to give his best if he was to maintain his exhausting workload. As was to be expected of a personable young man with a gift for evangelism who had travelled extensively throughout the Diocese, he had been approached by several parishes seeking a rector. In February 1937 he took up an appointment as the rector of the Parish of Shoalhaven in Nowra, where he had held a mission almost twelve months before in March 1936.

The Diocesan Yearbook for 1937 contains the following summary which covers all but the last few months of Begbie's work[18]:

Parishes visited	75
Missions conducted	56
Services conducted	1,012
Schools visited	107
Classes taken in schools	344
Approximate number of children reached through school and mission meetings	17,500

In his three years with the BDM, Alan Begbie had worked energetically and well. He had set a style and format for evangelistic meetings and placed an emphasis on ministering to people of a younger age that was to be a model for later Diocesan Missioners. Great impetus had been given through his missions to the formation of young people's fellowships. Later, Alan Begbie was to serve as chairman of the BDM.

With the outbreak of the Second World War in 1939 until its conclusion in 1945, the appointment of further Diocesan Missioners lapsed. However, in 1942 the Synod thought it desirable to increase the size of the Board from nine to fifteen members, even though it then exercised no functions. The members became responsible for ensuring that provision was made for the payment of the stipends and expenses of the staff.[19]

Hallelujah!—the work takes root

Archbishop Mowll maintained his desire to see further Diocesan Missioners appointed following the conclusion of Alan Begbie's term of office. He gave strong support to the BDM and the Youth Department in particular. He had a great longing for people to be converted to Christ. He himself had been a missionary in western China and he brought with him to Sydney that same zeal to see people won for Christ that had marked his own ministry on the mission field.

In July 1941, Mowll had a meeting with a thirty-one-year-old Church Army officer, George Rees, in the CMS rooms in Melbourne to sound out the prospects of Rees working in his diocese. The two men had not met before. Rees' work had come to Mowll's notice through reports from Alf Stanway (later Bishop of Central Tanganyika) and Marcus Loane.

George Rees.

Thomas George Rees was born on 26 August 1909 in Zeehan, Tasmania, the son of a mine manager. His family moved to Melbourne in 1913 and eventually settled in the suburb of Alphington. Rees first attended the local Presbyterian Sunday School and later St Paul's Church of England, Fairfield. He was converted at the age of twenty-one. At St Paul's, he became the scoutmaster of the Church's scout group and was also actively engaged in young people's work through the Church Missionary Society League of Youth. In December 1935, he was called to do the work of an evangelist. He resigned his employment of thirteen years as a salesman and went to St Luke's, Adelaide, for six months. In March 1937, he entered the Church Army and worked in Queensland and New South Wales before being commissioned in May 1938 as a Captain Evangelist and put in charge of the Church Army van in Tasmania. He travelled extensively throughout the island. Each year, for six weeks beginning in the last week of February, Rees commenced a circuit of the hops fields in the Derwent Valley. About 3,000 seasonal workers picked hops. Rees would work alongside them in the fields. The agreement he made with each one was that, as long as he continued to pick hops and put them into their basket, he could talk to them about the gospel. In the evenings, he held a service outside the pickers' huts near the hops kiln during which pictures were projected by means of a magic lantern.

At the time of his conversation with Mowll, Rees was ending a period of more than four-and-a-half years' itinerant work in Tasmania.

George Rees was offered the position of Diocesan Missioner on the condition that he attend Moore College and be ordained. He accepted. He came to Sydney and, during the period of his studies, first superintended the church at Ultimo and was then assistant minister at St Barnabas', Broadway, with Archdeacon R B S Hammond and later Archdeacon R B Robinson.

George Rees commenced work as Diocesan Missioner on 11 March 1946. There was no commissioning service. The Archbishop made a grant of £350 for one year to fund the work. There was no guarantee that further funding would be available after the first year.

Later in 1946, after Rees' appointment, Mowll invited Stuart Barton Babbage to his diocese to be the Diocesan Missioner in a special teaching capacity. Babbage was returning from missionary service in the Middle East as a senior chaplain with the RAF. In order that his and George Rees' roles would be clearly distinguished, Rees was to be restyled as the "Diocesan Evangelist". Babbage was duly appointed. After only a few months, he was invited to be the Dean of Sydney and accepted that appointment. D J Knox, as a member of the Standing Committee of Synod, suggested that the money earmarked for Babbage as the Diocesan Missioner should be used for Rees' support on the ground that Rees really occupied that position. This did not win the Standing Committee's approval and the funds went elsewhere.

At the end of the first year, George Rees was told by the Diocesan Secretary, H V Archinal, that no money would be forthcoming for the second year because a severe storm had badly damaged many of the Church's properties in the Glebe estate and substantial funds would have to be set aside for their repair.

George Rees' working conditions during that first year particularly, but also during the second year, would be a severe test of his commitment.

> That second year was very difficult, very, very difficult because we'd only been there twelve months and of course as income from missions wasn't so very great as yet, we hadn't the build up like we had later on. But the Lord marvellously provided. It's a mystery to me where the money came from, but not from the Diocese. They didn't have any interest whatever.[20]

Rees' fervour for evangelism, despite all the trying circumstances he faced, was such that he neither faltered nor ceased to be thankful to God for the richness of His blessing. He was to become widely known throughout the Diocese as "Hallelujah George".

Periodically, George Rees would be asked by the Archbishop or an Archdeacon, from concern for his welfare and the welfare of his family, whether he thought it was time for an appointment to a parish. He also received numerous inquiries from parishes concerning his availability for appointment. Although working in a parish would have provided far greater comfort and financial reward, again and again he rejected the idea and pressed on. "My aim, by the grace of God, was that the Board of Diocesan Missions should be established as a centre of evangelism in the Diocese."[21]

When George Rees commenced his work, the BDM owned no residence for its Missioner. This was not peculiar to the BDM. Not one similar diocesan organisation at that time owned a residence for its staff. Neither, although the whole Diocese was his mission field, did the Diocese provide him with a car. Rees and his wife, Freda[22], lived, by virtue of arrangements made by Mowll, in the precentor's lodge (480 Kent Street) at the rear of St Andrew's Cathedral. After almost three years, they were required to move. Rees' contemporaries from his years at Moore College—the class of '43—were to come to his aid more than once in many ways, including the matter of accommodation, over the next few years. Bernard Judd offered George and Freda the rectory at Hammondville. They lived there for the next three years.

Because of the uncertainty over the Missioner's accommodation, the BDM decided, following a BDM camp held at Lawson over the Australia Day weekend in January 1953 and attended by about 100 people of mainly eighteen to twenty years of age, to acquire a residence. The Lord had told Rees, in prayer and in thought, that if £200 was pledged by those present at the Lawson camp, he could go ahead. Rees did not reveal the amount. In the event, the amount pledged by the end of the camp was almost £220. A suitable house was found at 27 Bradman Street, Merrylands. After further appeals for donations, the funding arrangements were as follows:

Gifts	£800
Loan from Diocese (interest free)	350
Loan from Parramatta Building Society	<u>1,920</u>
	£3,070

The Building Society loan was in £10 shares and the repayments were about £16 per month. The period of repayment would be lessened if the share capital could be liquidated before the term of the loan. A share drive was made each year.

The Standing Committee of Synod was required to pass a mortgaging ordinance to authorise the borrowing. If the mortgaging ordinance were not passed promptly, the Rees family would be faced with the prospect of a period of homelessness. The Standing Committee eventually passed The Board of Diocesan Missions Mortgaging Ordinance 1953 on 27 April 1953.

During these years, it seemed that the Standing Committee, or its sub-committees, met only as the demands of business required. For many weeks, there was not sufficient business to justify the necessary meeting. Mrs Rees (and their three children) were forced to live with her relatives in Launceston, Tasmania. (She joked that the reason the Committee was called the "Standing Committee" must be because it never sat!) George Rees

Archbishop Mowll dedicates the Missioner's house.

55

lived in the rectories of parishes where missions were being held or in the rectories of his friends. Eventually, he was told "that the matter would be finalised the following week". He wrote to his wife telling her to join him immediately. He told her he would meet her at the station and take her to their new home. When he met her as arranged, his unhappy message was that the necessary meeting had still not taken place. Bob Gibbes of Guildford came to their aid. "We can't have you sleeping out on the grass!" he told them, and so, for the next few weeks, the Rees family shared the Guildford rectory with the Gibbes.

The house was dedicated by the Archbishop at a special service held on the premises on the afternoon of Saturday, 10 October 1953. By the time Rees's work with the BDM finished, the house had still not been fully paid for, but the substantial equity established in the property was to be of great help in future purchases.

BDM—what does it mean?

I used to often say to people for a bit of fun, "You know, you can find out what we are on the back page of the Sydney Morning Herald where it speaks of Births, Deaths and Marriages". I said to them, "The most important thing is to be born again, dead to sin and married to the Lord." But anyhow, there you are.
George Rees.

The Missioner's van.

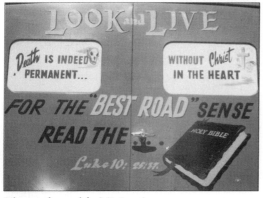
The rear doors of the Missioner's van.

Rees had no car during his first twelve months. All his travelling was done by public transport, otherwise he walked. Sometimes the rector of the parish would drive him home after the evening meeting, but frequently he was left to find his own way home. After twelve months, Mowll was able to provide him with a second-hand vehicle. It was an old CENEF wagon used during the Second World War. In September 1949 it was sold and a second-hand Morris Oxford van was bought in its place. Vic Hynds, a member of the BDM and an excellent mechanic, gave the Morris a life well beyond its entitlement. Subsequently, a young woman, converted through a mission camp at Kiama, donated £950 which was used to purchase a new mission van. Graham Wade had been strongly influenced at a mission at Summer Hill at the age of fifteen.

"Life, verve and enjoyment attracted me—creative storytelling as opposed to the dead boring sermon style of others", he remembers.[23] On one side of the van Graham Wade painted, "Victory is of the Lord" together with a picture of David slaying Goliath, and on the other, "The Lord is my Shepherd". Across the front was painted "Board of Diocesan Missions, Diocese of Sydney". There were two small windows in the back where other messages could be put. Written across both back doors was "For the best Road sense, read the Bible".

Disease of Sydney

We had obtained this sturdy second-hand car and had painted on it and at the front of it by my good friend, Graham Wade, "Board of Diocesan Missions, Diocese of Sydney". While sitting on the front seat one afternoon during a mission at St Thomas', Rozelle, waiting for the children to arrive, two youngsters came along and tried to read the sign. They started, "Board of Di..." ...and couldn't get out the "ocesan" so they just said "Missions". Then they started again, one lad in particular, started again. "Board of... " Got stumped. Then he went on to read "Diocese of Sydney" and got stumped again and said, "Disease of Sydney". I thought that was really tops and spoke of it in a report to Synod shortly after and hoped that we would indeed be a disease of Sydney—infectious disease, so far as evangelism was concerned, helping folk to realise how important it was in the life and work and witness of the church— very, very infectious indeed. But from the Synod's point of view little interest was taken in what I had to say and I thought to myself, "I think the disease here is sleeping sickness." Well, in all events, that's just something of the mood of the Diocese and I'm very grateful again to say once more the Archbishop (Howard Mowll) was very, very much involved all the way through in his own quiet and wonderful way.

George Rees.

Although Rees advertised his missions as being "For You and Your Family", his major impact in evangelism was the same as Begbie's, first children, then youth and young adults. Among the children, Rees had a particular appeal for young boys.

George Rees' first mission was at St Mary's, Balmain, from 17–24 March 1946.[24]

A mission ran in a parish from a Sunday (or a Monday) each day to the following Sunday. A programme of home visitation would often precede a mission. In the week before the mission, Rees endeavoured to take scripture classes at schools within the parish involved, both to introduce himself to the children and to publicise the mission. The teaching of scripture was a very successful strategy. A children's mission was held each afternoon from 3.45 to 4.45 pm. The beginning of a mission might see a slow start, but usually the children came in droves, rarely less than 60–70 each afternoon, commonly 150–200, and sometimes (as at Cabramatta and Canley Vale in 1954) in excess of 300. Attendances directly reflected the sizes of the school populations in the areas concerned.

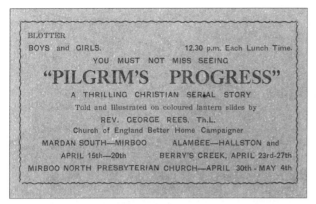

BLOTTER

BOYS and GIRLS.   12.30 p.m. Each Lunch Time.

YOU MUST NOT MISS SEEING

"PILGRIM'S PROGRESS"

A THRILLING CHRISTIAN SERIAL STORY

Told and Illustrated on coloured lantern slides by

REV. GEORGE REES, Th.L.

Church of England Better Home Campaigner

MARDAN SOUTH—MIRBOO   ALAMBEE—HALLSTON and

APRIL 15th—20th   BERRY'S CREEK, APRIL 23rd-27th

MIRBOO NORTH PRESBYTERIAN CHURCH—APRIL 30th - MAY 4th

Blotter given to school children when George Rees missioned for Walter Spencer at Mirboo North, Victoria.

In 1939, George Rees had obtained from England a set of 3¹/₄ inch glass lantern slides of "Pilgrim's Progress" showing Copping's paintings. "Pilgrim's Progress" had a special place in Rees' experience and ministry. As a Sunday School teacher at St Paul's, Fairfield, he had read all the books in the Sunday School library before coming to John Bunyan's allegorical journey of the man, Christian, from the City of Destruction to the Celestial City, carrying the burden of sin heavy on his back. The Lord had said to Rees, "This is you. You are the man with the burden of sin!" It was a means of his conversion. During his time in Tasmania, Rees had arranged for the slides to be hand-coloured for a shilling each. He used these slides very effectively as a serial through the week. C H Spurgeon, the great English preacher of the second half of the 19th century, was so enamoured with "Pilgrim's Progress" that he read it at least one hundred times during his life. If Spurgeon read it one hundred times, George Rees told it several hundred times and always with good effect.

The BDM had no projector. It had no equipment of any kind. In answer to prayer, a projector had been made available by the Presbyterian Church in Palmer Street, Sydney. The slides were supplemented with other teaching aids.

The children's missions in the afternoons were also used to advertise the evening sessions, to which the whole family was invited, but particularly youth. There was a conscious strategy of reaching parents through their children.[25] It was not a particularly successful strategy. With some exceptions, attendances by adults were invariably much poorer than attendances by children.

From Wednesday to the end of the mission, an emphasis was placed on making a personal commitment to Christ. As far as the children were concerned, a session for "Keenites" was held from 4.45 to 5.15 pm at which those who had attended the children's mission and who were willing to stay behind would be counselled. The emphasis on personal commitment increased as Friday approached. A commitment was not indicated by the raising of hands or by asking people to come to the front of the meeting. Rees gave his audience literature that they were to take home with them, including a committal form. He suggested that their commitment should be made at home, perhaps in their prayer time with their parents, perhaps quietly in the solitude of their bedrooms as they knelt by their beds. They were to make their commitment by asking Jesus to come into their lives as Saviour and Friend. They were then to fill in the form given to them for the purpose and to bring it back the following day. That day was the opportunity for them to confess openly that a commitment had been made. The Missioner would read out their names and they would stand as he did so. At first, anyone of the age of seven years or upwards could make a commitment, but because Rees experienced cases of children who made enduring commitments from the age of six, he lowered the age to six.

No prizes or other incentives were given for attendance or behaviour. If children were to come, George Rees said, they were to come because of the appeal of the gospel.

At the evening meetings, there was some singing of hymns and choruses, perhaps a solo. Coloured slides were again a feature. There would be a presentation of from 15 -20 minutes, often using a series of 35mm slides called "The Gospel in Wildflowers". George Rees was an ardent and gifted photographer. He had acquired a detailed knowledge of Australian native flora while working as a salesman for Law Somner, Seed Merchants, in Melbourne. Many of his photos of wildflowers and of places he visited in the course of his work were sold to the Australian Women's Weekly and published in its "Beautiful Australia" section. The payments he received financed his hobby. Rees had other themes he illustrated with his slides, such as "The Word from the Windows" (showing pictures of church windows) and "The Gospel in Stones" (testifying to the work of God in creation). He also developed other series that used commonplace things, such as soap, bread,

BDM bookmark.

matches, gloves and petrol slogans, as a starting point for introducing and illustrating the gospel message. Sometimes at an evening meeting, a film would be shown.

Children who were not already attending Sunday School were encouraged to do so and as many as possible were linked up with the Scripture Union Bible Reading Plan. Those who made a commitment were asked to respond to the gift of everlasting life in Christ by themselves making a gift. Money boxes were distributed seeking support for the Church Missionary Society and for the Bush Church Aid Society.

As time went on, Rees also introduced some slides showing places he had visited. He described the work he had done there as a means of increasing understanding of the BDM's role.

No charge was made to a parish in which a mission was conducted. In many places, particularly the inner city parishes, rectors were paid far below the minimum stipend recommended by the Synod. No offerings were taken up at any of the week night meetings so as not to embarrass those who had come. People were, however, given the opportunity to make a retiring offering at those meetings and a special thank offering was taken up on the Sunday evening at the close of a mission.

Christ in all

George, throughout his ministry, had developed the ability to use the commonplace to turn any conversation to Jesus. Familiar images and phrases became the basis for opening up the gospel. A "Miracle Margarine" container found in the gutter illustrated the miracle of Christ who rescued us from the gutter of sin. "Life. Be in it" became an illustration for the only life, the life in Christ. One morning, on the ferry to work, George, then eighty years of age and on his way to teach scripture at Woolloomooloo Public School, sat next to me and shared, not just with me but with all our fellow commuters, the lesson he had prepared. He had a huge poster of Centrepoint Tower to the top of which he had added a drawing of a cross. Above that was the caption "Christ—The Centrepoint of Life". Underneath were the words of a chorus he himself had written and which he was going to teach the children in his class that morning. Quite unselfconsciously, George sang it in his loud, true voice for everyone within earshot.

For many years, George had carried with him a Bible designed to fit exactly inside a matchbox. (The print was so small it could only be read with the aid of a magnifying glass.) In the box, there were also two matches, one live and one dead. If anyone asked him for a light, George would produce his matchbox, remove the Bible and the matches, and explain that, if it was a light you were after, Jesus was the true Light and you could either be alive with His light or you could be dead and in darkness.

Michael Orpwood

reminiscing about George Rees who, in 1986, came to live in Balmain within a few doors of the Orpwood home.

George Rees worked tirelessly with the typical restlessness of the evangelist. One mission followed hard on the heels of another. He had estimated that if he were to visit every church in the diocese once only for an eight-day mission, he would be fruitfully occupied for approximately twenty-two years. His labours were not limited to the Diocese of Sydney. He frequently ministered throughout all parts of New South Wales, in Victoria and Tasmania, and occasionally in the other States of Australia.

From 25 September–2 October 1949, Rees held a Mission at St Paul's, Oatley. He recalls that it was very fruitful. In particular, he greatly appreciated the assistance given to him by a Teachers' College student named John Chapman. He had no thought that John would succeed to his work.

In addition to parish missions, Rees conducted youth rallies throughout the year in the Chapter House adjoining St Andrew's Cathedral and at Bible Society House opposite in Bathurst Street. He held men's meetings and women's meetings. For four years, he conducted beach missions. He was regularly involved in running CEBS camps at the newly acquired Youth

Department properties at Port Hacking.

In 1954, George Rees was State President of Christian Endeavour. Christian Endeavour then had fifty branches in the Church of England in New South Wales with a membership of about 1,000. Rees spent many of his Saturdays in all parts of the State conducting Christian Endeavour rallies. He also had the opportunity to speak to the members of confirmation classes at the close of their time of preparation and to make a definite appeal to them to commit their lives to the Lord Jesus Christ.

From the context of his parish missions, Rees developed, as a supplementary work, a series of holiday camps for youth, mainly for those in their late teenage years. Many of these were carried out in conjunction with Graham Delbridge of the Youth Department. The pattern that became generally established for most of the next seven years was—St Michael's, Wollongong, for the Australia Day long weekend, Nowra (in a marquee) for Easter, Kiama or the Jamberoo showground for the June long weekend and the Campbelltown showground for the October long weekend. These camps were for evangelism, teaching and challenging youth for missionary service. Each was enthusiastically supported by the neighbouring rectors and their congregations.

A Turner begins to turn

I first became aware of the work of the Board of Diocesan Missions in 1947 at the first houseparty I ever went to, at Chaldercot. I was seventeen. I was not converted but I remember the Reverend George Rees who was the Diocesan Missioner at the time and the depth of challenge and impact of his message—even though I was fairly rebellious and unwilling to submit to the gospel at that particular point of time.

The late John Turner
who (apart from the six years when he was the Rector of Dapto) served from 1956 to 1990 with great faithfulness as a member of the BDM.
"Isn't that good," George Rees said when he read John Turner's testimony. "You know," he said, "I often used to tell people if they asked me what I did was that I was a fitter and turner—fitting people together in Christ and turning them from sin and death to the Lord".

At St Michael's, Wollongong, the parish hall was divided in half by a screen. One half was used to accommodate men who slept on straw-filled palliasses on the floor, the other half was used as the kitchen and dining area. Women were accommodated in the local Methodist and Presbyterian church halls. Each camp was attended by between 110 and 120 people. The highest attendance at the St Michael's, Wollongong, camp was on the weekend of 29 January to 1 February 1954 when 130 were present. Special literature was printed for counselling and referrals. The morning Bible studies at the Wollongong camp in 1954 were on Revelation 3.

61

From all these activities, George Rees recruited a group of about 300 young people originally called the "BDM Workers' Guild" but later renamed "The Ambassadors". They gave him systematic prayer and financial support and were his assistants in running camps and rallies. With their help, his work became self-funding after the first year. The Ambassadors undertook to hold boxes in which to place their donations. At the quarterly prayer and devotional rallies, the boxes were opened and the total donated through all boxes was announced. Rees was to work for a further nine years without any diocesan financial support. It was through the Ambassadors that he was able to find enthusiastic members for the BDM Council.

Replacement therapy

When I first started, the first Council meeting had just four people. Just four out of sixteen. Why? Because most of those appointed by the Synod, they didn't counsel. They didn't come along. So, as time went on, they still persisted in not coming and so we were able to write to them and suggest that we've got somebody now who would perhaps take a great deal of interest, they were busy in their parish life and not able to take such interest. And so gradually the Council became a very, very keen group of praying, giving, evangelistic people, young and old and a tremendous blessing. You know, when you go out and you do mission work, and you realise you've got such a backing, it's a tremendous thrill.

George Rees.

BDM Ambassadors' flag.

Support generally throughout the Diocese for Rees' work was poor, particularly in the early years. They were the years of greatest struggle. Somehow, there was just enough money to keep going, but never more. There was great indifference. Parishes were not supportive, nor was the Synod and its Standing Committee. George Rees did, however, receive strong backing from those he had been with in Moore College. His missions in the first two to three years were conducted mainly in the parishes of his fellow students. It was as the news of the success of these missions spread that other invitations started to come.

While institutional and general diocesan support was poor, several individuals showed a particular keenness for evangelism. Rees always received strong support from Mowll and was impressed with Mowll's enthusiasm for the spread of the gospel. He would meet with the Archbishop, usually every three months, in the tea rooms at CMS or CENEF and report to him on all areas of his work. Mowll was an interested listener and made many enquiries about the parishes Rees had visited. He always had prayer with Rees and he always had a word of encouragement. On several occasions, the Archbishop arranged accommodation for Rees and his family.

The real dynamic in the Diocese for evangelism throughout this period was David Knox, then the rector of Christ Church, Gladesville. At the time of Rees' appointment as Diocesan Missioner, Knox was the secretary of the BDM. He had always had a tremendous keenness for evangelism. He was influential in Alan Begbie's training and recruitment. He made many appeals to the Synod and the Standing Committee of Synod for support for the BDM's work.

Several others, small in number but important, also looked beyond the parish for the advance of the gospel. Graham Delbridge, often a co-worker with Rees, ministered to youth. T C Hammond, the Principal of Moore College, was a member of a co-ordinating committee that organised a city-wide mission by a number of evangelistic organisations, such as Campaigners for Christ, Open Air Campaigners and Scripture Union, and committed his students to the mission. R C M Long, rector of St Michael's, Wollongong, and rural dean who, over a period of five years, organised rural deanery youth weeks throughout the south coast each year was another. Clive Steele was a very supportive member of the BDM and a member of its governing body for many years.

The Cinderella of the Diocese

I well remember a special night in the Cathedral in connection with the preparation for the coming of the Billy Graham Crusade in 1959 and in the clergy vestry, there we were, robed for the service. Canon D J Knox turned to me and said, "Well, George, at last we're not the Cinderella of the Diocese". And that was true. I do feel, by the grace of God and in His goodness, the Diocese from then on began to support the work, subsidise the work, putting it down as one of the organisations for which the Diocese should undertake.

George Rees.

At the time of his conversation with George, David Knox was 84. He died in 1960 at the age of 85.

After nine years of solid work, George Rees left the BDM in March 1955 to take up the national directorship of Christian Endeavour in Australia. He had been appointed State President the year before. However, following the earnest persuasion of Mowll, he accepted appointment instead as the rector of St Columb's, West Ryde. Summarising the years of ministry from 1946–1954, George Rees wrote in "The Ambassador", the BDM's quarterly news bulletin, in March 1954:

All told during the past eight years, 4,401 addresses have been given to aggregate attendances of 270,273 people. Decisions registered for conversion and dedication totalled approximately 5,215; of that number 3,660 were children.

CHAPTER THREE

1   Stephen Judd & Kenneth Cable, *Sydney Anglicans*, Anglican Information Office, 1987, p 176.

2   Marcus L Loane, *Mark These Men*, p 23.

3   Loane, *Mark These Men*, p 25.

4   Phillip J Heath, *Trinity: The Daring of Your Name*, Allen & Unwin Australia Pty Ltd, 1990, p 79.

5   Heath, *Trinity: The Daring of Your Name*, p 97.

6   Trinity Grammar School Council Minute Book, p 183, quoted in a monograph in the Trinity Grammar School archives of R Marsh, *The Headmastership of Dr G E Weeks*, 5 March 1993, p 49.

7   Marsh, *The Headmastership of Dr G E Weeks*, p 56.

8   Janet West, *Innings of Grace—A life of Bishop W G Hilliard*, Trinity Grammar School, 1987, pp 69,70.

9   First Report of BDM to Synod, Year Book of the Diocese of Sydney, 1930, pp 384,385.

10   C E Latham & Alan Nichols, *Trinity Grammar School—A History*, The Council of Trinity Grammar School, 1974, p 46.

11   Heath, *Trinity: The Daring of Your Name*, p 106.

12   Report of BDM to Synod dated 25 September 1930, Year Book of the Diocese of Sydney, 1931, p 449.

13   Loane, *Mark These Men*, p 41.

14   Judd & Cable, *Sydney Anglicans*, p 245.

15   Loane, *Mark These Men*, p 48.

16   Loane, *Mark These Men*, pp 110,112.

17   Interview with Effie Begbie by Matthew Pickering. Transcripts of Matthew Pickering's interviews are in the records of the Department of Evangelism, St Andrew's House, Sydney.

18   Year Book of the Diocese of Sydney, 1937, p 370.

19   Diocesan Missions Ordinance Amending Ordinance of 1942.

20   Interview with Matthew Pickering.

21   BDM Newsletter April 1949.

22   Freda is a diminutive of Mrs Rees' Christian name, Alfreda.

23   Letter from Graham Wade in the records of the Department of Evangelism.

24   Margaret Rourke (nee Grieve), the aunt of the author's wife, was converted at this mission as well as others, including Rita Quintrell.

25   Article prepared by Rees for publication in the *Australian Church Record* of May 1948 "A Little Child Shall Lead Them".

John, aged 17.

THE CINDERELLA OF THE DIOCESE 1955-1966

From the ends of the earth

George Rees was succeeded as Diocesan Missioner by Bernard William James Gook. Like Rees, Bernard Gook was a true evangelist and an endlessly energetic enthusiast. Both men delighted in seizing any opportunity to speak for Jesus. Both had strong confidence in the power of the gospel of grace. Both were well used by God in His salvation work.

George Rees was a Tasmanian, but Bernard Gook was from the opposite end of the globe, the European Antipodes. He was born in England in 1919 at Norwich, Norfolk, and moved to London with his parents at the age of two.

Bernard's father was a publican, at one stage being the licensee of four public houses, as well as having other business interests. He had considerable wealth. He had built the family home at Watford but, as is commonly the case with a man who is preoccupied with his property, there was not much home life. As money was no object, the young Gook was sent to Berkhampstead, one of England's public schools. He did not make the most of the educational opportunities the school offered him. His natural preference was for sports. He also got into the wrong company. At the age of about sixteen, the school asked him to leave. Bernard's father, about to depart on a cruise with his wife, was furious. He told his son that if

65

Bernard Gook.

he hadn't found a job by the time they returned, he would not be welcome under their roof. Bernard Gook cycled around the city until he found a job as an office boy.

The year following the termination of his schooling was an eventful one. One day, as he was watching some tennis players in a local park, Bernard was approached by a man, Ray Bywaters, who was a parishioner of St Mary's Church, Watford, and who worked in the Crusader Bookshop opposite St Paul's Cathedral. This man had a great mission to the local youth. He had a model railway in his attic and invited the neighbourhood boys to his home to play with it. On Saturday he ran a Crusader class and taught them the Bible. He invited Bernard to his Crusader class. Bernard went. It was the first time in his life that he had come under any Christian influence.

The parish church of Watford was a thriving church. It held two evening services in order to accommodate all those wishing to attend. Many of the young parishioners were given training in evangelism and took the gospel to the streets of Watford. Later, when its vicar, Mr Earnshaw-Smith, was appointed to All Souls, Langham Place, they took the gospel to Oxford Street in London. Bernard helped to start the All Souls Sunday School.

Bernard Gook now experienced a time of great turmoil. He found himself being pulled powerfully in opposite directions. The attraction of the old life was very strong, but the new influence was proving stronger. One day, at the Crusader class, he gave his life to the Lord and started to attend the Watford parish church. His parents expressed their strongest anger and disapproval. Bernard's father had wanted his son to follow in his footsteps as a publican.

At about this time, Bernard's father told his son that, as he owned a fish and chip shop at Twickenham that was temporarily without a manager, he could work there and learn that trade. Bernard did so for a short period. He sold fish and chips during the week but, on Sundays, he used the shop to run a Sunday School. He then worked for two years at John Dickinson's Printing Works. At this time, he also began his public evangelism. On one occasion his father had heard that he was going to be speaking at an open air meeting in Watford. He vowed to stop him. His threat proved hollow. In the end, all he did was to walk past in silence.

Bernard Gook was coming more and more to realise that he did not want to spend the rest of his life in an office or as a publican but desired rather to undertake some form of full-time Christian service. His first thoughts were to join the Church Army. Again, his parents expressed their violent opposition. His mother would bang on his bedroom door if she thought he was praying. She would often seize his Bible and throw it out. Despite his parents' animosity, Bernard approached the Church Army and began a period of weekend training. A great friend of Bernard's, Douglas

Clark, who had been converted with him at Watford, had gone to Oakhill College to study. He asked Bernard why he shouldn't consider Oakhill, too. Bernard Gook was very reluctant. He said that he had left school at sixteen without having matriculated and that it would be too hard. Clark continued to press him. After much struggle and self-searching, Bernard eventually approached a dubious principal of Oakhill College, Prebendary Hinde, and was accepted as a student for matriculation. Bernard's father relented in his opposition to his son's ambitions and agreed to pay the first year's fees. Before that year was out, Bernard's father was discovered to have cancer and had died.

Following his father's death, Bernard's mother was forced to sell the house at Watford and to move into one of the two remaining public houses, the businesses of which she had inherited from her husband. They took up residence at the Surrey at the Elephant and Castle intersection in East London.

An activist rather than an academic, Bernard Gook battled on. His motivation was his overwhelming desire to be an evangelist. After two difficult years, he matriculated and was able, at last, to begin his study of theology.

Bernard's inspiration at Oakhill was the Reverend Alan Stibbs. During the five years that Bernard spent at college, Stibbs gave him a thorough grounding in the Scriptures as well as great personal encouragement.

After Bernard had studied for two years, the War broke out. Bernard applied to join the army. On the morning he was due to leave, the Principal called him in and said he had just received a telegram from the Houses of Parliament to say that students at theological colleges were not required to undertake war service. Bernard was disappointed at this news. He saw it, nevertheless, as God's way of guiding him to finish his training and he stayed at college. He became an ambulance driver instead. He studied during the day and at night he was engaged in rescue work, freeing people from the rubble of buildings destroyed in the blitz.

The other ambulance drivers with whom he worked were toughened, older men, past the age when they could consider active service. They resented their twenty-year-old colleague whose capacity to serve his country was something denied to them. During the blitz, while Bernard was taking refuge with them at nights in an air raid shelter, he would regularly kneel in prayer beside his bunk. The other men threw things at him as he prayed. They took up a petition asking to have him dismissed. Bernard bravely asked permission to address them. His request was granted. He told them that they were mistaken in believing him to be a conscientious objector (he sensed that was the source of their hostility) and that he was a theological student. It was an opportunity to proclaim the gospel. From that moment, the attitude of the men began to change and Bernard Gook became a counsellor and mentor to them. He shirked none of his share of responsibility or any of the dangers of the blitz. Together, he and the other men experienced some terrible disasters.

During the blitz, the Surrey at the Elephant and Castle suffered a direct hit. Bernard's mother had escaped to the safety of the air raid shelter in her nightdress, but all their personal possessions were destroyed. Because of the bombing, they were forced to move to Croydon to the remaining public house she conducted.

Bernard's mother ran the public house and her son tried to help her as much as he could during his holidays. Croydon was where the identical twin sisters, Joyce and Joan Clapham, lived. Mr Clapham invited Bernard and his mother to join the Clapham family for Christmas dinner in their home. On Christmas Day 1942, Bernard and Joyce Clapham met for the first time. Later, they would marry.

Bernard Gook remained at Oakhill and finally completed his General Ordination Exam in 1943 at the age of twenty-four. He was ordained as a deacon that year and as a priest the following year. He obtained an appointment in West London as curate of St Luke's, West Kilburn, in the Diocese of London from 1943–45 and afterwards as curate of the Cheadle parish church from 1945–48. From 1948–50, he was the Secretary of the Young Churchman's Movement (the junior branch of the Church Society) and honorary curate of St John the Baptist, Beckenham. Bernard Gook's work with the Young Churchman's Movement took him all over England to conduct teaching and evangelistic missions. He also participated in a number of Inter-Varsity Fellowship missions with Howard Guinness. In 1950, Bernard was appointed vicar of a parish in the east end of London, St Luke's, Walthamstow, in the Diocese of Chelmsford. His bishop was the Bishop of Barking, Hugh Gough.

The diversity of Bernard Gook's background, education and experiences had given him the ability to relate to people of all descriptions, although he seemed to have a particular rapport with working-class people. It was to be a valuable preparation for his ministry as an evangelist.

While Bernard was at Walthamstow, Archbishop Mowll wrote to L F E Wilkinson, the new Principal of Oakhill College, asking him if he knew of anyone who might accept appointment as Diocesan Missioner in his diocese. Wilkinson thought of Bernard because of his work with the Young Churchman's Movement and passed his name on to Mowll. Mowll in turn wrote to Bernard and asked him if he would consider the position. Bernard was eager to accept. He had been at St Luke's for five years, he was keen to be an evangelist but, in that role, there was uncertainty as to where his future lay. With now a wife and four young daughters, it would be quite an undertaking. Bernard and Joyce talked and prayed earnestly about the prospect. They also sought more information from Archbishop Mowll but found him, in the busyness of episcopal life, to be an uncertain correspondent. They turned to an old friend, Eric Pitt, then the Dean of Sydney. Bernard had conducted missions for Pitt when Pitt was the vicar of St Matthew's, Rugby. The Gooks went to Australia House and generally tried to find as much information about Australia as they could.

Joyce Gook did not want to be separated from her twin sister, Joan, with whom she was very close. Their parents were now both dead and there were no other family members. Joan Clapham was single and working as a teacher. She applied to the New South Wales Education Department for a teaching position. Bernard wrote to Howard Mowll and accepted the appointment. For a long time, they heard nothing. Another English clergyman, David Harris, was in a similar position. He was so anxious for news from the Archbishop that he sent him a telegram with the text "Like cold water to a thirsty soul, so is good news from a far country!" (Proverbs 25:25).

Arrival in the New World

We had a very difficult voyage with four young children because they put us on H Deck which was below the water line. When we arrived at Pyrmont, we were met by members of the Board of Diocesan Missions—the last Diocesan Missioner, George Rees, the Secretary and a few others. All we had to do when we docked at Pyrmont was to walk up to the house! We knew what sort of area Pyrmont was because we had got a book of photographs of Australia with all the beautiful bays and beaches and bush and harbour and there was just one photograph which was industrial—power station, sugar refinery and the boats—and underneath it said "Pyrmont". We all sat down and laughed at that stage. We've never been able to get out of the inner city.

We walked up to the house at Pyrmont and unfortunately, because of the mix-up (as to who would be appointed to succeed George Rees), nobody had prepared for us. Some local people came and had afternoon tea. Of course, they wanted a rector but they weren't exactly going to get one.

At night, as we didn't have any furniture because there was a dock strike, we finally put the children to sleep on the floor of the dining room. The next morning when we woke up, they were covered with flea bites. The house was absolutely filthy because the poor last man, who must have been eighty-odd, lived alone in the house for twenty years and at that time the fallout was tremendous. There was the power station, the sugar refinery, the railway yards and the boats. The dirt was indescribable. We couldn't even see the windows in one of the rooms for the cobwebs, it was so dirty. Some young Board of Diocesan Missions supporters had started to decorate and they'd done one room beneath the picture rail and above the picture rail was dirt an inch thick. But Geoff Fletcher who was on the Board at the time, when he heard about the fleas, he arrived with a huge tin of flea spray and sprayed everywhere. The family still call him the flea man. My sister and I started to scrub.

Bernard said he would go out and get a radio and communicate with this strange land we knew so little about. We just could not believe our ears when the first tune it played was "Count your blessings name them one by one". This amazed us as there were so few Christian radio stations in England. I said there must be a message here. We must count our blessings. The Lord had provided us with a lovely big house and we just had to scrub it.

Two weeks later, the Archbishop asked Bernard how his wife was enjoying Australia. He said, "Well to tell you the truth, she hasn't got out of the front door yet, she's still scrubbing". The next morning, a firm of cleaners sent by the Archbishop arrived on the doorstep. Archbishop Mowll was very kind and took a great personal interest in the family from that time onwards.

We were very happy there, although it was very dirty. We'd put the baby out in the pram and when we picked him up, you could see where he had been lying!

Joyce Gook

Bernard Gook's widow.

Eventually word came that the Archbishop had appointed Bernard Gook the rector of Pyrmont. Bernard was concerned. He thought he was being asked to do two jobs and that he could not function effectively in a parish if he were to be continually absent conducting missions. However, Mowll's reason for the appointment was simply to provide the new Diocesan Missioner and his family with adequately-sized accommodation. The Gooks had indicated that the BDM's two-bedroom house at Merrylands would be inadequate for three adults and four children. The Pyrmont rectory had recently become vacant. The Archbishop added that Pyrmont had only a few families and he undertook to provide assistance to run the Sunday services. It was an undertaking that was to have an interesting outcome.

Bernard and Joyce Gook and Joyce's sister, Joan, came to Australia as permanent residents under the immigration scheme for £10 each, arriving on 2 October 1955.

While Mowll was negotiating with Bernard Gook, the members of the BDM, in total ignorance of the Archbishop's initiatives, were negotiating with another clergyman, Walter Spencer. Their negotiations were well advanced. They were dismayed when they were informed of Bernard Gook's appointment by the Archbishop. It was understandable that the appointment of an unknown Englishman was, at first, less than wholeheartedly received.

Unlike most previous missioners, Bernard Gook did not commence his ministry with a formal commissioning. Although he was a complete outsider, he was soon booked up. In fact, being an outsider was no disadvantage. At that time, Australians generally felt that people from overseas had a greater answer. Bernard Gook was different from those who had done their training at Moore College. His voice was a fresh voice. He was an interesting speaker. His illustrations were always well chosen, lively and arresting and often about people whose lives had been touched in one way or another by the gospel. He was warm and folksy. He got on well with people of all kinds, students, workers, the wealthy. Unlike many Anglican ministers, he had a very good rapport with those among the less well educated. After his English experiences, Bernard thoroughly enjoyed working in what was a predominantly evangelical diocese.

Evangelism within the Diocese was still done principally by means of the week- or two-week-long parish missions that had been so well established under Alan Begbie and George Rees. Bernard Gook slotted easily into this pattern of work. His style was different from that of Rees and he had different preferences. While Bernard aimed his work at the whole family, he sought to reach them, not mainly through the children as George Rees had done, but through the men.

Also, he did not care particularly for Rees' mission van. By now, it had come to be adorned with a remarkable collection of texts including one designed to condemn the vices of drunkenness and extol the virtues of temperance—"Where there's a swill there's a sway". The old van which was fast approaching the end of its useful life was replaced with a VW micro bus. The new vehicle was used to transport people to and from missions and to collect people to take to meetings during mission times. It was invariably carrying literature for distribution at meetings. Bernard always had a book stall as well as a collection of Bible study notes, tracts and similar material to be given away.

A mission would normally run for eight days straight, but sometimes longer, starting on a Saturday night with a formal service for which the clergy would robe and at which the Missioner would be commissioned for the mission, usually by the Archdeacon or some other appropriately significant church dignitary. The Missioner preached at all Sunday services the next day. Meetings would then follow each night of the week in the church. At these meetings, there would be a time of singing (as lively and as up-to-date as Gook could persuade the parish to accept), perhaps a testimony or a book review and then the Missioner would speak. Bernard's common topics were "Sin" on Monday, "Repentance" on Tuesday, "The Death of Christ" on Wednesday, "Faith" on Thursday and "Commitment" on Friday. The talks were all based on a story from the Bible and Bernard had his favourite themes. He liked to stress that we cannot buy our way into the Kingdom of God. Some favourite stories were Naaman the leper (2 Kings 5) and Simon the Pharisee (Luke 7:36–50). Bernard Gook invariably gave his personal testimony on the Friday evening. Each night an appeal would be made for people to come forward to accept the Lord. Those who responded completed a card and were given the booklet "Beginning with Christ". On Saturday there might be a film, such as a Billy Graham film. The Missioner would then speak at another round of services on the final Sunday. On that Sunday, emphasis was given to encouraging the new believers to take the next step. It was strongly recommended that they join a Bible study group and look to contribute in some way to the ongoing life of the church. These follow up meetings were generally called "What next?"

Bernard often called his missions "Key missions". He placed great emphasis on the need for careful preparation. He had designed three leaflets to advertise a mission and these were delivered at least to all the nominal Anglican families but, if there were enough workers involved in the preparation, to every house in the parish. The first leaflet was delivered six weeks, the second four weeks and the third two weeks before the mission.

Many of Bernard's missions drew large attendances. This seemed particularly to be the case in country areas. A ten-day mission at Nowra in May 1958 with Ray Bomford called "Operation Friendship" was attended by 5,500 adults and 1,500 children. Attendances at individual meetings ranged from 125 to 450. About sixty people were brought to Christ. Another ten-day mission in Lismore in March 1959 also called "Operation Friendship" was an outstanding success. Bernard Gook said "From almost every point of view the Lismore Mission was the most successful individual Parish Mission

A Prayer for the Missioner and his Helpers.

Bless, Good Lord, Thy Servant, BERNARD GOOK, strengthen and inspire him in connection with the Operation Friendship which he is about to conduct within the Parish; provide him with prayerful, earnest and willing helpers in his task; and incline the godly and the ungodly, the faithful and the wayward, to hear him. Help his helpers to make ready the way for the Mission, so that the seed may be sown upon good and well-prepared ground, and bring forth fruit for the extension of Thy Kingdom, and to the Honour and Glory of Thy Name, through Our Lord, Jesus Christ. Amen

A prayer for the Missioner.

71

I have ever been privileged to run".[1] It had received wide prayer support and had been preceded by excellent innovative publicity. There were never less than 500 people at any of the meetings, often 700–800, and on the final night there was an overflow congregation in St Andrew's Church of 1,100. The total attendance was just on 13,000. 210 people came forward and received a copy of "Beginning with Christ". Bernard concluded that "Country centres are certainly eager to tackle Evangelism on a big scale".[2]

There were also missions other than parish missions. Howard Guinness had left England in 1949 to become the rector of St Barnabas', Broadway. Bernard Gook joined him in several missions conducted at the University of Sydney during the 1950s although Bernard expressed disappointment at the lack of any vision of the Evangelical Union for evangelism at the University at that time. He found that, while the students were very interested in attending "deep and earnest Bible studies", their desire to engage in evangelism was another matter.

After a mission, Bernard spoke at whatever individual meetings could be fitted in until the following Saturday when the next round of missioning would begin.

An important innovation of Bernard Gook's was the involvement of Moore College students in his missions. The idea came from his English experiences with Howard Guinness where he had seen the value of including students in this work. The first mission in which students participated was in May 1956 at St Stephen's, Willoughby, when the rector was Archdeacon R B Robinson and his curate was John Turner.

In May 1957 there was a totally new initiative. The whole of the College went to the South Coast for a mission in May. Not only the students, but all the College faculty as well as some of the younger clergy in the Diocese who showed an enthusiasm for evangelism, were involved. There were twelve missioners and thirteen teams of students. They covered the centres stretching from Waterfall in the north to Kiama in the south. John Turner commented:

> I can remember that week. Bernard Gook himself missioned at St Michael's, Wollongong; Marcus Loane, who was then the Principal of the College, at St Stephen's, Port Kembla; Broughton Knox, who was the Vice Principal, at St Mark's, West Wollongong; Reg Hanlon at Fairy Meadow; and I was at Austinmer and Thirroul. I think one young Donald Robinson was at Figtree which in those days was called West Kembla.
>
> The Moore College mission on the South Coast that year was such a success that it was repeated again in 1958 further down the coast but, this time, we had only three missions and we didn't involve the College faculty as far as I can remember. We divided the College into three teams. Bernard Gook himself led a team at Nowra, Ray Wheeler at Huskisson in the southern part of the parish, and I led a team in Bomaderry in the northern part of the parish. Both those missions, the '57 in Wollongong and the '58 in Nowra, really set the tone for the involvement of College students in practical evangelism.[3]

THE CINDERELLA OF THE DIOCESE: 1955-1966

Through the Willoughby mission, Bernard Gook and John Turner formed a strong friendship. Turner became the godfather to Bernard's and Joyce's only son, Roger, born in October 1956. Bernard also asked John Turner if he would be his colleague in the BDM. John Turner welcomed the idea but the Archbishop, because of the shortage of clergy, would not agree.

Bernard Gook at Wollongong.
John Turner and John were both present.

The great missions of George Rees and Bernard Gook during the 1950s and particularly the involvement of the Moore College students in some of these missions meant that many of the newly ordained clergy had acquired a vision for evangelism. It was a factor that contributed to the momentous Billy Graham Crusade in 1959. Indeed, as the time for the Billy Graham Crusade approached, there seemed to be an increasingly widespread openness to the claim of Christ.

> Looking back upon the Missions and efforts of the past three years, I do know that we have made more progress during the past twelve months than at any other time. We have seen a larger number of definite decisions for Christ, and better personal contact has been maintained with a good number of these folk. Larger numbers have attended throughout the whole ten days (of a Mission), and an increased percentage have asked for our News letter and begun to pray for the work.[4]

Invitations for missions were constant. While they came predominantly from within the Diocese of Sydney, they came also from places outside the Diocese, such as Adelaide and Ceduna in South Australia, Wagga Wagga, Tweed Heads and Lismore in country New South Wales, Brisbane and Melbourne. The members of the BDM clearly preferred their Missioner to direct his attention and energies to the area within which he was employed to work. They were not particularly supportive of initiatives directed to a wider mission field. An uneasy difference existed about the rightful place of work outside the Sydney Diocese. This was an issue that would not be resolved until some years after John Chapman had joined its staff.

In June 1956, Bernard, with his typically expansive vision and having the fresh perception of a newcomer, wrote a lengthy and impassioned letter to Archbishop Mowll setting out a rough blueprint for a comprehensive diocesan plan for improving evangelism.[5] Some of the points he included were:

- parishes should be elevated to a status of permanent mission
- lack of adequate training led to a lack of manpower
- too many younger Christians in fellowship groups lacked real commitment
- the standard of preaching needed to be raised
- quality youth camps should be conducted.

73

He proposed a meeting for wide-ranging discussion between representatives of the BDM, the Youth Department, the Board of Education and other diocesan groups. Impatient for change, he introduced some reforms of his own.

Bernard Gook's years as a parish clergyman had given him an understanding of the hopes and disappointments, the pressures and isolation of the parish clergy for whom he worked. He saw their loneliness and lack of fellowship. He saw the size of their workloads—Ray Bomford in Nowra with fourteen different centres to maintain, Bryce Wilson in the burgeoning parish of Yagoona. He also sought to raise the level of parish evangelism and to make it a regular part of parish work. Together with Basil Williams, the rector of St Alban's, Five Dock, he began to organise regular gatherings of clergy at Gilbulla at which they could come together and discuss evangelism and other matters of mutual concern. The conferences were held two-monthly on Mondays, the "clergy day off". Over the years from 1956 to 1958, thirteen conferences were held. A number of clergy would come and bring their wives. Sometimes thirty people came, sometimes fifty, sometimes as many as ninety. Usually there would be a speaker for the men and a separate speaker for the women. Invariably, there was the opportunity simply to talk to one another about matters of mutual concern.

Throughout the second half of the 1950s, the BDM's financial support continued to be uncertain. There were times of bare adequacy, times of reasonable comfort and times of want. Bernard continued the practice of holding quarterly rallies of the BDM's supporters in the Chapter House at which the boxes of donors were opened. He was able to increase the number of boxholders.

By April 1957, the BDM had purchased its first tape recorder. By August of that year, Bernard was able to report "...it may thrill you to know that at the present moment our financial position as a Board is the best it has ever been for years with all bills paid and a very substantial balance in hand".6 By October, "The balance in the bank continues to be maintained and has encouraged the Board to go ahead with requesting the Archbishop to appoint an assistant to me to help cover the large number of requests for missions in the forthcoming year".7 By February 1958, however, the situation was that "there now seems little chance of any permanent help from an ordained assistant this year".8

In March 1958, the Board agreed to purchase a house at 51 Ashley Street, Chatswood, a few doors from the home of the Board's Honorary Treasurer, Ron Bailey. Bernard and his family took up residence on 21 May 1958.

On 1 August 1958, the BDM received its first significant diocesan grant. £400 was provided from the income of the Glebe Administration Board for one year towards the stipend of the Missioner. A further £500 was promised for the stipend of an assistant if one were to be appointed. The grant was to be reviewed when the year was up. It came by way of replacement for the stipend Bernard had received as rector of Pyrmont, a position he had relinquished when he moved to Chatswood.

By September 1958, the financial circumstances of the Board had deteriorated alarmingly. It had defaulted on the repayment of a personal loan of £300 used in the purchase of the Chatswood home and it had other outstanding accounts estimated to be about £250. After audit, the deficit was found to be closer to £1,000. Bernard wrote to the Board's supporters in his News letter of 12 September 1958:

> I can assure you that the situation is really urgent—it is only through a cheque in today's post that salaries and stipend can be met this month, and we thank God for this provision at the right time.

Family movements

After three years, Bernard approached the Board and said he thought perhaps the time had come that the Board might buy a house for the Missioner somewhere else. Pyrmont was in an isolated position for me with no transport, five children and no church fellowship. My sister had married John Brook who, for the previous year had been the senior student at Moore College. He had several times taken Keith Gowan's place as catechist. We couldn't understand why John had been so keen to come and take services with so few people!
John became the curate at Holy Trinity, Adelaide. When, Archbishop Mowll visited Adelaide, he asked Joan if she were missing her sister. She said she was. Several days later, I received an air ticket for Adelaide. The Archbishop was always concerned for clergy families.

Joyce Gook.

The BDM made immediate application to the Standing Committee of Synod for £250 of the Assistant Missioner's provision. It submitted that, because of the Missioner's commitment to the forthcoming Billy Graham Crusade, involvement in parish missions would be suspended, there would therefore not be work of a kind appropriate for an Assistant Missioner and there would be no income from parishes to meet the Missioner's stipend. In the event, the whole of the Assistant Missioner's provision was made available and an immediate loan of £300 was also arranged to enable repayment of the personal loan.

Evangelism on a shoestring

I remember the Board didn't even have a workable typewriter in the office and the facilities were very poor. They had no headquarters. In fact, when we went to Chatswood, there was a little shed out in the back garden which we made into an office and at that stage Bernard had some secretarial help. So the office for the Board of Diocesan Missions was in a shed out in the back garden in Ashley Street.
I remember that after the St Ives mission, there was a lady called Nan Arndell who, with her sister, had come into a real faith through the mission. Nan wanted to come and help in the office. She came along but, at some stage during the morning, she put her head inside the house and decided she was much more needed in the house than in the office! For someone with six children and no relations, she was a godsend. She became a great friend and confidante.

Joyce Gook.

In 1954, before leaving England for Australia, Bernard had witnessed the Billy Graham Crusade at Harringay. It made a deep impression on him. His great zeal for evangelism made him eager to see vast numbers of men and women swept rapidly into the Kingdom. He was often frustrated to be working with people who were "fairly enthusiastic but inexperienced"[9] and who did not share his breadth of vision and sense of urgency. Crusade evangelism on a big scale and carried out by a team of highly professional specialists became a consuming hope for his own public evangelism. The prospect of a Billy Graham Crusade in Sydney heightened his hope. He longed to establish the kind of team that comprised an advertising manager, an administrative organiser and other key personnel. With such support, the evangelist would be set free to prepare fully and to stay fresh.

> Billy Graham could not possibly succeed in the way that he does without all the preparation and follow-up which is done by the full-time group of experts on his team. For our missions to succeed (and I mean this in the sense of reaching large numbers and seeing definite conversions to Christ, and new members in the church) we too must have an adequate team. I feel so strongly about this at the present time that I am wondering whether I ought to organise Parish Missions on the scale so far planned after the Billy Graham Crusade in May. Maybe we ought to have less actual missions, so that we can have bigger united efforts organised on a larger scale which will in turn attract far more the average non-Christians. At these bigger efforts we could have planned groups of counsellors, ushers and choir members, and maybe a permanent leader for the choir.[10]

From 1 December 1958 to 30 June 1959, Bernard was set apart to be the Church of England representative for the Diocese of Sydney with the Crusade team. Officially, he was Diocesan Representative and Liaison Officer with the Billy Graham Crusade Office. His responsibilities were to stimulate interest among Anglicans for the Crusade and, as a member of the follow-up team, to be responsible for seeing that all Church of England inquirers were shepherded into the fellowship of their home churches and were there welcomed and taught. In particular, a Bible study course was to be developed for the newly converted "to lay special emphasis on Confirmation and its importance; The Sacraments, their significance and importance; the history of the Church of England; and Church Membership, its privileges and responsibilities".[11]

The Standing Committee agreed to pay the BDM £1,000 for the period from 1 March to 31 August 1959 on the understanding that its Missioner would devote himself exclusively to the Billy Graham work during this period. Bernard Gook did so. He worked with great dedication and great enthusiasm.

> I spent the majority of the time during the four weeks of the Crusade in the Follow-up Office where the decision cards were processed. On most nights I also co-operated with the Counsellors as an Adviser, and so had the joy of meeting many enquirers for myself. The number of enquirers associated with the Anglican Church reached a figure of round about 25,000.[12]

A few days prior to the Billy Graham Crusade in Sydney, Bernard had been in the Diocese of Armidale. He visited Narrabri, Warialda and Moree. He wrote of his meetings:

> The response was obviously very much smaller in the little town of Warialda, but at Narrabri we had nearly 600 people present and at Moree about the same number. After the showing of the film "Souls in Conflict" I gave an address, and at the end we had thirty-one respond at Moree and fifty-one at Narrabri. The local Clergy and ministers were thrilled at this excellent response and the outcome of the Moree visit is an invitation to run a big combined mission there, during the first week of August... It is good to know that two or three of our enthusiastic BDM supporters, including the Rev. John Chapman, are preparing for this Mission.[13]

Bernard Gook was not to participate in the Moree mission. His newsletter of 26 May 1959 contained a final dramatic entry under the heading "STOP PRESS":

> Just as this letter was ready for posting, negotiations ended between myself and the Billy Graham Organisation with regard to the position of Director of the "Hour of Decision" office here in Caltex House, Sydney. I have accepted the offer of this position, as it will give me the wider scope I have been seeking for some time now. A tremendous number of letters is received at the office each week—just 6,000 last week—indicating the blessing of the programme to thousands. There is a lot of personal counselling to be done by correspondence, but I have also the privilege of passing on the genuine enquiries and seekers to local counsellors in the district where the person lives.
>
> I shall also be introducing "Hour of Decision" Rallies by the showing of Billy Graham films, and there will be freedom for me to run my own Missions anywhere in the country, under my own name. This means that 'though I have resigned from the post of Diocesan Missioner in the Diocese of Sydney I shall still be able to run parish missions in the Diocese, subject to the Archbishop's approval.

Bernard Gook's resignation took effect from 13 July 1959. Archbishop Gough immediately wrote to Bernard advising him:

> I shall, of course, be very happy to give you a licence authorising you to officiate throughout the Diocese, and I shall be glad for you to carry out your preaching commitments already made, except in the case of definite missions. The Board of Missions feels that it would be better actually for you not to continue to take missions in the Diocese, but to leave this work for your successor.[14]

Some rather pointed correspondence then passed between the BDM and its former employee. The members of the Board believed that Bernard's successor would find it difficult to establish himself as Diocesan Missioner while missions arranged through the BDM were carried out by his immediate predecessor and while the income derived from these missions was redirected to the "Hour of Decision" funds.

Bernard's plans for his own missions with the Billy Graham organisation did not materialise. The local denominational churches were quick to point out that that organisation existed to supplement and reinforce their work. They did not wish to see a separate and parallel work undertaken that could be an incursion into their established role. In the end, the job for which Bernard had held such hope was reduced to one of routine administration. Office work held not the slightest appeal for him. He had a warm love for people. From the end of 1959, he accepted appointment as the rector of St Barnabas', Broadway, and Archbishop's chaplain to the University of Sydney. He ministered there for eight years before moving to St John's, Darlinghurst, where he served for another sixteen years. Bernard Gook died on 16 November 1993.

After Billy Graham—consolidation through teaching

On 1 September 1959, David Milroy Hewetson was appointed Acting Diocesan Missioner. Born on 28 July 1929, David had attended Trinity Grammar School where he was converted. For two years before his appointment to the BDM, he had been the acting rector of Holy Trinity, Miller's Point. The Church Missionary Society had seconded him to the Church Mission to the Jews and assigned him to work in Ethiopia. He was having difficulty in getting a visa. It took two years for the visa to be granted and by that time David had decided against Ethiopia. The delay was propitious. The Lord had other work for him to do. As Alan Begbie, the chairman of the BDM, explained in a letter to its friends:

...His Grace the Archbishop (Hugh Gough) requested the Board to give consideration to the nomination of a successor to Mr Gook who would hold the post for six months, giving His Grace time to look into the whole matter of evangelistic work, a work in which he has had so vital an interest in England, and time to think of a permanent successor to tackle the job within the Diocese.

...Mr Hewetson has a special ministry in teaching, and it is felt that for this period, immediately following the Graham Crusade, there are many parishes that need just that kind of specialised ministry for their people, and particularly those who came into blessing as a result of the Crusade.[15]

David was commissioned at St Philip's, Church Hill, on 28 September 1959. He took up residence at Ashley Street.

David Hewetson saw his role clearly:

May our prayer be for the following months, Paul's desire for the Ephesian Church (Ephesians 1:18) that the eyes of new converts and old may be enlightened by God's Spirit to know how great is the hope of their calling. Their need is not to be led into new and ecstatic experiences, but rather to learn to more-deeply appreciate the experience which has already become theirs by opening their lives to Christ.[16]

57,000 people had gone forward in response to Billy Graham's call in Sydney. Before, and particularly during the Crusade, the Diocese had been saturated with evangelism. Nurture and consolidation were now the priorities.

The six months of David Hewetson's appointment were extended to fifteen months. In that period, he conducted teaching missions on practical aspects of the Christian life in thirty-five parishes from one end of the Diocese of Sydney to the other, sometimes visiting a parish more than once. He also spoke at houseparties, Sunday deputations and other occasional meetings.

A teaching mission usually ran for five consecutive days, beginning or ending on a Sunday. The same group attended each night. David says:

> What we did was sing a few hymns. I gave an address. In fact, I gave a series of addresses. I simply taught the basics of victorious Christian living, or at least, some of the basics of victorious Christian living, and we had a very good response as a result of that. I always did a question/answering session and I simply walked up and down and gave out pieces of paper and a pencil and took questions and then answered them from the floor. And we always sold books.[17]

St Thomas', Kingsgrove

I personally benefited greatly from David Hewetson's ministry in that one of the churches that had the largest number of referrals from the 1959 Billy Graham Crusade was St Thomas', Kingsgrove. Ray Weir was the rector at the time and David Hewetson conducted a teaching ministry there a few months after Billy Graham that really had the most remarkable effect on the lives of many people. Ray Weir moved to Manly a few months after that and Dudley Foord came to Kingsgrove. And you can see why, with the teaching ability of Dudley, it was to become one of the strongest parishes in the Diocese in the next five years. It was my privilege to follow Dudley and to see much of the fruit of what had happened at the '59 Crusade and the teaching mission of David Hewetson which so many people referred to constantly as being such a significant thing in the early days of their Christian life.

The late John Turner.

As the Board's involvement in the Billy Graham Crusade had formally ended, the Board was now cut off from diocesan funding and responsible for raising its own income again. At the end of 1960, its bank account had a healthy credit.

David Hewetson relinquished his position with the BDM on 1 December 1960 just after his marriage to Ann Caiger and prior to their preparation for an overseas appointment with CMS. They departed for Tanganyika (soon to be reconstituted with Zanzibar as Tanzania) in January 1961. David's ministry with the BDM had been a short but significant one.

Moving closer to the centre

Archbishop Mowll had been keen for evangelism. While not personally involved in the BDM, he was strongly supportive of its missioners and its members. He trusted them and delegated an area of his concern for evangelism to them. After Hugh Gough, Mowll's successor, had established himself and had turned his mind

Geoff Fletcher, as General Secretary of CMS NSW, tied the knot in St Stephen's, Willoughby, at Ann and David Hewetson's wedding on 19 November 1960.

to the future of evangelistic work, he invited A W Goodwin Hudson, the vicar of All Saints', Woodford Green in Essex, to become the third co-adjutor bishop of the Diocese and the Director of Evangelism. It was through Goodwin Hudson that the new Archbishop would focus his concern for this area of ministry. In the process, the BDM's status underwent a subtle shift. For the moment, it had a leader with access to the Archbishop, financed by the Diocese and with a presence in Church House at the centre of diocesan administration.

The Board and its partners welcomed Goodwin Hudson as Director of Evangelism and chairman of the Board at a public meeting in the Chapter House on 15 June 1960. He continued as its chairman until his resignation and return to England four years later on 30 July 1964.

Arthur W Goodwin Hudson.

Goodwin Hudson had had some success in England in media evangelism. On his arrival in Sydney, he was keen to gain access to television. Because of the quota requirements concerning religious broadcasting, he was successful in presenting a regular epilogue at the conclusion of an evening's telecast.

The new Director was not to be the Missioner although he did conduct occasional missions. The Board sought another evangelist. The BDM had a few names on its shortlist. Among them were those of Geoffrey Fletcher, then the General Secretary of the New South Wales Branch of the Church Missionary Society and a member of the BDM, and a Victorian clergyman, Walter Spencer.

Geoff Fletcher, when approached, did not rule out the possibility of his appointment at a future date. He felt he should serve some time in a parish first as he had been out of parish work for ten years. He was geared in his thinking to missionary administration, recruitment and funding. He wanted an opportunity to experiment in a parish with ideas to reach those outside the church and to evangelise the nominal church member.

At the time of George Rees' resignation, the BDM had been negotiating with Walter Spencer, while Archbishop Mowll had been pursuing Bernard Gook. The BDM was still keen to obtain Wal Spencer's services if it could. Again, the BDM sounded him out. Wally Spencer was then the vicar of St George's, Bentleigh, in the Diocese of Melbourne. He replied that he could not consider the appointment for at least twelve months. He felt it would not be fair to leave his parishioners at

Bentleigh after just three years. The BDM accepted that and obtained his agreement to an appointment from 1 March 1962.

Canon Rudolph F Dillon was appointed Acting Diocesan Missioner for the period from 1 March 1961 to 28 February 1962. A commissioning service was held for him in St Andrew's Cathedral on 8 May 1961. If Rudolph Dillon was the short-term compromise, it was a good compromise. He was a senior clergyman, an examining chaplain to the Archbishop and an army padre. He had a wealth of pastoral experience. He was a powerful preacher, a renowned evangelist and an able teacher. He was a man of drive and initiative. Before joining the BDM, he had been sought after by many parishes to conduct evangelistic missions and teaching missions for "the deepening of the spiritual life".

Rudolph Dillon, 1960.

In announcing the appointment, Goodwin Hudson expressed the BDM's view concerning the true place of evangelism:

> We have all too often been sidetracked into placing secondary works in the place of the primary obligation of proclaiming by every means the Gospel of Jesus Christ. Every Christian a Proclaimer should be the emphasis of the Church in every generation. I am hoping to design a new approach to Missions with Mr Dillon, using a military term, "Missions in Depth"—a scheme to involve the whole Church Membership, before a mission is attempted. However small that known membership may be, there should be a total involvement for only those who are convinced they should take this Holy task in hand. Nevertheless, we must encourage everyone to regard the winning of others for Christ as the Priority Job.[18]

The Board reverted to its traditional staple, parish missions. They continued to be the principal means of reaching the lost. As before, a mission began with the Missioner's formal commissioning in the sponsoring church and usually ran from Sunday to Sunday. A more concerted effort was now made to engage the whole parish in the enterprise and to prepare more thoroughly. A thank offering to defray the BDM's expenses was taken up at the final meeting.

> Mr Dillon's first task as Diocesan Missioner was to compile four comprehensive handbooks designed to implement our Diocesan ideal of "Mission in Depth", to deepen and stimulate the Christian commitment of Church members and "Mission in Breadth", to reach those outside the Church with the Evangel of our Lord Jesus Christ. These handbooks were titled "Evangelism in Depth" which was a manual of Preparation for a Mission, covering every aspect of Mission Preparation and Scheduling; a Counsellor Training Course, "Methods of the Master"; a "Home Fellowship Course" for nurturing and strengthening new converts; and a Training Course for "Lay Evangelism".[19]

The handbooks were quickly prepared and became the standard manuals for the conduct of parish missions over the next five years.

Evangelistic missions were now supplemented with Teaching missions. Rudolph Dillon was soon fully booked. In his Missioner's Report for November 1961, he observed, "One overall comment on these missions is the noticeable effect of the 'Mission in Depth' preparation. This systematic preparation by BDM is beginning to take effect and in itself is conducive to our desired aim of getting parishes started in the principle of 'Continuous Evangelism'."

In 1961, the Board was caught up in another Sydney-wide crusade. Leighton Ford and Joseph Blinco spoke at "Crusade '61" at the Sports Ground in November. 97,000 people attended, with over 2,800 making responses. Of these, 58% professed a Church of England affiliation. Many who responded showed the strong appeal of Leighton Ford's message for teenagers, the group with whom he most sought to communicate. For the Diocese of Sydney, after a steady groundswell, the last three years had been years of exceptional reaping.

During Lent 1962, under the title "A New Thrust in Evangelism", each rural deanery held a weekend conference to improve the evangelistic thrust of their churches. Goodwin Hudson conducted these conferences.

Rudolph Dillon passed from the employment of the BDM to become the first Director of the Church of England Chaplaincies of the Home Mission Society. In 1967, he became the BDM's chairman for a brief period.

The end of the first era...

Rudolph Dillon's successor, Walter Spencer, was born on 10 November 1919. At the time of his appointment as Diocesan Missioner he was forty-two

Walter Spencer.

years old. While he was not Sydney-born or Sydney-trained, he had several connections with the Sydney Diocese. He had come to Marcus Loane's notice while serving as the organising secretary for the Church Missionary Society in Western Australia from 1955–1958. The two men had formed an acquaintance over those years. Wally Spencer had a longer and closer association with George Rees. Their friendship stemmed from the time when they were neighbours in Melbourne, sharing a back fence. George had been Wally's scout leader in the St Paul's Fairfield 1st Scout Troop. Wal had also attended some young people's camps in which George was actively involved. It was following a camp taken by George that the fourteen-year-old Wally Spencer decided to give his life to the Lord. George had spoken on the story of blind Bartimaeus. He had drawn on the verse, "Master, let me receive my sight" (Mark 10:51). On the way home, George asked Wal if he was a Christian. Wal had said "Yes" but in his heart he knew it was not the truth. That night, he knelt by his bed and prayed Bartimaeus' words.

After his conversion, Walter Spencer became actively engaged in the life of his parish and in the ministry of the League of Youth. He worked as a fitter and turner until the age of twenty-five before studying at Ridley College in Melbourne as a candidate for the Diocese of Gippsland. He was ordained deacon in 1948 and priest in 1949. He then served in the parishes of Foster and Mirboo North. He completed a ThSchol in 1953 and served for a short time as Director of Religious Education in the Diocese of Gippsland. He was an examining chaplain to its bishop. Then followed his service with the Church Missionary Society in Western Australia and after that his four years as vicar of St George's, Bentleigh.

Following his appointment as Diocesan Missioner on 1 March 1962, Walter Spencer was commissioned at a service in St Andrew's Cathedral on 12 March 1962.

Rudolph Dillon had his own accommodation in Hurstville and did not occupy the BDM's residence at Ashley Street, Chatswood. During 1961, the Chatswood property was sold. In preparation for Walter Spencer's arrival, the Missioner's accommodation was upgraded. A new residence was purchased for £7,500 at 13 Alpha Road, East Willoughby. It was partly financed by a bank loan of £4,200. The Missioner continued to work from an office of sorts at his home.

The Board's secretarial assistance since Bernard Gook's time had been provided, sometimes voluntarily, sometimes for remuneration, by a series of capable and dedicated women. For the most part, the standard of service was commendable, but a sudden crisis when important letters were not sent out before the events to which they related, and when records of the names and addresses of the Board's supporters were temporarily lost, heightened the need for fully professional assistance.

In commenting in its annual report in March 1962 on its increased financial commitments, the Board stated, "It is clear that greater Diocesan financial support must come if the Board is to continue unhindered in its commission to evangelise". By September, the BDM was facing the prospect of increasing its deficit by £65 a month. Walter Spencer, "with some timidity" was deputed by the Board to inform the Synod that year that "Under the circumstances, the only thing left open to us, is to come back to the mother who begat us, this Synod, and state our needs, and look hopefully for a generous expression of mother love".[20] Following Synod, £900 per annum was voted to the BDM from the income of the Glebe Board. Despite this grant, the BDM ended its financial year £400 in debt. By 1964, after further lobbying in Synod, the BDM was placed among the diocesan organisations receiving annual grants from the taxes, called assessments, raised from parishes.

Cinderella redressed

The BDM has been described as the "Cinderella of Diocesan organisations". I think that this title is not altogether inapt. You will remember that, beneath the rags and tatters, Cinderella was a beautiful girl. While members of the BDM are not girls, nor could they lay claim to physical beauty, yet there is that inherent in our charter to which beauty is ascribed by God, who "looks on the heart". "How beautiful are the feet of them that preach the Gospel of Peace, and bring glad tidings of good things" (Romans 10:15).

We do not suggest that other Diocesan organizations are ugly sisters, or that they have big feet; but we do look upon Synod as the fairy godmother who will introduce us to "Prince Charming". Prince Charming, of course, is none other than the Standing Committee of the Diocese. We know that it will not be love at first sight, because there have been other introductions. But we do trust that this introduction will lead to a happy marriage, which will bring forth a nice fat cheque, which, in turn, will remove the embarrassments which exist today.

Walter Spencer

speaking in the 1962 Synod to motion 38/62 requesting the Standing Committee to consider the special financial needs of the BDM.

On his arrival, Walter Spencer inherited some of the appointments that had been made through Rudolph Dillon but there was a brief lull in new engagements until the news of Walter's arrival had spread. He preserved the now well-established pattern of parish missions of from seven to ten days' duration. A few months before a mission, he generally held a "Meet the Missioner" service in order to introduce himself to the parish and urge them into action. A month or so after a mission, he returned for a "Mission Echo" service. Missions continued to be conducted at the rate of about twenty each year. At a mission, the evangelist continued to urge unbelievers "to ask Jesus into your heart". Revelation 3:20 was a popular authority.

Over the next two years, the Board's programme of development for increased evangelistic outreach basically involved the further elaboration and refinement of what had been its core ministry for the previous thirty years. The mission handbook had grown to be a sophisticated manual. It outlined courses in the theology and practice of evangelism for parish members. There were diaries for prayer and forms of prayers. There were suggestions for home visitation and ideas for publicity. There were preferred musical items for the choir. There were programmes for counsellor training and follow-up. The lists grew longer and longer. No point was too small.

In October 1963, in an article for the Australian Church Record, Walter Spencer reported:

During the nineteen months since he arrived, Mr Spencer has conducted twenty-six missions at which he has preached to over 27,000 people. Something like 550 Inquirers have been counselled, of whom about 400 have registered first decisions for Jesus Christ.[21]

The screening of Christian films that was such an important adjunct to Bernard Gook's ministry continued under Walter Spencer. In September 1964, eighteen months after the Missioner had first requested it and when the appeal of this medium had probably begun to wane, the BDM purchased a 16mm sound projector.

As had been the practice with previous missioners, Walter supplemented missions with a wide variety of individual engagements—guest services, youth fellowship teas and various forms of teaching.

Board of Diocesan Missions

(Sydney)

"Entrusted with the Gospel , so we preach " (1 Thess. 2:4, R.S.V.)

DIOCESAN MISSIONER
Rev. W. Spencer Th.Schol.
13 Alpha Road,
WILLOUGHBY.
Phone 95 4984

BDM letterhead.

Walter Spencer's appointment had been for two years with the option for an extension for a further year by mutual agreement. The option was taken up resulting in his appointment continuing until the end of February 1965. At the beginning of 1965, the Board was actively considering a successor. There were two forthcoming events that particularly engaged its attention. Firstly, a World Congress on Evangelism was to be held in Berlin in October and November 1966. It aimed to gather together leaders in evangelism from all over the world. The Anglican Church in the Diocese of Sydney might expect to be invited to send two or three delegates. Secondly, Billy Graham had been invited to conduct a second Sydney Crusade in April 1968. It was reasonable to assume that the BDM's Missioner would be fully involved in some capacity with the organisation of the Crusade and its aftermath as Bernard Gook had been in 1959. The members of the Board were keen to see the appointment of Geoffrey Fletcher. In March 1965, it resolved not to reappoint Walter as Diocesan Missioner when his term expired in February 1966. It left his actual finishing date flexible, recognising that it would depend on Walter's ability to obtain a parish appointment. The Board's decision was publicly announced. However, shortly after the decision was taken, it appeared the Archbishop would not agree to Geoff Fletcher's immediate appointment for the reason that he had completed only one year as rector of the parish of Northbridge. Agreement was eventually reached in November 1965 for Geoff to begin after the following Easter. In the interim, the Board requested Wal Spencer to continue. Geoff Fletcher eventually commenced as Diocesan Missioner on 1 May 1966.

Walter Spencer completed his duties with the BDM on 26 May 1966. He was inducted as the rector of St Stephen's, Mittagong the following day. He spent six years at Mittagong and later served as a prison chaplain at Long Bay and, for ten years, was the rector of St Saviour's, Punchbowl. Walter Spencer died on 13 December 1992 at the age of seventy-three.

CHAPTER FOUR

By the mid-1960s, the first era in the history of the BDM was completed. The forty-three years from 1927–1966 had produced a foundational legacy of faithful gospel preaching. Prayer support had been organised. Recognition had been won that the BDM was a legitimate diocesan organisation worthy of annual financial investment. A house had been acquired for the Missioner. All this had been achieved within a single generation through the successive ministries and the encouraging support of some exceptional evangelists whose lives were lived at the heart of God's sovereign work. A new era awaited.

---

1   Bernard Gook's News letter dated 26 May 1959.
2   Bernard Gook's News letter dated 26 May 1959.
3   Interview with Matthew Pickering.
4   BDM Newsletter dated 31 December 1958.
5   Letter dated 15 June 1956, a copy of which is in the records of the Department of Evangelism.
6   BDM Newsletter August, 1957.
7   BDM Newsletter October, 1957.
8   BDM Newsletter February, 1958.
9   Letter to supporters dated 31 December 1958.
10 Letter to supporters dated 31 December 1958.
11 Letter from W Ostling, Hon. Secretary, BDM, to Bishop Kerle, Bishop Coadjutor of Sydney, dated 11 December 1958.
12 News letter dated 26 May 1959.
13 News letter dated 26 May 1959.
14 Letter from Hugh Gough to Bernard Gook written in early July 1959 and quoted in Bernard Gook's letter to W Ostling, Hon. Secretary, BDM, dated 14 July 1959.
15 "A Letter to All the Friends of the Board of Diocesan Missions from its Chairman" dated 31 August 1959.
16 BDM Newsletter dated 17 September 1959.
17 Interview with Matthew Pickering.
18 BDM Prayer letter dated 24 April 1961.
19 Annual Report to Synod of the Board of Diocesan Missions for the year ended 31 March 1962.
20 Walter Spencer's speech to the 1966 Synod, a copy of which is in the records of the Department of Evangelism.
21 *Australian Church Record*, 11 October 1963, p 2.

John, 1969.

RETURN TO SYDNEY

...and the dawn of the next

From the mid-1960s, demand for parish missions began to wane. Attendances at them fluctuated but generally were smaller. It became increasingly difficult to bring the unchurched to church. The number of those making commitments at parish missions dwindled correspondingly. With increasing frequency, the majority of those who accepted Jesus Christ at these events were under the age of twenty-five years; commonly they were teenagers. While there was a growing perception that the traditional methods of evangelising were starting to lose their appeal, particularly for adults, the old ways were maintained. Evangelism was becoming defensive. The BDM's Missioner had, for example, written in August 1965, "...it seems to me some consistent, new approach needs to be found to counteract the demoralising, enslaving influence of the licensed clubs".[1] There was a need for new ideas and fresh thinking.

Geoffrey Mitchell Fletcher was to occupy the position of Diocesan Missioner from 1 May 1966 to 1 July 1969, a period of just over three years. A thinker, innovator and strategist, he would, during that period, cause the place and practice of evangelism in the Diocese of Sydney to be radically altered. These three years would be as dynamic and formative as any in the brief history of the BDM. The stunted diocesan offspring would undergo a wholesale transformation. With rare vision, enormous flexibility and with no model of any kind from which to work, Geoff Fletcher, together with the BDM's incoming chairman, Dudley Foord, established a new foundation for its work. Geoff was also instrumental in recruiting to the service of the BDM a man who was to be the outstanding leader in evangelism in the Diocese for the next quarter of a century.

Geoff Fletcher.

During the Second World War, Geoff Fletcher served with the AIF Artillery and the RAAF as a pilot and flying instructor. After the War, he entered Moore College intending to train as a missionary pilot. He graduated and was ordained deacon in 1947 and priest in 1948. His wife's health prevented him from going overseas. He had served in the parishes of St Andrew's, Summer Hill, St Barnabas', Broadway, and Kingsgrove with North Bexley before becoming the General Secretary for New South Wales of the Church Missionary Society. He served CMS for ten years in that capacity. While with CMS, he went on a world tour of missionary work in Malaya, Pakistan, India, Kenya, Tanganyika, Uganda and the Middle East. He also visited England, Canada, America and New Zealand. Before his appointment as Diocesan Missioner, he had been the rector of St Mark's, Northbridge for two years. He had been a member of the BDM from 1951 to 1963.

Geoff Fletcher was appointed on an annual stipend of $2,910 plus a monthly travelling allowance of $72.50. These were the same rates Walter Spencer had received and were those applicable to chaplains employed by the Home Mission Society. The Board's Alpha Road property was sold for $15,750 and another property purchased at 9 David Avenue, North Ryde for $14,400.

At Northbridge, Geoff Fletcher developed a number of initiatives that became useful during his term as Diocesan Missioner. Geoff recalls:

I divided the parish into twenty areas and appointed a host for each area. He was, wherever possible, a nominal church member, preferably known to neighbours, secretary of the golf club, or identified locally apart from church. He was given a list of the Anglicans of his area and asked to invite them to his home on a given night for an informal meeting with the rector. No extra chairs were to be provided. Many sat on the floor, including myself.

The evening started with a five-minute talk leading to questions and discussion. No attempt was made to evangelise during the evening but, at supper, I made a personal lunch appointment with every man in the room. This led to all kinds of lunch experiences, some at a city club or a restaurant or a cut lunch, with the proviso that no phone interruptions were acceptable. Once I was in my car with a painter who was working on a school building. This was where "one-to-one" evangelism took place. Whatever the outcome, the name was added to a list of invitees to a Saturday morning breakfast at Coles in Pitt Street about every quarter. The manager of Coles was originally one of the lunch appointments.

This idea was carried over into early "missions" and led to a series of house meetings rather than the regular parish mission series of church meetings.[2]

As another Northbridge initiative:

I conducted a door-to-door survey and personal evangelism effort. This was fruitful but frustrating, so little time was available in the midst of all the other demands of a parish and the man of the house was not easily contacted this way. This was when a spate of books was emphasising the role of the laity and I realised the importance of lay training.[3]

From the beginning of the 1960s very little evangelism, apart from parish missions, had been undertaken in the wider Anglican Church. Christians were losing meaningful contact with non-Christians. Evangelistic initiative was very much in the hands of the local clergyman. The average parishioner was not equipped to answer the questions his or her neighbours were asking and, consequently, was reticent to engage them in conversation about spiritual issues. Many parishioners were not always prepared to give an answer to a neighbour who might ask them "to give the reason for the hope that you have" (1 Peter 3:15).

After his arrival as Diocesan Missioner, Geoff Fletcher conducted a few missions in the old style.

Normally when a new missioner was appointed, many of the parishes which routinely held missions, having had one or two with the previous missioner and exhausted his repertoire, tried out the newcomer. It didn't take long to discover that missions meant a sign announcing the event which effectively warned the outsider (presumably your main target) that they're after you, steer clear! You could tell a parish that had endured a mission by the fact that the faithful were very tired! In some instances, I suggested house meetings, but these were usually arranged by the rector in the home of one of his trusted stalwarts and might as well have been held in the rectory or even in the Church itself.[4]

Several delegates of the Anglican Church in Sydney were invited to the World Congress on Evangelism in Berlin at the end of 1966. They included Dudley Foord, Bishop Jack Dain, also a member of the BDM, and Geoff. At Berlin, Dudley Foord and Geoff Fletcher found they were sharing the same hotel room. Very late one night, the two men discussed their vision for the future of the BDM. They canvassed various needs—a change of name from "Board of Diocesan Missions", moving the operational base from the suburbs, raising financial support and finding another worker. [5] During this conversation it was as if, in God's providential care, the glass slipper was at last placed on the foot of the Cinderella of the Diocese.

Cinderella—from the scullery to the castle

In accepting the Board's appointment as Missioner, I insisted on a few changes. I would not work, as my predecessor Wally Spencer had, from a shed in the backyard of his suburban home. Evangelism had been somewhat of a Cinderella in the Diocese despite the Diocese's reputation as a stronghold of evangelistic fervour. Even the name of the Board (Board of Diocesan Missions) was confusing, suggesting either that people sent you old clothes or posted you overseas. I requested the name be changed to "Department of Evangelism". I was told that wasn't possible as the diocesan grant, small as it was, was made to the Board of Diocesan Missions and nothing should be done to disturb this tradition lest we lose the grant. I suggested then that, for the time being, the Board set up the Department of Evangelism as I had in mind a wider approach to evangelism than the customary parish mission.

If evangelism was "top priority" for the church, then its Department should have the Archbishop's address and phone number. The old Church House (at that time between St Andrew's Cathedral and the Sydney Town Hall) was the original residence of the Dean and was strictly limited for the purposes of the largest Anglican Diocese in the world. However, a disused lavatory at the rear of the building was remodelled and was put to our convenience! In addition, we were connected to the Church House exchange and had the same number as the Archbishop both for address and phone. Psychologically this was significant, even though more comfortable and prestigious premises might have been found elsewhere.

Geoff Fletcher.

Through his reading and thinking on evangelism, Geoff was convinced that the newly styled "Department of Evangelism" should be involved in training the huge reservoir of lay potential rather than, or if necessary in addition to, the provision of a star evangelist performer. He was seeking lay evangelism methods that could be applied in a denominational church context and that would lead to a clear presentation of the gospel to the unconverted.

> If there is one emphasis more than another, easily discerned in the Spirit's message to the Church worldwide today, it is that of lay evangelism. Now, I know that is no new thing—it is as old as the New Testament Church when first the Holy Spirit was given, poured out upon **all** flesh so that every believer might truly be a priest and a prince. But God is rebuking today the concept of priesthood which has so limited outreach that a full theological course is regarded as an imperative prerequisite to the simple sharing of Christ—and this is not the view of clergy alone—it is the accepted emphasis of most of the laity who tend to use it as a refuge from the real responsibility of every Christian.[6]

Most of the literature on lay evangelism available in Australia at the time came from the USA. Australian Anglicans began to look to the USA, in addition to the United Kingdom, for ideas. The allocation for Geoff Fletcher's travel to the Berlin

Congress had been sufficiently generous to allow an itinerary across the USA. With careful planning, a visit to many evangelism centres was possible.

On his way to Berlin, Geoff conferred with the Director of Evangelism for the Missouri Synod of the Lutheran Church, Charles Mueller, author of the recently published "The Strategy of Evangelism". He called in on the Navigators at Colorado Springs. He visited the Dallas Diocese, the Southern Baptists and the Methodists at Nashville. He attended two conferences in England. The second of these, called together by a Latin American group, promoted a development called "Evangelism in Depth". It gave Geoff some useful ideas. In each place, however, the answers obtained were incomplete.

> The most fruitful contact was Campus Crusade at Arrowhead Springs, California. Initially a university campus ministry, concepts they had developed had been adapted by some very enterprising laymen to provide an Institute (or group teaching) programme for use in a church context. Although booked to return via Asia from Berlin, I rescheduled myself to return via California so I could attend their first Pastors' Institute for Evangelism. This was a very exciting week-long training programme attended by 400 clergy. It appeared quite adaptable to our church evangelism plans and included practical application in a visitation session. Having been sickened over years by seminars which theorised on possible ventures, it was a great adventure to be part of a training session which actually had you out doing it! I returned motivated and seething with plans and visions.

> Towards the end of 1966 when I returned from Berlin, I had a speaking engagement at the Mt Tamborine Convention in Queensland. On the way to the Convention I found not only was I sharing the transport with the other speaker but he had prepared to cover the same Scripture passages as myself. He being an ex-Bible College Principal, I had no desire to gather up the fragments that remained after he had covered the ground. I found myself somewhat anxiously wondering what God was doing to me. It was then I decided to follow the topic sequence used at Arrowhead Springs but with exposition of Scripture rather than the use of the topic. This was the birth of the Institute lectures which I used for about ten years.[7]

Lay Institutes For Evangelism trained people to evangelise with the aid of two small booklets "Have You Heard of the Four Spiritual Laws?" and "Have You Made the Wonderful Discovery of the Spirit Filled Life?" Large scale visitation programmes were organised at which the trained lay evangelist first sought to arouse a person's interest by taking a survey of the person's views on religion. From this, the evangelist endeavoured to share with the person the "Four Spiritual Laws". These were set out in a booklet, simple in its format and language, that ultimately allowed the person to pray a prayer committing his or her life to Christ.

Lay Institutes began in Australia with a houseparty at Katoomba over the Australia Day long weekend in January 1967. Geoff gathered a group of about sixty people, mainly CMS associates, at the CMS Conference Centre. "We had a training series, then went visiting. All were scared, all apprehensive, but none could believe how rewarding it became. One gentleman, a diplomatic service veteran, admitted to having witnessed meaningfully for the first time in his life." The next training session was held at Dundas over the following Anzac Day weekend.

Geoff Fletcher's involvement in the further development of the Lay Institutes ministry had to be laid aside for nine months between November 1967 and June 1968 because of the 1968 Billy Graham Crusade. The Crusade was held at the Sydney Showground over nine days in April 1968. During those nine months, Geoff was caught up in the preparation, progress and follow up for the Crusade in his capacity as chairman of the Follow-up Committee. Although not having the impact of the 1959 meetings, over 516,000 people attended the Crusade or heard Billy Graham's messages on landline. There were in excess of 24,000 inquirers, 74% of whom were under the age of nineteen years. 50% of inquirers expressed their denominational preference to be Anglican.

After the work of the Follow-up Committee was completed, Lay Institutes were resumed. They were held at regular intervals in central and outer Sydney, in Melbourne and other capital cities.[8] In preparation for them, Geoff ordered about $8,000 worth of materials to be printed, the greatest single item of expenditure in the history of the BDM to that time and well beyond its ordinary capacity to repay. It was novel for participants in a training course to be expected to purchase their own materials. The Lay Institutes attracted eager crowds. Those held at St Andrew's Cathedral in Sydney and at St John's, Toorak, in Melbourne were attended by over 3,000 people. The costs incurred were recovered. But far more importantly, many ordinary Australian people made an initial planned attempt to evangelise in the supportive environment of a training programme. For some it began a life-style sharing of their faith that continued over subsequent years.

Geoff found that he was giving less and less attention to the home meeting evangelism that had been in his mind when he joined the BDM.

At the beginning of 1968, Geoff had given the Bible studies at the CMS Summer School at Burleigh Heads in southern Queensland. John Chapman was there. The two men talked about their work. They shared their frustrations concerning the ineffectiveness of traditional parish missions as well as the different ideas they were developing for reaching non-Christians by moving away from events centred on the church building. Geoff shared his vision for motivating and equipping the laity to engage in personal evangelism. John spoke of the way in which he was starting to develop home meetings evangelism. It was a significant conversation. John's ideas struck an immediate chord in Geoff Fletcher. The discussion between them would lead, very quickly, to an offer of employment being made to John by the BDM/ Department of Evangelism to bring his home meetings strategy, called dialogue evangelism, to the Diocese of Sydney.

DEPARTMENT OF EVANGELISM

1st FLOOR
91 BATHURST STREET
SYDNEY, N.S.W. 2000
TELEPHONE 61 3235

BDM/Department of Evangelism letterhead.

John's invitation and arrival

On Friday 22 March 1968, a meeting was held of the Executive of the BDM/Department of Evangelism. Those present were Dudley Foord, chairman, Bishop Jack Dain, Ron Bailey and Jack O'Connor. The minutes record that:

Bishop Dain proposed and it was unanimously resolved that we extend an invitation to the Rev. John Chapman of Armidale Diocese to join the staff of the Board.

For at least three years the appointment of a second missioner had been a strong hope of the Board. Throughout its forty-year history, it had only ever been able to support one missioner, if one could be found, but the opportunities for evangelistic work had not diminished. At the time at which the demands of parish missions had peaked, it had begun pressing its case in the Synod for additional funding. It had achieved a measure of success. Among its guidelines for possible future action the Board had listed "House meeting development as a way to the outsider". It had done so because of Geoff Fletcher's initial thoughts when accepting appointment as Diocesan Missioner. John's recent work in Armidale exactly answered this description. The Board wanted him to come to Sydney to be engaged predominantly in organising home meetings.

When John had first gone to the Diocese of Armidale, he had thought the whole of his working life would be spent there. It seemed that so much needed to be done in order to establish a lasting foundation for strong clear Biblical teaching on a wide front that it would take, not just the working life of one person, but of many. A return to Sydney had never been within his contemplation. A number of events conspired to cause him to change his mind.

On 17 July 1967, John's father died. Then, early in 1968, his mother had a slight stroke. She made a good recovery but her doctor thought that part of her worry was that she lived so far from her two sons, John's elder brother Jim having married and long since established his home in Canberra. John asked his mother if she would like to live with either of them but she emphatically declined the offer. John was and always had been very close to his mother. He was naturally concerned for her. It was following these events that the offer of employment with the BDM/ Department of Evangelism arrived. John says, "The thought of leaving Armidale had never crossed my mind until the offer arrived in the mail. I am

Mum and Aunt Vera.

sure that I would not have given it much thought except for Mum. When it came, it seemed like an answer to prayer."

The situation in Armidale had changed more rapidly and more deeply than John and his friends had ever anticipated. With Clive Kerle's remarkable election, what had seemed a lifetime's work did not seem to be that any more. The urgency had passed. The future was full of hope and possibility. John spoke to Clive Kerle about the offer and Clive Kerle warmly supported the view that John should take it up.

The offer had come from Marcus Loane, now Archbishop of Sydney, as the appointment lay within his hands. In his letter, the Archbishop had suggested that John should meet with him and discuss the offer before he decided whether or not to accept it. John, since his sole year at Moore College, had maintained his friendship with Marcus Loane. Whenever John was in Sydney he had called to see him. Marcus had been greatly interested in what was happening in Armidale and on every occasion had given John his strong encouragement. However, certain perceptions of John had been formed. "John," Geoff Fletcher says, "had developed a reputation as being somewhat radical as far as 'rocking the boat' was concerned. This excited both of us, the Archbishop and me, for very different reasons."[9] When John called to see the Archbishop in his office in the old Diocesan Church House alongside St Andrew's Cathedral, John happily anticipated there would be a continuation of their dialogue. He was not prepared for what transpired. "Marcus said," as John recalls, "in no uncertain terms, that he had enough troublemakers in the Diocese already without having to import them from other places!" In a state of shock, John went downstairs to the basement of the building where the BDM had its office to report what had happened to Geoff Fletcher. Geoff roared with laughter. "Don't you understand, Chappo," he said, "that you never get encouragement from bishops. Not from bishops or administrators or committees. They seldom encourage the free spirit of the evangelist. Do you or do you not want a big platform from which to preach the gospel? Forget about anything else." In fact, Marcus Loane, after John had accepted his invitation, gave John every encouragement throughout the remainder of his episcopacy and could hardly have been more supportive.

At its meeting in April 1968, the BDM resolved that:

a) Mr Fletcher be designated "Director" of the Board and any other full-time Missioner as "Missioner" and that both, by reason of their office, attend all Board meetings.

b) The "Missioner" is to be responsible to the Board, as is the Director.

c) The Director is to draw up a programme in consultation with the Missioner for presentation to the Board for approval.

Before this time, the BDM's staff had not attended Board meetings but had submitted a written report.

John commenced his duties with the BDM/Department of Evangelism as a Missioner on 1 October 1968. He was then thirty-eight years of age. His annual salary was $2,950, with a car allowance of $850 and an appropriate residence and superannuation provided. Initially, it was proposed that he would live in a rented home unit. Geoff Fletcher comments:

The Board was concerned that in their delicate state of wealth they couldn't afford to buy another house. I suggested that if they sold mine and bought a new unit for John they would avoid expensive maintenance and I would get a war service loan and they could pay me rent. They saw this as a great favour on my part and I fancied similarly until some years later as the real estate market took off I realised what a great favour the Lord had done me.[10]

The Department sold its David Street residence and purchased a new unit at 17 Cambridge Street, Penshurst, for $12,200. John was to live there for the next twenty-three years.

What do I do?

John has often recounted how, when he arrived at the Department of Evangelism, he asked Geoff Fletcher, "What is my job description?" "Evangelise Sydney" was the reply. "Is there anything more specific?" John asked. "If I have to tell you that I've got the wrong man," Geoff replied.

So John was back in Sydney. He returned with the same phenomenal energy and deep commitment to the cause of the gospel that he had shown since the time of his conversion and that he would continue to show throughout the next twenty-five and more years.

Director

John's diary quickly filled. By November 1968, he reported to the Board that he had spoken at many meetings since he took office and will commence a teaching mission at Wentworthville late November. This will take the form of home meetings where three Christian couples are asked to invite three non-Christian couples for discussions. Ten missions have been arranged for 1969. Dialogue evangelism had been placed squarely on the Board's agenda.

In the meantime, with the arrival of a colleague, Geoff Fletcher pursued the Lay Institutes ministry almost exclusively. The BDM now faced a hard decision. Lay Institutes was fast growing beyond the ability of the BDM to support it from its limited resources. Should it embrace this work or should it break with it and let it develop as it might? In the context of this major issue, some smaller issues were also raised. For example, a few within the Church expressed unease concerning the Lay Institutes' booklets. It was alleged they lacked the element of repentance. Some questioned the use of a survey to initiate conversation. Others objected to the "canned pitch" approach. There was also a degree of concern that the Lay Institutes ministry was too interdenominational and extended too frequently to places outside the Diocese of Sydney.

I was conducting Institutes for training laymen in most Australian States with several different denominations as well as having overseas commitments. Clearly something had to be done. So I approached the Archbishop with the concern that the baby had become a monster. Did he think I should kiss it goodbye or go with it? He suggested the programme may lose its momentum if I pulled out but the Diocese would not be able to fund me if I decided to operate separately. I reminded him that I had been a missionary society secretary for ten years assuring young people that if they were in God's programme He would underwrite their support and it looked like he was saying "Have a crack yourself, mate!"[11]

In December 1968, matters came to a head. The members of the Board at the time were the Reverends Dudley Foord (chairman), Owen Dykes, David Hewetson, Milton Myers, John Turner and Clive Steele, Bishop Jack Dain, Canon Alan Begbie and Messrs Eric Bird, Ron Bailey, Wilbur Gates, Frank Taylor, George Wilton, Laurie Wood and Jack O'Connor.[12]

At a meeting of the Board, Geoff sought leave of absence for six months to develop Lay Institutes For Evangelism. He proposed to take the leave over the course of the next calendar year as occasion called. He suggested his salary be halved. He proposed that the arrangement be reviewed after twelve months. Following discussion, the Board's meeting was adjourned for a week. At its resumption, it was moved that Geoff Fletcher resign as Director and undertake responsibility on a part time basis for lay training in evangelism in the Diocese of Sydney. "At the request of the Chairman, Mr Fletcher then left the meeting and a lengthy and lively discussion followed."[13] The motion eventually was carried. Geoff Fletcher tendered his resignation as Director that day. Because a number of training programmes in Sydney Anglican churches were planned for the first half of 1969, his resignation was dated to take effect from 1 July 1969. A difficult issue had been resolved without rancour or breach of fellowship. Lay Institutes For Evangelism became a separate body, later incorporated as LIFE Ministries, with Geoffrey Fletcher its National Director.

The subsequent development of a number of tracts and methodologies for use in personal evangelism in the Diocese of Sydney and their impact in the lives of many of its people can be traced to Geoff's introduction and energetic sponsoring of the "Four Spiritual Laws".

In his final report to the Board as Director, Geoff wrote:

While the development to Lay Institutes was far from my mind at the time of accepting the appointment, I am grateful to God for this development and the tremendous opportunity for ministry this has afforded.

He added prophetically:

...I have come to appreciate even more than previously the ministry of your new Director. I feel sure that the Board is looking forward to its most exciting days.

Later he commented:

I resigned from the Board confident in the thought that though John Chapman had once told me he wasn't an evangelist, I was handing over to the best Anglican evangelist I knew who, once he began putting a hook on his line, surprised himself and became a blessing to countless others.[14]

The Board recommended to the Archbishop that John be appointed as Diocesan Missioner and Director of the Department of Evangelism. The minutes of the Board meeting held on 11 March 1969 record that "a letter was received from the Archbishop duly appointing Mr Chapman to the position of Director of the Board and it is to be further noted that this appointment dates from 1 July 1969 for a period of two years. In this connection it was resolved that we arrange a Commissioning Service on Tuesday 8th July." The service was duly held in St Andrew's Cathedral at 5.30 pm on that day and Bishop Dain was the preacher.

At the same time, a week long crusade was being prepared at St Andrew's Cathedral to be conducted by Maurice Wood, Principal of Oakhill Theological College, London. Within the space of seven years, the movement in evangelism would be reversed as Sydney evangelists, led by John, began to conduct crusades in London.

Future directions

John, in his report to the Board in June 1969, put forward a suggested programme for 1970:

Stimulation for Evangelism

I believe that as well as the Board doing direct evangelism it should engage in stimulating others throughout the Diocese to engage in evangelism more.

This stimulation needs to be along two lines:

i)   **Techniques:** We need to show how the maximum evangelistic use can be made of the existing opportunities (particularly for clergy and in every day life for lay people) as well as the making of more opportunities.

ii) **Deepening of Christian Commitment**: No-one, whether a clergyman or a lay person, will engage in evangelism with any real zeal unless there is an increasing and deepening love for our Lord and for the lost. I do not believe we should assume that this is present among our people.

This simply expressed programme was in many ways the blueprint for the years to come. It embodied those elements that have always been at the centre of John's work. The gospel was the primary focus, always the gospel. As many people as possible, clergy and lay, were to be trained and stimulated to be its servants. Ways had to be found to do this. Those ways had then to be taught and applied. Opportunities were to be sought and each opportunity given was to be taken. Alongside this was the insistence on personal holiness. Personal holiness had to be comprehensive; it had to pervade the whole of the believer's life. There needed to be holiness in capacities and holiness in relationships. John would model all his work for the Christian family, his own holiness no less. It was a remarkable, ever-present quality embodied transparently in his life.

Call to prayer

John has been a friend for more than forty years and his influence has extended into many areas of our personal and family lives. Forty years is a long time and there are many stories, some highly amusing, that we could tell.

However, the episode that sticks firmest in the mind isn't funny, nor is it one where John did or said something in our presence. It was, rather, a hidden act which we only found out about afterwards.

Briefly, what happened was that he was to be our guest at a meal at Stanwell Tops. We had gone down the previous day to prepare the site. Tired after the effort, we had all gone down to the beach to refresh ourselves. Debbie, one of our twins, aged four, and as always, adventurous, had borrowed her elder sister's bathing cap and gone out into the lagoon. What we saw as Elisabeth practising breathing was, in reality, Debbie about to drown. She did.

After an initial searching, along beach and lagoon, and the enlisting of many to help, her limp body was trodden on and she was brought to shore, eyes wide, clinically dead it seemed. After mouth-to-mouth, and oxygen, a faint flush appeared on her cheek. She was rushed, unconscious, to hospital with the "drowning team". We held no hope at all for her recovery.

John was phoned, to be told the meal was off, and why. He said little. But, unknown to us, he phoned up every Christian whom he knew or thought would pray and asked them to do just that. A great reservoir of prayer must have erupted. And Debbie eventually came out of coma and revived, undamaged. Today, she is a godly young matron with children of her own.

The nexus between our prayers and our loving Father's activity is a closed book to our intellect, mine anyway. But when prayer is made, He acts. In a sense, we believe we owe our daughter's life to those prayers. Of all the things that John has done for us, it is in the calling of others to pray that we stand most in his debt.

Royle and Junee Hawkes
—a remembrance.

Bible studies

When Geoff Fletcher left the Department of Evangelism, John took over a weekly lunch hour Bible study that Geoff had conducted in the basement of Church House. It was attended by a small group of faithful folk. In 1969, John Reid was appointed Archdeacon of Cumberland and arrived to occupy an office in Church House. The new Archdeacon was keen to begin a Bible study ministry in the city. The two Johns met in June and discussed whether they should pool their energies into a united effort. They agreed to do so.

The first of the new lunch hour Bible studies was given in the Chapter House on 17 July 1969. Eventually, the meeting moved to the Lower Chapter House and, after the opening of St Andrew's House in 1977, to the Auditorium in that building. In due course, this Bible study gave rise to three other weekly Bible studies in the city and three in the suburbs. Groups were established at St James'

Hall in Phillip Street (later moving to the adjoining University of Sydney Law School) and at Scots Church at the corner of Margaret and York Streets. The ministry team at St Phillip's, Church Hill, under John Jones, picked up the concept and introduced a similar work. In the suburbs, there were Bible studies at Chatswood, Bankstown and North Sydney. The North Sydney meeting was later merged with the ministry of St Thomas', North Sydney, under the leadership of Simon Manchester.

The Bible studies, generally expository but occasionally directly evangelistic, gave a strong and clear focus in the heart of the Central Business District of Sydney to the critical importance to the health of the city and its people of listening to the Word of God as part of a regular pattern of behaviour. Their endurance over many years was made all the more remarkable by the fact that the two Johns and the others who took them did so in their "spare time". Many of the addresses given at these meetings were recorded and sold in sets as "Tapes that Start Talk".

Bible studies brochure.

John Reid says, "I never recall anything but cordial and effective co-operation in the years that followed. Over a period of time, we brought in others to assist us but John and I carried the load between us. I thought John was probably at his best as an expositor. He did it with accuracy, reverence and humour. He was never afraid to tackle difficult books."[15]

Go to the great city

Twenty-five years ago John Chapman and I took over the Bible Study group which Geoff Fletcher had run in a loose connection with the Department of Evangelism. Under John's leadership it grew until we averaged about a weekly attendance of 100 and we extended to Phillip Street and York Street. There were these three regular groups with about 200 a week. It was a good partnership. Quite a few clergy took six-week series and overall the standard was excellent. However, when John took the studies, the numbers inevitably increased. People responded to his carefully prepared material, with good exegesis and practical (and often humorous) application.

I always thought he made a major contribution to the life of the city by his leadership here. Of course he did other significant things but I was grateful for what he did in teaching the Bible in the City of Sydney.

John Reid

a former Chairman of the Board of the Department of Evangelism and a Board member
for over ten years.

The Prayerletters

George Rees had produced the first BDM prayerletters shortly after his appointment as Diocesan Missioner. They had been a valuable means of stimulating interest in his work and gathering support for it. Subsequent missioners had continued the practice. The prayerletters were almost invariably records of events past and summaries of events to come, often with a report of some notable act of grace or kindness on God's part. John's prayerletters also had those features but he added a new element. He prefaced each one with a short exposition of a passage of Scripture, generally in the classic three-point form, on a theme related to the gospel. They were sermonettes. John has written more than seventy of these over the years. Many people have found them of great value. Some clergy have preached them. John's first such message in the quarterly prayerletter after becoming Director (his second contribution to the prayerletter since joining the Department) is a typical example. It has not lost its relevance.

DOES IT REALLY MATTER?

From time to time I suppose you ask yourself the question about Evangelism—"Does it really matter?" It's hard work—it's exacting—you see little results for your labours—you wonder if it matters—if it *really* is worth the effort. In 2 Thess. 1:5–10 we are told of the starkness and reality of the return of our Lord and of the ensuing judgment. Three different aspects of this passage are worth noting.

1. **Basis of Judgment** v.8

The vengeance of God will be inflicted on "those who do not **know** God and upon those who do not obey the gospel of our Lord Jesus".

2. **Consequence of Judgment for the Unbeliever** v.9

What could be more terrifying—"to suffer the punishment of eternal destruction"—to lose everything that matters—to be cut off from every aspect of God's goodness and "to be separated from the presence of the Lord" in the great eternal loneliness. Hell is a reality. It does matter if men and women hear the gospel, because this gospel is the "power of God unto salvation to everyone who believes" (Rom. 1:16).

3. **Results of that Day for the Christian** v.10

Unlike the unbeliever the Christian man longs for the day when Christ returns and the delight of that moment is expressed here by the Apostle—"to be glorified in his saints and to be marvelled at in all who have believed".

Reflections

After being with the Board for just over a year, John wrote, "It has been a year full to overflowing with activities and opportunities to preach the gospel. To those of you who pray for me, let me say how much I appreciate this act of fellowship. The work has been varied and exciting—houseparties, dialogue missions, conferences."

The foundations of a significant ministry in a new setting had been quickly laid. Many of the distinctive elements that would continue and be developed in the years to follow had been set in place.

The first encounter

How could I forget it? It was one of the really big events of my life. My very first encounter with John. It happened at an Australia Day Convention at St Matthew's, Manly. It was in January, 1970.

There was something unusual happening in my life at that time. There was nothing funny about going to Manly on a public holiday, particularly in the middle of summer—but it seemed a waste to spend it in a church! (Actually, I had started going to church, but tentatively, and certainly not on public holidays and definitely not for the whole day.) What sort of fanatics were these "friends" from the office who had dragged me along?

If I remember rightly, the main speaker was a visiting Englishman, the author, Alan Redpath. He spoke in the morning. I'm afraid I can't remember his topic or even one word of what he said about it. Somehow, I don't think my friends were too worried. They had no doubt as to who they really wanted us to hear. Chappo spoke after lunch.

The afternoon was getting pretty warm and we'd been going a couple of hours. To tell you the truth though, I was transfixed. Chappo, that day, must have set an all-time-speed-speaking record—even for Chappo. I have never heard anyone speak so fast! For style, the nearest thing I can compare it with are those pianists who play Rachmaninov's "The Flight of the Bumblebee" and make it sound like a 45 rpm being played at 78. I'd swear John never took a breath. He wouldn't have had time. He did the whole of Romans 1–8 in about one minute flat. (The time shot by so fast, I'm sure it couldn't have been more than a minute. Well, not much more.)

I can remember every word he said. (Well, perhaps not *every* word, and I did go for the next few weeks to the Lower Chapter House where he repeated his talk over the slightly more reasonable period of six successive Fridays, and I have heard it a couple of times since then, and I have pinched every bit of it and taught it myself once or twice as well as used little bits of it here and there on other occasions.) The most wonderful thing was that I actually understood what he was saying. It was so clear. You couldn't have any doubts. It all made sense. And it made you feel as though you might be able to understand the Bible yourself if you were to read it. It was also at times very funny. Who could have guessed that anything to do with the Bible and that wasn't totally blasphemous could get a laugh? When you're under conviction, with your friends looking sideways at you, let me tell you that the chance to laugh can be a wonderful release from the tension.

It was about a week later that I made my first public profession of faith in Jesus.

Michael Orpwood
Board member from 1977 and Chairman from 1981–1991.

Chapter Five

1. Missioner's report to BDM meeting of 10 August 1965.
2. Interview with Matthew Pickering.
3. Interview with Matthew Pickering.
4. Interview with Matthew Pickering.
5. The name of the Board of Diocesan Missions was not formally changed to the Department of Evangelism until August 1978 with the passage of the Department of Evangelism Ordinance 1978 (No. 25 of 1978).
6. Geoff Fletcher's comments in the BDM/Department of Evangelism Prayerletter written while "in flight over Newfoundland" on 18 November 1966.
7. Interview with Matthew Pickering.
8. See, for example, the report of the Lay Institute held at St Alban's, Lindfield, in June 1967 in *Southern Cross*, August 1967, pp 5–7.
9. Interview with Matthew Pickering.
10. Interview with Matthew Pickering.
11. Interview with Matthew Pickering.
12. John Turner, Clive Steele, Ron Bailey, Laurie Wood and Jack O'Connor, in particular, gave long and faithful service as Board members through the ministries of a series of Diocesan Missioners. In each of the cases of Turner, Bailey and O'Connor, it was of not less than 30 years.
13. Minutes of BDM meeting held on 18 December 1968.
14. Interview with Matthew Pickering.
15. Letter from John Reid to the author dated 5 December 1994.

John, 1970s.

DIALOGUE EVANGELISM

Genesis

In 1956, the city of Melbourne hosted the Olympic Games. The staging of this event helped prompt the introduction of television into Australia, the first public broadcast being made from TCN–9 in Sydney on 16 September in that year. The television revolution was emphatic. Television was enthusiastically embraced throughout the whole of Australian society. Everyone seemed utterly entranced by the medium. It became a centrepiece of family life. It had a powerful impact on the lives of communities. It changed the way in which many things were done, including evangelism.

Week-long parish missions centred on the parish church had been conducted throughout the Armidale Diocese on traditional lines during Bishop Moyes' episcopacy and were continued during the early years of the episcopacy of his successor, Clive Kerle. With the advent of television, the previous patterns of society began to change markedly and it became increasingly difficult to sustain meetings every night at a church. As more and more households gained access to the television channels and were able to afford the cost of a TV receiver, more and more people became reluctant to leave the comfort of their homes in the evening to go out to competing events.

The parishioners of Wee Waa had worked hard in preparation for a mission to be conducted by John and the Bishop in their parish during 1965. Throughout the week of the mission, the church people attended the nightly meetings but, no matter how hard they tried, practically no-one else could be persuaded to come. The group who met on Wednesday night was identical with the group who had met on the previous Sunday morning. Traditional methods of evangelism were proving fruitless. Clive Kerle was determined to find another way.

Prior to its constitution in 1953, the University of New England had been a university college of the University of Sydney. In 1950, four Christians at the university college had, following the pattern of the older and more established Australian universities, formed the New England University College Evangelical Union.[1] Like other EUs, its members held a daily prayer meeting and a weekly Bible study. A Christian fellowship group had existed for a number of years at the Armidale Teachers' College and the EU combined with it for "public meetings whenever a suitable visiting speaker appeared"[2] as well as for houseparties and church services. In its fledgling years, it was natural that the EU should look to Sydney for support.

The New England University College Evangelical Union remained small and inward-looking for ten years until a mission by Dudley Foord in 1960. Then it found it could not cope with rugged converts like Ian Hore-Lacy. Twelve months later, Stan Skillicorn's week of witness blitzed the EU out of its complacency. By mid-1962, it had nearly trebled in size and half the new membership were new Christians.[3]

Both Dudley Foord and Stan Skillicorn had been at Moore College in John's sole year as a student there. John, naturally, was fully involved in each mission.

The centre of the picturesque campus of the University of New England straddles a small hill. In 1960, the University was largely residential with several of its colleges over a kilometre from the main teaching area. In planning the 1960 mission, it was seen that while evening meetings were highly desirable, most students would not bother to climb the hill at night to attend a Christian meeting. Some colleges had a tradition of gathering in a floor common room for a coffee break during the evening and this suggested the idea of holding two or three supper meetings each night. Much hard work was done by the organisers and supporters of the mission to cook appealing items to entice attendance. At these supper meetings the Christian faith was discussed in an informal way, following something of the seminar format that the students regularly experienced in their studies. The format worked well. The students appreciated the casualness and informality as well as the opportunity for conversational interchange.

Following the Wee Waa mission, Neville Collins, the vicar of Baradine, requested a mission be held in his parish. John told him that no more traditional missions would be conducted but that he was interested in trying a new experiment he had discussed with Kerle. "If we're not going to do any more of the old-style parish missions," John had said, "why not try something like the supper meetings we do at Uni?" John asked Neville Collins if he could find a few graziers with large lounge rooms in their homes who would be prepared to invite some of their friends in over a couple of evenings to meet the Bishop and to talk about Christianity. It was proposed that the Bishop and John would then engage in discussion about the fundamentals of the faith with those who had gathered in the same way as the university missioners had done with the students at the University of New England. Collins agreed.

They were all astounded by the response. People were happy to offer their homes. Their friends were glad to accept the invitations extended to them. The gatherings were natural and uninhibited. Conversation flowed. Perhaps another method of evangelism had been found that could help bring the gospel to unbelievers. They applied the approach in another parish, and then another. At times there would be between twenty-five and thirty people present, many of whom would not be churchgoers. A rough format emerged. Clive Kerle decided that they would keep talking on the first night until those present actually heard them say that all people were sinful. On the second night, they dealt with the remedy for sin, the death of Jesus Christ. They were so excited by the results of the early meetings that, by 1967, missions in the new style were being held all over the Diocese. The basis of the evangelistic strategy that would later be more fully shaped and would come to be known as "dialogue evangelism" had emerged.

Neville Collins says:

> There was a great warmth about the gatherings and a great willingness to discuss the issue and to raise some of the hindrances to becoming Christian. It became quite formational for me as I had struggled to find an appropriate model for reaching outsiders (or unclear insiders!). I discovered that the only previous model I had thought about, Maurice Wood's attempt in high rise London, was a little irrelevant in north-west New South Wales.[4]

John says, "I have never had an original idea in my life. But like most of us, I am a good revisionist. Dudley Foord really 'invented' dialogue evangelism. I just adapted it to meet a different situation." But there can be little doubt that John saw the potential of the method and its implementation and development in his hands was wonderfully inventive. Perhaps Dudley Foord, too, was a revisionist. Following a mission conducted by George Rees at St Mark's, Harbord, in September 1947, Rees had written in his monthly report:

> A "squash" held in a home on the Saturday night proved well worthwhile, and considering the success of such in previous Missions, I am seriously considering the possibility of more such evenings during a Mission and less services in the Church. I would covet your prayers with regard to such, because we have found them a better means of reaching the outsiders than the Church services.

Nothing further seems to have developed.

At the beginning of 1968, John attended the CMS Summer School at Burleigh Heads. It was there he discussed his work with Geoffrey Fletcher, the Diocesan Missioner from the BDM/Department of Evangelism in Sydney. Their discussion led to the offer of employment being made to John to bring dialogue evangelism to the Diocese of Sydney.

Importation into Sydney

When John joined the staff of the BDM/Department of Evangelism, he imagined his work would consist exclusively of doing dialogue meetings. He expected they would occupy each night of the week. He took to the work with a will.

Within a few weeks of his appointment, John had accepted an invitation to take a teaching mission at St Paul's, Wentworthville. While it retained some elements of the traditional parish mission, it provided his first opportunity to introduce some dialogue meetings as well. He suggested that, on the three week nights during the week of the mission when there was no public meeting, one Christian couple each night might invite three non-Christian couples to their home for discussion. The home meetings would commence with John giving a simple presentation of the gospel in not more than ten to fifteen minutes. The rest of the evening would be open for questions and discussion. With further refinement, the gospel presentation John developed for this purpose would later be published as part of a correspondence course on the Christian faith and later still as a separate tract.

When John reported to the Board in November 1968, ten missions had already been arranged for the following year. It was intended that these would develop the dialogue evangelism format a little further. On the first four nights of the week (Monday—Thursday) home meetings would be held for not more than about fifteen people in each home to allow ample opportunity for discussion. The people who went to these meetings would be encouraged to attend public meetings to be held in the church or parish hall on the following Friday, Saturday and Sunday. These would also be very simple in form, with time for questions at the end.

The late 1960s was the era when almost any event was described as a "Something-In". An American TV show, Dan Rowan's and Dick Martin's "Laugh-In", was widely popular. Demonstrators who occupied the premises of some organisation by way of protest staged a "Sit-In". John Lennon and Yoko Ono took to their bed to hold a "Love-In" for peace. The Board sought to keep abreast of popular culture. The home meetings were called "Talk-In on Christianity" and the public meetings "Teach-In on Christianity".

- Dissatisfied with your Christian experience?
- Want a better grip of Bible truths?

COME TO ST. PAUL'S

TEACHING CONVENTION

WITH REV. JOHN CHAPMAN

of Board of Diocesan Missions, formerly Director of Christian Education in the Diocese of Armidale, and a first-class Bible teacher.

NOVEMBER 20-24, 1968

THEME: "The Key to Happiness", from Letter to Philippians

- Wednesday, 7.45 p.m.: "The Gospel and the Man of God" (Phil. 1:1-30).
- Thursday, 10.30 a.m.: Ladies' Morning Tea — 6.30 p.m.: Men's Buffet Tea — 7.45 p.m.: "Greatness Through Humility" (Phil. 2:1-11).
- Friday, 7.45 p.m.: YOUTH NIGHT. "The Christians in the World" (2:12-29).
- Saturday, 7.45 p.m.: FAMILY NIGHT. "Knowing Christ in His Power" (3:1-11).
- Sunday, 8 a.m.: "Jesus the Lord" (Romans 10:9) — 11 a.m.: "What is Spiritual Maturity?" (Phil. 3:12-4:9) — 5 p.m.: YOUTH TEA. "The Christian and the Unbeliever" (Matt. 9:35-38) — 7.15 p.m.: "Giving and the Spread of the Gospel" (Phil. 4:10-23).

ST. PAUL'S CHURCH OF ENGLAND, PRITCHARD ST., WENTWORTHVILLE

Bushell Press — 648-2531

Brochure for St Paul's Wentworthville Teaching Convention.

John, as was natural for him, shared his experiences among his circle of friends. Some of them asked if they could try their hand at this new form of evangelism too and so, during 1969, John explained what he did to men like Ken Short, David Hewetson and John Reid. They quickly took up the work.

Through these early experiences, some basic principles for the new form of evangelism emerged. It utilised established friendships. The meetings took place in a friend's home. This would help those who felt shy about attending a church building. A strong emphasis was given to naturalness and informality. The approach adopted the casual Australian style of ready acceptance, friendliness and lack of pretension. Consequently, if the clergy took the role of dialogue leader, they were not to wear their clerical collars. Christians, apart from the leader, who might be present were not to have their Bibles with them. They were not to present themselves as specialists and hold the floor on all subjects. They were not to make their guests feel so different and so ignorant that they felt excluded from the discussion. An "outsider" led the meeting so that there might be an opportunity for frankness as well as privacy. Groups were small to allow maximum participation. There was time for prolonged conversation and time to correct wrong and misleading ideas of Christianity. As well as saying what the gospel was, it was necessary to say what the gospel was not. Hosts and hostesses had an opportunity to be further identified with the gospel among their friends and in their neighbourhoods.

Early experiences also showed that only about one-third of those who attended the home meetings attended the public meetings later in the week. To stem the leakage and as a form of follow-up, a correspondence course was offered. Prospectuses for these courses were available for distribution at the end of each meeting.

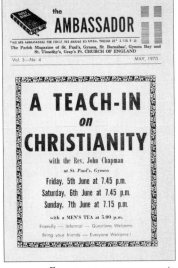

Front-page announcement in "The Ambassador".

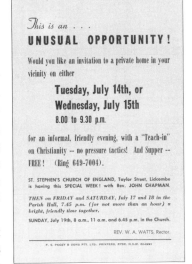

St Stephen's Lidcombe invitation.

The correspondence course had been developed by Alan Nichols (then the Director of the Anglican Information Office) through a body set up for the purpose called the Anglican Inquiry Centre. It had not been developed with dialogue evangelism in mind. For a number of years the Roman Catholic Church had been offering, with some success, a course explaining the Roman Catholic faith. It was decided that an Anglican course should be offered to match it. John was a member of the organising committee. After the committee had chosen the topics to be dealt with, they could not agree on which members should write the pamphlets for those topics. They had a draw from a hat. John drew No. 1—Man and His World—and No. 6—What is a Christian? When the series had been put together it was offered publicly. After a few months, a man came into the AIO office wanting 100 copies of No. 6. He was told that the pamphlets comprised a set and that the sets could not be broken. He was asked why he wanted them. "It's because I was converted when I read it," he said, "and I want to give a copy of it to all my friends". Alan Nichols made a quick and inspired decision. "We can't risk people dropping off and not getting to No. 6 in the series," he said. "Let's make it No. 1." Dialogue evangelism happily appropriated the course for its own purposes by offering it to everyone who had attended a dialogue meeting. As well, at the suggestion of Ken Short, "What is a Christian?" was separately published for use as a tract.

The scriptural truth that underlay dialogue evangelism was that "faith comes from hearing the message, and the message is heard through the word of Christ" (Romans 10:17)—that "there is only one method of evangelism, that is, the faithful explanation and application of the gospel".[5] Proclamation was a basic principle of evangelism that John was to stress again and again. In the first pamphlet he prepared to explain dialogue evangelism, John commented:

"Why," you ask, "should we be concerned about evangelism?" Simply stated, the answer to this question is:

a) I should be concerned because God is
    —John 3:16, Luke 19:41–44
b) I should be concerned because I should love my neighbour
    —Mark 12:31
c) I should be concerned because, as men and women come to know the grace of God, He is glorified
    —2 Cor. 4:15

In the last three months of 1969, missions were conducted at Gunnedah, Balgowlah, Canley Vale and Carlingford. At them, sixty home meetings, now called "dialogue meetings", were held and around 300 non-church members and 750 church members had been involved.

Towards the end of that year, John Reid suggested that, as the method was straightforward and easily taught, a special focus could be given to dialogue evangelism throughout the Diocese in the following year during Lent. He suggested to John that he train enough leaders to do ten meetings a week in every parish in the Diocese over that period. John estimated that it would need 300 leaders per night to have one meeting per parish per night—a total of 3,000 to do the whole task! John Reid's suggestion was not immediately pursued.

For 1970, twenty dialogue missions were planned. Prayer was asked that God would provide sufficient men and women to staff the proposed 400 dialogue meetings that would be held, based on the 1969 results. It was anticipated that 1,700 non-church members and 2,500 church members would be involved. In view of the workload, John and Geoff Fletcher recommended to the Board of the Department the appointment of another missioner. In a report to the Board dated

10 February 1970, Geoff Fletcher wrote:

In 1969, our Director, the Reverend John Chapman developed dialogue evangelism in this Diocese. Today he has twenty-nine trained assistants and is completely booked out until February 1971 and is receiving an embarrassing number of further invitations.

In order to meet the demand, John organised the first formal and systematic training for dialogue leaders. The course began at Moore College on Saturday, 21 March 1970. It ran over four Saturdays and each session had two components—training in apologetics and training in small group dynamics.

SATURDAY 21st MARCH
9.30 am—12.30 pm

Bible Study: Rev. D Cameron

Seminar: "Why Christians Believe in God"
—Dr D B Knox

Group Life: "Communication"
—Rev. J Chapman

SATURDAY 6th JUNE
9.30 am—12.30 pm

Bible Study: Rev. D Hewetson

Seminar: "Historicity and Canonicity of the New Testament"
—Rev. Canon D W B Robinson

Group Life: "Creative Use of Opposition"
—Rev. J Chapman

SATURDAY 18th APRIL
9.30 am—12.30 pm

Bible Study: Rev. K Short

Seminar: "The Nature of Evil"
—Rev. B Smith

Group Life: "Barriers to Communication"
—Rev. J Chapman

SATURDAY 18th JULY
9.30 am—12.30 pm

Bible Study: Ven. J Reid

Seminar: "Authority and Inspiration of the Bible"
—Rev. P Barnett

Group Life: "Setting Norms in Groups"
—Rev. J Chapman

Extensive experience gained from the many dialogue meetings subsequently conducted taught John that the same questions were asked at them again and again. How do you know that God exists? How do you know what God is like? Why do the "innocent" suffer? What happens to the person who has never heard of Jesus? Is the Bible accurate and reliable? Aren't all religions equally valid? Don't all good people go to heaven? Do I have to go to church to be a Christian? Isn't faith all psychological? Later dialogue leader training courses were modified to reflect this experience.

Within the first few months of 1970, fourteen parishes had requested missions for 1971. John reported, "We have more work than we can cope with. Please pray that God will raise up a man to help in this important work." Finding a man was one thing, paying for him was another. For another person to be employed, the Board's income would have to double. Providentially, at this time, gifts from individuals and from parishes increased significantly. The Department's income in fact doubled.

During the annual week of mission of Moore College and Deaconess House held at St Mary's during August 1970, eighteen dialogue meetings were held. In following years, dialogue evangelism came to be a regular part of College missions.

Other missions in other parts of the Diocese also came to include the dialogue evangelism format.

Expansion—"Christ Cares" 1971, 1972 and 1973

John Reid's ambitious hopes for the diocesan-wide application of dialogue evangelism remained undiminished. In June 1970, on his initiative, the Standing Committee of the Synod of the Diocese set up a small committee to promote a programme of outreach, to be called "Christ Cares", during Lent 1971. It was proposed to conduct some 580 dialogue meetings in fifty-eight parishes. The Department of Evangelism would be the mainstay of this Lenten programme. The plan was to hold almost 100 meetings a week for the six weeks of Lent. At least 150 dialogue leaders would be needed. Special courses to train them began later that year at Burwood East, North Ryde and Westmead. In the event, eighty-five of those who undertook the training indicated their willingness to help as dialogue leaders. The Department's staff also worked for just over a month with three sessions a week to prepare hosts and hostesses for their role in the work. Each participating parish was left to arrange its own weekend programme to conclude the mission week.

Christ Cares logo.

These widespread home-based missions were a significant evangelistic thrust. People were converted. The interest of many others was stirred. The understanding of a host of Christians was sharpened and their confidence in God's saving power was strengthened. By May 1971, at the completion of the series, 130 people had enrolled to do the correspondence course and in some places small groups, often based on the homes of the original hosts and hostesses, continued to meet to deepen their understanding, some of them transforming into regular Bible study groups. It was almost as if, during Lent 1971, a vast audit of the church had been carried out.

By February 1971, another staff worker had been found. Brian Telfer, a former school teacher, had been working for the previous two years in the Diocese of Armidale as an assistant to Peter Chiswell (now a Canon) at Gunnedah. Brian

The Telfers in 1971.
Jonathan, Brian, Kathryn, Judy, Susan. Martin was subsequently born on 20 September, 1974.

Telfer, while a student at Moore College, had worked on some Church of England Boys Society camps that John had conducted in his time in Armidale as Youth Director and subsequently Director of Christian Education. More recently he had come to John's notice through John's friendship with Peter Chiswell. Brian was to be largely responsible for the dialogue evangelism work of the Department so as to give John the opportunity to concentrate on teaching missions and attempts to stimulate evangelism among the working population of the city.

Brian Telfer was commissioned at a service conducted by Bishop Dain at St Thomas', Kingsgrove, on 23 February 1971 at which the Department's chairman, Dudley Foord, was the preacher. Brian was the last staff worker of the Department to have the commencement of his ministry marked in this way.

Because of the increase in demand for dialogue meetings, a new series of meetings to train dialogue leaders was planned for six weeks in June 1971. Two sessions were held each Thursday, one in the morning in the Lower Chapter House and the other in the evening at Moore College. Seventy men and women were trained at these and many subsequently became active in leading dialogue meetings in parishes and elsewhere.

John and Brian dialogue

The first half of the first session for training prospective dialogue leaders was used to teach us a simple gospel outline in non-technical language. Its essence was—Jesus is Lord through Calvary. John would first ask us to say what we thought a Christian believed and, as we waffled around with vague notions of God's love, he would suggest the blind alleys up which our waffle would lead us and, instead, would guide us in a surer approach. For homework, we had to practise our statement of the gospel so that we could tell it to the person sitting alongside us at the next meeting.

In following weeks, after doing our practice, the first half of the evening was used to outline a response we might offer to one of the handful of questions that came up again and again at dialogue meetings. Brian Telfer would usually take the role of the unbeliever and John the defender of the faith. The interchanges could be hilarious, Brian enjoying the opportunity to be particularly rude and forthright and John remaining brilliantly cool and incisive, enjoying the mental and verbal sparring. The second half consisted of advice on how to handle a small group, such as making eye contact, parking one question while dealing with another, hearing the question behind the question and so on. (I had seen John at work with a number of groups. He seemed so natural I had never suspected how thoughtfully and carefully he had worked at his technique.)

I was so excited and so stimulated by what I learned each night that I wanted to rush straight out into King Street and grab the first person walking by and say "Did you ever wonder why the innocent suffer?" (or whatever it was we had been dealing with). "Well, let me tell you this!"

Michael Orpwood

recalling dialogue leader training at Moore College at the evening meetings in the winter of 1971.

In 1971, an invitation was issued to John to dialogue with a group of men who worked in one of the large firms of solicitors that practised in the city. This led to the formation shortly afterwards of a second city Bible study (to complement the one that three years before had made its home in the Chapter House) as well as a small supporting prayer group.[6] This Bible study met in the Phillip Street area, either at St James' Hall or in one of the lecture theatres in the Sydney University Law School, over the next twenty years.

The initial "Christ Cares" programme was such a remarkable success that it was decided to repeat it again in 1972. By November 1971, the preparations were well in hand. A Bible study course entitled "Evangelism: What? Why? How?" comprising four separate studies was published for use in preparing parishes and other groups for their missions. The 1972 programme ran in forty-five parishes in the Diocese from mid-March to the beginning of May.

A family outing, 1976.
Left to right: Back row: Elsie Fletcher, Junee and Royle Hawkes, Muriel Chapman, Helen and Phillip Jensen. Front: Bronwyn and Deborah Hawkes, Matthew and Ruth Jensen and "Mardi" Law

Brian Telfer resigned from the Department in May 1972 to take up a position as Chaplain at The King's School. His vacancy was filled in February the following year by Phillip Jensen, then Assistant Minister at St Matthew's, Manly. Phillip Jensen was a graduate of the University of Sydney with an honours degree in geography. He had been converted, as had his wife Helen, at the 1959 Billy Graham Crusade, Phillip in Sydney and Helen through listening to the Crusade broadcasts on a landline at Broken Hill.

On St James' Day 1972, John Reid was consecrated a bishop. In the prayerletter for October 1972, John Chapman wrote:

> ...as I move around from place to place, I am greatly heartened, not only by the opportunities to preach the gospel, but by the number of people I am meeting whose first encounter with Christianity was through dialogue meetings and who have subsequently been converted. Bishop Reid told me that in his first Confirmation there was a man who had been converted in the "Christ Cares" campaign.

The "Christ Cares" campaign was repeated again in 1973. Phillip Jensen had the task of organising the meetings and allocating dialogue leaders for the homes of the participating hosts and hostesses.

In May 1973, John reported to the Board of the Department the results of a survey he had made of this work since he had joined the Department in October 1968.

> It is gratifying to me to see that we have missioned in this way in 155 parishes in our Diocese, which constitutes about one-third of the parishes. (Because there are still the other two-thirds, we ought not yet to look for "new fields" as if dialogue evangelism had "had" it, although it seems

essential that we should look for some way of consolidating the work begun in these.) In these 150 parishes, we have been in about 1,500 homes which constitutes an outreach to about 15,000 non-churchgoers.

Phillip Jensen had developed a publication that sought to answer the types of questions most commonly asked by people at dialogue meetings as well as setting out the substance of the gospel. For a university mission in mid-1973, some ilustrations in a cartoon-style format were added by Peter Oram. The publication and illustrations were combined in a booklet called "I Object". When released towards the end of 1973, the booklet had instant popular appeal.

The "Christ Cares" ministry was not continued in 1974. On further reflection it was felt that the technique, at least temporarily, had been worked out in those areas that were prepared to employ it. There was no need to train more leaders and those who had participated as hosts and hostesses found that they were unable to persuade their friends back to dialogue meetings after more than two or three occasions. In the following year, intensive dialogue evangelism gave way to a more broadly based programme of parish evangelism entitled "Encounter '75".

DO GOOD PEOPLE GO TO HEAVEN?

ONLY BAD PEOPLE GO TO HEAVEN./

Illustrations from "I Object" (artist: Peter Oram).

Exportation abroad

In September and October 1971, John visited Christchurch and Auckland, in New Zealand, to speak at public evangelistic meetings and to introduce dialogue evangelism. The invitation had come principally from L E Pfankuch of St John's, Woolston, and the Dean of Holy Trinity Cathedral, Auckland, John Rymer, formerly the University Chaplain at the University of New England in Armidale. Not only did this mark the first exporting of this evangelistic technique overseas, it was John's first overseas trip in a teaching capacity.[7] Both these commodities would prove to be very exportable!

John abroad

One of the great milestones in John's life was the discovery of the joys of travel. Overseas speaking engagements provided many opportunities to develop this interest. He would say, "If it's more than 1,000 km, I don't even have to pray about it. It's a call that must be obeyed. The answer is 'Yes!'"

Russell and Kay Clark
who, when with CMS in Hong Kong, enjoyed some memorable visits from John
en route to the UK.

CHAPTER SIX

In July 1974, John went as a delegate to the International Congress on World Evangelism in Lausanne, Switzerland. The Congress gathered people from all over the world whose principal focus was evangelism. John had been invited to give demonstrations of dialogue evangelism. Copies of a pamphlet outlining dialogue evangelism, "What is a Christian?" and "I Object" were distributed to each person attending the demonstrations. In connection with this visit, the Board of the Department decided that John should take the opportunity to observe evangelistic work in the USA, Canada and England, to undertake some speaking engagements and to train people in dialogue evangelism. In New Jersey, he visited a church that had a large team engaged in door-to-door evangelism. In Philadelphia, another had started five satellite "home" churches that catered for outsiders. At St Helen's, Bishopsgate, in London, John was impressed with the lunch time services conducted by its rector, Dick Lucas. He returned home invigorated and stimulated with many new ideas.

A year after attending the Lausanne Congress, news was received that Harry Robinson, the rector of Little Trinity, Toronto, whom John had first met in 1960 and who had attended one of John's workshops at Lausanne, had just finished conducting a training course on dialogue evangelism at a clergy conference.

Throughout the 1970s, John introduced dialogue evangelism to many parts of Australia, to parts of North America and at St Helen's in London. He also began annual dialogue leader training at the Sydney Missionary and Bible College at Croydon that would continue for the next twenty-five years and beyond.

By 1981, John gave this summation:

We originally began the series of home meetings called dialogue evangelism because we simply could not get unbelievers to come to guest services at our church. However ten years later we were able to get people to come to church and so the guest service became an effective method again. We were in a new social and spiritual climate. In the late 1960s, the guest service only gave the *illusion* of evangelism. In the early 1980s, it was *real* evangelism.

It should be noted that the effectiveness of all evangelistic methods changes from time to time, place to place, and person to person. What works in one place may not work in another. What does not work at one time is often tailor-made for a new situation. One person may use a method which another never can. However, the first question always is "Are there unbelievers present?" If not, the method is wrong.[8]

Dialogue evangelism never ceased to be a useful evangelistic technique. It also generated a host of other initiatives. So many other good things John would later undertake in ministry had their foundation here. Many people came to know the Lord. Others were trained in personal evangelism and were thrust into immediate service, quickly gaining confidence as they saw the power of the gospel demonstrated. Some who had attended the training sessions but who had no real desire to become dialogue leaders were strengthened in their faith through an understanding of apologetics. This eventually led John to develop a range of evangelistic and teaching resources. It stimulated him and later staff members to pursue several new means of engaging in personal evangelism and to offer training courses to equip people in their use. It gave John his first exposure on the international stage and, through the contacts he made, widened his evangelistic opportunities into many parts of the world. Travel enabled him to gain stimulation from the work of others, to draw on their ideas and to be refreshed. Dialogue evangelism was a fruitful doorway into many lives—both Christian and non-Christian—and a starting point for many rewarding endeavours.

$^1/_4$ million for "private tract"

A tract never intended for general publication has reached a circulation exceeding 250,000 in less than 10 years. The Director of Evangelism in the Diocese of Sydney (the Rev. John Chapman) said that he first wrote *What is a Christian?* as the sixth lesson in a correspondence course offered by the Diocese. Response was so encouraging that it was printed in booklet form and has since been translated into Greek, Italian, Spanish and Chinese.

"The booklet really explains the main points preached in public sermons recorded in the book of Acts," Mr Chapman said. "Those familiar with 'dialogue evangelism' will recognise them immediately. It has been a tremendous encouragement to hear over the years of people converted through its use."

One minister (the Rev. Trevor Middleton) said that he had distributed over 3,000 copies of the tract in his parish of Oak Flats, south of Wollongong. "We encourage each member of the congregation to carry a copy or two for personal evangelism," he said. "Several people have definitely come to Christ in recent months through the use of this tract."

Mr Middleton said that he had visited a couple after learning that the husband had terminal cancer. Both husband and wife had objected to the material in *What is a Christian?* as he went through it with them. Mr Middleton undertook to visit them the next morning when he found them still in their night attire. Neither had slept and he was warmly welcomed. "I threw Mr Chapman's little book down in a rage," the husband said. "I thought, 'What more can God expect me to do than what I've already done?'" However, they again read the booklet and discussed it, and by the time Mr Middleton had arrived, each had found peace with the Lord.

"That man became a missionary to his family and to the whole community," Mr Middleton said. "I have rarely known such a true and definite change. He was an encouragement to me and to all who visited him."

Mr Middleton said he had used the booklet for hospital visitation, in school work and even with hitch-hikers. He generally went through the main points with those to whom he had given a copy.

The booklet deals with a description of the Christian person, an outline of the Christian life and the basis of assurance.

Australian Church Record, 5 November 1979.

What is a Christian?[9]
by John C Chapman

Let us begin by noting that the world and everything in it, including people, belong to God. What we do in God's world and with it, is important to God. He has never lost interest in His world, not in any part of it. Some people think that God made His world and then grew tired of it but this is quite contrary to what the Bible says (Psalm 104).

Jesus—the Master of the world

When God created the world He did it so that Jesus Christ would be Master of it. "All things were created through Him (Jesus Christ) and for Him" (Colossians 1:16). Jesus Christ, through His death and resurrection, has become Lord or Master of the whole creation (Philippians 2:10–11). He has, therefore, the *right* to control everything in the world, including the lives of men and women. They should recognise Him as their Master and God. They should worship and obey Him. This is what is meant by the statement "Jesus Christ is Lord". It is believing this and acting on it which makes a person a Christian.

Rebels!

Men and women everywhere are rebellious to the idea that their lives should be controlled by Jesus. They want to be independent. They want to be free from His rule and authority. They see themselves to be "master of their lives and captain of their souls". They make the mistake of thinking that their lives are their own to do with as they like.

They reject Jesus as their Lord—sometimes passively, sometimes actively, but whether actively or passively—they reject Him. Consequently they do not bother about obeying His laws. They act in a way which shows they are self-centred in their approach to life. It is this *spirit* of rebellion which allows some people to murder, commit adultery, steal. The same spirit of rebellion causes others to be puffed up in pride, eaten up in jealousy and fritter away their life in selfishness. Different people show different symptoms of this rebellion but *all* are rebellious. The fact of the rebellion in us all is real. The Bible calls this spirit of rebellion *sin*. It makes no effort to minimise the seriousness of it. It sees it to be the root cause of all the problems which we have in trying to live in relationship with each other (wars, strife, divorce, race riots).

But the worst feature of sin is that since it is a rebellion against Jesus Christ's right to control our lives and since Jesus *is* Master, then sin has consequences of eternal magnitude. One day Jesus will return and overthrow all who remain rebellious to this rule (2 Thessalonians 1:5–10). Sin does matter because it wrecks life here and now and if unforgiven will take a person to hell.

Stop the revolution

God in His love and mercy does the only thing that we would expect Him to do. He commands everyone everywhere to stop rebelling against Him and turn back and obey Him. This is what the Bible means by the term "repentance". Paul tells us that God commands all people everywhere to repent because He has fixed a day when He will judge the world (Acts 17:30).

Because of our sin, we do not have the ability to repent unless God gives us this ability as a gift (John 6:44) and we should consequently beg God to have mercy on us and to give us this gift so that we can stop rebelling and submit to Jesus Christ as Lord.

Amnesty is granted

When people repent, they are granted an amnesty by God. They are not punished for their acts of rebellion as they ought to be. Indeed, they are treated as if they never were rebels. We don't deserve this treatment and it could never have been ours except for the death of Jesus Christ on our behalf. When Jesus died, He took the punishment which mankind deserves because of its sin (1 Peter 3:18). He was punished for sinful people so they could be set free from the punishment which they deserve. This is the measure of the love of Jesus Christ for us: He loved us and gave His life for us (1 John 4:10).

A new beginning—it is possible!

When anyone stops rebelling and allows Jesus to control their life, this is a clear indication that God has changed them and made them into a new people. They may feel the same, look the same but they act differently, and they act differently because they are different. They now want to please Jesus—before, they wanted to please themselves. Now they want to obey Jesus—before, they ignored and disobeyed Him. This changed behaviour stems from a changed attitude to Jesus and this changed attitude is what the Bible calls being born again (John 3:1–15; 2 Corinthians 5:17). This change is something which God does and is sometimes referred to as having Christ living in us (Galatians 2:20) and sometimes as having the Holy Spirit dwelling within (Romans 8:14).

It is, of course, important to realise that in submitting to Jesus' control a person does not lose his or her own identity. Rather, they become more complete as human beings. Before they were slaves to sin, now they have found true freedom. For it is in Jesus' service that "perfect freedom" is found.

What is a Christian?

A Christian, then, is someone who recognises that Jesus Christ has the right to control his or her life. They recognise that they are rebels against Jesus Christ and deserve to be punished. A Christian believes that Jesus Christ died for him or her on the Cross taking the punishment which their sins deserved. A Christian is a person who has responded to God's call to repent. They have turned from rebelling against Jesus and submitted to Him. This person knows that he or she has been forgiven. They know that God has made them a new person and that Jesus lives in their life. They know this because they see their changed desires, attitudes and behaviour. This person trusts God with his or her life.

Mistaken ideas!

It will be clear from this that a person does not become a Christian merely by living a good life as such, or being a good father or mother, an honest person in the community, or even making great sacrifices for others. It is possible to do all these things and still be rebellious to Jesus. In fact, it is often true that the better people are the more difficult it is for them to realise that they need to be forgiven. They tend to think that they are good enough. A Christian is not just a *good* person. A good person, no matter how good he or she is, needs to be born again and forgiven. Christians will try to be good and obey Jesus not *so* they can be forgiven but because they *have* been forgiven.

Neither should we fall into the snare of thinking that a regular churchgoer is necessarily a Christian. There's nothing wrong with going to church, in fact, there's every reason why a person should go regularly, but this is not the thing which causes a person to be a Christian. It is possible to be baptised, confirmed and receive Holy Communion regularly and still not submit to Jesus. However, when a person repents and hands the control of his or her life over to Christ, that person *will* attend church every Sunday not so he or she will become a Christian but because they have become one. They will want to meet with other Christians to pray, to be taught and to praise God. There is nothing wrong with being good or going to church. They just are not the ways a person becomes a Christian.

How does a person become a Christian?

Basically, people become Christians when God changes them and makes them new people (2 Cor. 5:17).

However, they have to do something themselves. They make a response. That response is what the Bible calls repentance and faith. To respond in repentance and faith, a person would pray a prayer something like this:

Lord Jesus,
I recognise that You are God and have the right to control my life. I have rebelled against You, sinning in thought, word and deed, sometimes unconsciously, sometimes deliberately. I'm sorry for this and ask You to forgive me. As best I can, I will turn away from rebellion and obey You. Thank You, Lord Jesus, for dying for me on the Cross. Please come into my life and take complete control of it.

How does a Christian behave?

The Christian now sets out to serve the Lord and, to do that, he or she will need to be a regular and careful reader of the Bible. We cannot know how to please our Lord or obey Him unless we know what kind of a person our Lord is. We can only find this out through the Bible. New Christians are advised to begin with one of the Gospels and then to read the Acts of the Apostles and then the other books of the New Testament. Christians also start to pray. They develop their new friendship with Jesus Christ in prayer. As we read the Bible, God speaks to us. We speak to Him in prayer. It is essential also for Christians to have fellowship with other Christians and they should link up with a church where they can help others and be helped themselves to grow up to be like their Lord.

How can a person be sure?

Several things assure the Christian that he or she is a real Christian. Firstly, God's promises about forgiving them and receiving them are true and can be relied on. Secondly, their changed attitudes toward God, sin and the world assure them that God has made them new people. When God does this, it is forever (John 6:37–44). Thirdly, there are times when Christians feel the wonder of God being their Father. Paul tells us that this is the Holy Spirit bearing witness with our spirit that we are God's children (Romans 8:15–16). A person knows he or she is a Christian because they do not want to go on in sin any more. They have a new love for all people. All of these are gifts from God.

Are they then perfect?

You may think having read the above that Christians are perfect. Far from it, but they do long for the day when Jesus will return and then they will be perfect (1 John 3:2). Although Christians have turned their back on sin and the *aim of their life* is to obey Jesus, because they are still sinful they do, from time to time, sin against Jesus. Such people wish they hadn't sinned and immediately repent and resolve not to fall again. They are unlike non-Christians whose whole lives are rebellious to Jesus, and who don't care when sin grieves God but only worry when they themselves are hurt or upset by it. In this the Christian can be distinguished from the non-Christian even though they both commit acts of sin.

1   John and Moyra Prince, *Out of the Tower*, Anzea Publishers, 1987, p 36.
2   Prince, *Out of the Tower*, pp 36–37.
3   Prince, *Out of the Tower*, p 37.
4   Letter from Neville Collins to the author dated 14 September 1994.
5   Dr J I Packer—as quoted by John in the original training notes.
6   Over the years, the members of this group included Gavin Lawrie, Jim Mitchell, Garry Pritchard, John Russell and Stephen Toomey.
7   In 1960, John had travelled to the Pan Anglican Congress at Toronto, Canada, as the sole clerical representative of the Diocese of Armidale. After attending the conference, he flew on to England and returned home via East Africa, India, Hong Kong and Malaysia, visiting and encouraging many friends.
8   Chapman, *Know and Tell the Gospel*, p 140.
9   John C Chapman, *What is a Christian?*, AIO, 1969.

John, Paul Barnett and some great ones—
1974.

UNIVERSITY MISSIONS

Not my right

For a man with high intelligence, penetrating insight and commanding wisdom, John Chapman, for a very long time, was strangely modest when confronted by members of the academic community. There was a degree of insecurity somewhere deep within him—perhaps stemming from his humble antecedents and from what he saw to be his lack of formal education, both general and theological—that cautioned him about taking the stage normally occupied by those whose academic qualifications were manifest and superior to his. Perhaps, in a moment of confrontation, he had experienced that the learned and wise can be cuttingly dismissive: "What is this babbler trying to say?" (Acts 17:18). Under God's grace, the inappropriateness of John's self-assessment would eventually be demonstrated without equivocation.

By 1960, New South Wales had three universities. The oldest and the first university in Australasia, the University of Sydney, had been established by an Act of the State Legislature on 1 October 1850. It had been given power to establish colleges and, under that power, had established the New England University College at Armidale in January 1938. The College became the University of New England on 1 February 1954. The second university to be established was the New South Wales University of Technology. It was constituted on 1 July 1949. Its name spoke of the intention of its founders to place special emphasis on science and

121

technology and so meet the increasing demand in Australia after the Second World War for technologists and applied scientists. By 1958, it had grown to embrace a broader academic scope. Its name was changed to the University of New South Wales. As was the case with the University of Sydney, the University of New South Wales had also been given power to establish colleges. It had established a college at Newcastle in 1951 (it became the University of Newcastle in 1965) and another college at Wollongong in 1962 (it became the University of Wollongong in 1975). Gradually other universities emerged, Macquarie University in 1964 and, with the conversion of a variety of tertiary institutions, the University of Technology, Sydney, on Australia Day 1988, the University of Western Sydney on 1 January 1989, Charles Sturt University later in that year, the Australian Catholic University in 1990 and Southern Cross University on 1 January 1994.

John's first involvement in proclaiming the gospel to students on university campuses came with the missions conducted in Armidale at the University of New England by Dudley Foord in 1960 (the mission that, in its supper meetings, saw the birth of dialogue evangelism) and Stan Skillicorn in 1961.

Reassurance

I have often recalled the first (supper) meeting (at one of the colleges of the University of New England in 1960). John was to speak and I was chairing it. He called at our house near Uni to pick me up. Both of us were very apprehensive about how we would cope and were imagining all sorts of difficulties and embarrassments. As we opened the door into the chilly Armidale night he turned and said—

"OK, we believe the Lord wants us to do this don't we?"

"Yes."

"Right then, if He wants us to do it He will give us all the ability we need."

This is a principle I have used for reassurance very many times since.

John Wheeler

who, with his wife Dorothy, were members of the Graduates Fellowship of AFES in Armidale.

The period from the late 1960s to the early 1970s was a volatile one in Australian life. This volatility was reflected as strongly among university students as among any other section of the community. In 1965, the Australian Prime Minister, Sir Robert Menzies, had committed Australian troops to fight in the Vietnam War. The youth of the country were conscripted to the army. During this period, the women's movement became more vocal and more militant over a range of issues, including contraception, abortion and equal opportunity in employment. In 1971, Dr Germaine Greer published "The Female Eunuch". Aboriginal activists under the leadership of people such as Charles Perkins grew more demanding in their claims for recognition and for land rights. South African sporting teams met fierce opposition from anti-apartheid protesters. It was a time when it was good to have a cause. It was a time for protest marches and the burning of effigies.

In this atmosphere, John, not long after his return to Sydney, was asked to address the students of the University of Sydney. There was a single public meeting. Dr Barry Newman shared the occasion with him. In a letter to the Board of the Department in July 1970 recording the event, John wrote:

> I celebrated my fortieth birthday (23 July 1970) by speaking at a front lawn open air meeting at Sydney University. (*And then, with typical Chapmanesque understatement, he continued*) I wouldn't have thought that there were any more than 1,000 listening and on reflection I can't think of a finer way to have entered into middle age. When the President of the Evangelical Union wrote to me and thanked me for coming, he expressed the hope that when I reached my eightieth year I would still be preaching the gospel, to which I give my own hearty "Amen". My real hope, however, is that our Lord Himself might have returned before another forty years.

It might have been thought that such a large attendance and John's positive response would be interpreted as confirmation of God's approval for his involvement in a ministry of this kind to university students. What more was needed to overcome the evangelist's doubts as to the significance of this field of mission and his ability to there proclaim the gospel of grace? The truth was that John had stepped into an arena whose audience reacted strongly against anything they saw to be traditional, conservative, hierarchical and authoritarian. These qualities the church epitomised. Its message was greeted with derision. John encountered great hostility from a number of the students. It was an experience he would not quickly forget. It fuelled his doubt. He was not a university man and he felt very much that he was out of place.

John undertook no further university work until 1976 when, on three successive Tuesdays in March, he conducted evangelistic meetings for undergraduates at the newly constituted University of Wollongong at the invitation of the Wollongong University Christian Union. It was symbolic of the CU's desire to place evangelism at the top of its programme from the inception of the new institution. During March and April of the same year, he gave some Bible studies on Romans 1–4 at the University of New South Wales as part of a ministry begun by Phillip Jensen who had been appointed as the chaplain of that University after leaving the Department of Evangelism in 1975.

Sydney University—1977

By 1976, the mood among university students in Sydney had changed remarkably. The collective memory of each intake of undergraduates is brief and so the great causes of the first half of the decade were almost a distant memory for many of them. Australia's combat role in Vietnam had ceased by the end of 1971. A year later, the election of Australia's first Labor government in twenty-three years under Mr Gough Whitlam had brought the prospect of advancement on women's issues and aboriginal rights. Whitlam's sacking as Prime Minister by the Governor-General, Sir John Kerr, on 11 November 1975 had enraged many and had momentarily divided the nation. Environmental concerns were now finding expression by an increasing number and social issues, such as no-fault divorce, engaged the attention of others. By 1977, anger was abating and conservatism was taking over. The overwhelming interest of students was becoming the pursuit of materialism. But while the mood had changed, there was still strong antagonism towards the gospel.

The principal Christian group at Sydney University in 1977 was the Evangelical Union. It had an interdenominational membership of about 225. Its members were mainly conservative evangelicals but included some liberal evangelicals. It had not been active in evangelism since the 1970 mission and a number of its members were becoming openly critical of this failing.[1] In particular they were challenged by the work of two organisations based in the United States of America that had started to engage in personal evangelism on campus of the kind known as "cold" or "stranger" evangelism. The Navigators using their tract "The Bridge to Life" and Campus Crusaders (known in New South Wales as Student Life) with their tract "The Four Spiritual Laws" approached individual students at random seeking to lead them to Christ.

The 1976 Annual General Meeting of the EU had been held in the back hall of St Barnabas', Broadway. This Anglican parish adjoins Sydney University and has had a long association with it. At the meeting, the retiring President, Larry Hand, moved a motion that the EU consider a return in 1977 to a traditional public mission. There was tension among Christian students over the issue of evangelism. Some strongly supported personal evangelism but opposed public evangelism as it was seen to be too threatening. The Student Christian Movement and the liberal

John at Sydney University, 1977.

evangelical members of EU were totally opposed to any public proclamation of the gospel, viewing it as patronising and paternalistic. Hand's motion, despite opposition, was carried.

The incoming President of the EU was an undergraduate in the second year of a four-year social work course. Adrian Lane had been converted as a student at The King's School. His conversion had come through the ministry of Christian teachers, including Rod West (later the Headmaster of Trinity Grammar School) and the School's chaplain, Brian Telfer. Brian had gone to The King's School after leaving the Department of Evangelism in the middle of 1972. Adrian Lane warmed to the idea of a mission. He contemplated it with a mixture of naive confidence on the one hand and apprehension on the other.

He was more than prepared to give it a go but he was totally inexperienced in organising anything like it. Everything was new. The EU needed to undergo a massive shift in its culture and it needed to do a lot of hard preparatory work. Adrian also recognised that to be authoritative about anything, particularly an issue expressed so narrowly that it asserted the exclusiveness of Jesus Christ as the means of salvation for all, was thoroughly unfashionable.

An evangelist had to be found. Adrian Lane as a sixteen-year-old had first met John in 1972 at a Crusader camp at Galston on the north-western outskirts of Sydney. Adrian was then in the fourth year of secondary school and was not a Christian. At every mealtime he had sat next to John and bombarded him with questions. Why this? How that? Question followed question. But each question had been met with a better answer. Now, in October 1976, he invited John to be the missioner.

John quickly declined the invitation. He gave many reasons. He was not a university graduate. He had only been to a technical college and done woodwork. He felt that without a university degree he did not have the right to come. He would lack acceptance among the students. His message would not be heard. The rejection he had experienced in 1970, he pointed out, confirmed this clearly. He suggested that Adrian look elsewhere. The suggestion was peremptorily dismissed. Without any understanding of the significance of what he was doing, Adrian Lane said:

"Look. Uni students are just ordinary people who need to hear the gospel. You just have to talk to them as ordinary people. And since when did anyone have to be a university graduate to be an evangelist? I am looking for an evangelist. I want the best evangelist available in Australia. And I want you."

"But don't you see, the gospel has to have credibility," John said.

"The gospel's got its own credibility," Adrian said. He rebuked the older man. "You need to repent of that attitude!"

John was barely convinced. After considerable persuasion and negotiation, he reluctantly agreed but only on the condition that Paul Barnett, then the rector of Holy Trinity, Adelaide, accompany him. Paul was a longstanding friend and confidant, a former rector of St Barnabas', Broadway, and, more particularly, a university graduate and a university lecturer.

While missions were part of the EU's history, the members of the organising committee were totally inexperienced in public evangelism. They knew no models. It was all unexplored territory. Adrian Lane says:

We followed the major model of the world. If anything happened at Uni, it happened on the Front Lawn. That's how you interfaced with your culture at that time. That's where the AUS (the Australian Union of Students) had its rallies. That was where effigies of the Vice Chancellor were burnt. It was the public forum—like the Areopagus. And the University was one of the places where the current issues of the day were debated. It was a bit like a boil. It was a place for the discussion of ideas

125

and we wanted to be part of that. We wanted to say that the gospel was one of the issues of the day. It was a very conscious thing to do it in public.[2]

Paul Barnett strongly shared this view. During his days at Broadway, he had seen the Front Lawn used for the Vietnam demonstrations and for a succession of political purposes, but never for the gospel. He felt that it was very important for Christians to take their turn. While the committee, with Paul's support, insisted strongly on the inclusion of some public outdoor meetings as a witness to the world, John continued to resist. Both evangelists were fearful of having to face the crowd. Open air meetings strongly lacked the element of control. They felt much more comfortable about the meetings to be held indoors.

The committee decided the mission needed a theme or title. They appropriated the message of the freeway sign "Go Back—You're Going the Wrong Way". Adrian Lane recalls, "It is interesting that at the time, this title was fairly confrontational in a similar way to the way that protests on campus had been confrontational".

A month before the mission began, John again intimated his apprehension about the venture. In the BDM's Prayerletter for May 1977, he wrote:

Some of the meetings will be held on the Front Lawn (you know how I love speaking in the open air!) and some will be in the Carslaw Lecture Theatres. Please pray for the Committee who are working on plans for this and also for Paul and myself as we prepare.

John, Allan Blanch, Paul Barnett.

In order to introduce John and Paul Barnett to as many students as possible prior to the mission, a number of ventures were initiated in which they were featured. Firstly, three church services of a kind that would now be called "seeker" services were held at St Barnabas', Broadway. The members of the church, its rector, Allan Blanch, and its other staff members keenly supported the mission. These services were as novel as they were experimental. They were carefully designed to be simple in their format. They did not use the prayer book. Music was carefully chosen having regard to its accessibility to non-Christians. Some Christian students gave their testimonies. Secondly, the EU had traditionally conducted a public lecture programme on campus at lunchtime every Wednesday during the three terms of the academic year. Two lectures each term were made evangelistic and at some of them John was able to be introduced to the EU members. Thirdly, John produced a ten-minute motivational tape that was played to good effect at EU faculty group and cell group meetings.

The mission ran in the middle of winter from 29 June to 7 July.

MISSION PROGRAMME

Wednesday, June 29	**Jesus – Other than Ordinary?** *John Chapman and Paul Barnett* *1 pm: Front Lawn*	Tuesday, July 5	**Your chance to Speak. Are you prepared to stand up for what you think?** Have a go at John and Paul for two minutes and they have two minutes in return. *1 pm: Front Lawn*
Thursday, June 30	**Man or God? – Rediscover Jesus** *John Chapman* *1 pm: CLT 4 and 5*		
Friday, July 1	**Who does Jesus Think He Is? The Sayings of Jesus** *John Chapman and Paul Barnett* *1 pm: Front Lawn*	Wednesday, July 6	**Why Should You Go Back?** *John Chapman* *1 pm: CLT 4 and 5*
		Thursday, July 7	**It's the Real Thing – What being a Christian is all about** *Paul Barnett* *1 pm: CLT 4 and 5*
Monday, July 4	**People in Rebellion. Where do you stand in relation to God?** *Paul Barnett* *1 pm: CLT 4 and 5*	Each Day	*2 pm–3 pm* *John Chapman and Paul Barnett will be available for questions.*

Extract from "CLEARWAY" the Mission newspaper.

The first of the meetings held in the open on the Front Lawn of the University attracted over 1,000 students, the largest gathering of students on campus since the Vietnam moratorium meetings. John's nervousness as he spoke could be heard clearly in his voice. It was tight, high-pitched and his delivery was very fast.[3] Good attendances continued throughout the mission. Carslaw Lecture Theatre No. 4 which was the main indoor venue seated about 400 and was full on all but one occasion. The overflow watched the proceedings by closed circuit television in the adjoining Carslaw Lecture Theatre No. 5. One front lawn meeting was held on a particularly cold day. It brought the comment from John that "Most martyrs die by fire or the sword, but I think I'll be the first martyr to die of frostbite!"

The planning for the mission was resourceful and its execution thorough. John's and Paul's evangelism was full of meat. They both proclaimed the gospel clearly and simply, they did not hesitate to present the challenge of commitment and they gave the Christian body a sure defence of its faith. In his report summarising the mission, John wrote:

> The members of the EU had done a truly wonderful work in publicity and especially in bringing their friends to hear the gospel. Some meetings were held on the Front Lawn and were attended by large numbers (1,000), others were held in Lecture Theatres and were smaller (300–600). In addition eleven dialogue meetings and seven barbecues were held. During the week we heard of many people who were converted. I cannot remember when I was associated in a venture where God blessed us as He did in this one.[4]

The follow-up programme for the mission successfully used some basic Bible studies for new believers that had been put together principally by Phillip Jensen and Colin Marshall in preparation for the 1979 Billy Graham Crusade. These were later developed into the introductory series "Just For Starters".

"As a consequence of this mission," Adrian Lane says, "we came to realise that evangelism is a whole process and that we have to be working regularly with our friends in this process. As it takes place, so people are converted before missions and during missions and after missions. In fact, the most successful missions are always those in which people are converted just before or right at the beginning because they hear the gospel in time to be discipled through the mission. They are also keen to bring their non-Christian friends to hear the gospel and they are ripe to do that."

The effects of the mission were not limited to the University of Sydney. Immediately after the mission, some of the EU members spoke of it to the Australian Fellowship of Evangelical Students in Melbourne (representing the EUs of three Melbourne universities) and Adrian Lane gave a report at the AFES annual conference at Stanwell Tops in January 1978. As a consequence, the EUs of other Australian universities took up the challenge of public evangelism "and the domino effect... rolled the wave of missions round Australia twice".[5]

John and Adrian Lane, Gordon-Conwell Theological Seminary, 1990.

The success of so much of the experimentation associated with the conduct of the 1977 mission made it a stimulating and exciting time—a positive time. It reflected a movement away from a rather defensive attitude towards public gospel ministry to an approach that was more enterprising and more entrepreneurial. There was a new enthusiasm. John would later acknowledge that this mission began a new era in his ministry in the public proclamation of the good news of Jesus. It caused him to think that there could be a place for crusade evangelism as well as personal evangelism. Other influences, including the Billy Graham Crusade of 1979, would carry his thinking further. While not destroying the haunting doubts about his entitlement to minister to university students, it began a slow process of growth in confidence to do it. As had been the case with dialogue evangelism, another significant evangelistic work was born in an initiative taken on a university campus.

University of New South Wales—1978

At the beginning of August 1978, John and Paul Barnett conducted a two-week mission at the University of New South Wales organised by Phillip Jensen.

The mission was called "Cross-Talk". If John was not sufficiently apprehensive at the prospect of another bout of university encounters, while returning home from a meeting of the Standing Committee of the Diocesan Synod the Monday night before the mission began, he was involved in a car accident in which his car was written off. Neither John nor Tony Lamb, who was travelling with him, was injured.

The mission was highly successful. It consisted of meetings held on the Library lawn, other meetings in the form of lectures and seminars, and dialogue meetings. Many undergraduates were converted and linked with Bible study groups. As a means of follow-up, an evangelistic houseparty was also arranged at the end of that month. Throughout it all, John "was specially conscious of God's presence and care".

John and Paul Barnett, University of NSW, 1978.

Sydney University—1980

John returned to Sydney University at the end of June 1980. It had long been part of the general policy of the EU (though not always implemented) that a mission of some form be held on campus every three or four years so that each student generation would have an opportunity to publicly hear the gospel of salvation. 1980 also marked the 50th anniversary of the founding of the Sydney University EU by Howard Guinness. The prospect of a jubilee mission had a strong appeal. Dr Bill Andersen, a senior lecturer in Education with a long and distinguished association with the EU, had also made a personal recommendation to hold a mission in the jubilee year. Other members of the academic staff, including Jan Hext, Alan Craddock and Ted Fackerell, gave their support.

This time John's co-missioner was Phillip Jensen. At Phillip's suggestion, the Sydney University EU entitled the mission:

NO CHRIST, NO LIFE

KNOW CHRIST, KNOW LIFE

It was a thrilling time. All the lessons of 1977 had been well learnt. The details of the earlier mission had been thoroughly documented by its administrative co-ordinator, Rosemary Waugh (later Rosemary Pidgeon). Rosemary, the Student Worker at St Barnabas', Broadway, was again the co-ordinator of the 1980 mission.[6] The Christian students had worked hard for a full year in preparation. In addition, the first week of the mission coincided with the period set aside for missioning by the students and faculty of Moore College which adjoins the University. A team of twelve students under the direction of Peter Jensen participated in the work.

CHAPTER SEVEN

The students at Sydney found the mission's title to be intriguing. In pre-mission publicity, it had been disclosed in four parts, starting four weeks before the mission with the words "No Christ". Another part was added each week as the mission approached. It provoked some typical undergraduate responses. Bogus slogans appeared, including "NO BRIAN, NO LIFE" inspired by the Monty Python film "The Life of Brian" and "NO RONALD, NO HAMBURGERS" derived from a rather more obvious source.[7] Three broadsheets were produced, one of which captured a great deal of interest. It included a Bible quiz compiled by Phillip Jensen that caused many to discover to their surprise how poor their understanding was of the greatest book of all.

The University atmosphere had changed since 1977. All the meetings were indoor meetings. Lunchtime meetings were held in the two Carslaw Lecture Theatres as in 1977 and evening meetings were held in a more informal atmosphere in the Menzies Common Room at the Women's College. Each missioner prepared four talks and gave each one twice, once at the lunchtime meeting and once in the evening.

Phillip Jensen took the more negative "No Christ: No Life" part of the slogan to assert that to say "No" to Christ was to say "No" to life. His talks were publicised as:

CHRIST AND... WORK—in the land of the seven-day week
　　　　　　　SEX—in the land of the lost weekend
　　　　　　　LEISURE—in the land of the long weekend
　　　　　　　DEATH—the land without weekends

John took the more positive part of the slogan "Know Christ: Know Life". His talks were based on four passages from John's Gospel and were called:

CHRIST AND... LIFE'S SATISFACTION (John 4)
　　　　　　　LIFE'S DIRECTION (John 9)
　　　　　　　REAL LIFE (John 10)
　　　　　　　LIFE FOREVER (John 11)

A leaflet containing the Bible passages for each talk was prepared and distributed at each meeting. For a long time, John had argued that whenever the Bible was expounded, the hearer should have the passage open in front of him or her so as to be able to check whether the teaching accurately matched the text. His principle was now implemented. The leaflets also had a space for taking notes, they publicised the next day's talk and Phillip's included the prayer he prayed at the end of the meeting.

Lunchtime attendances averaged about 700 and the evenings about 250. After students filled the two lecture theatres to capacity to hear Phillip speak on "Christ and Sex" and reports of his talk were published in the "Sydney Morning Herald"[8] and telecast on the current affairs programme "Willesee at Seven", John stoutly declared that from then on he was planning to call all his talks "Christ and Sex". On one of the days, the former Australian Prime Minister, Gough Whitlam, happened to be at the University speaking to the members of the Labor Club. As there were fewer at Whitlam's meeting than at the mission, newspapers the following day headed their story "God Got More Than Gough".

As an immediate consequence of the mission, about thirty-five people were converted and forty others expressed a desire to learn more about the Christian faith. The mission also created a continuing climate for evangelism. In the week that followed the mission, Student Lifer's doing "cold" or "stranger" evangelism at lunchtimes reported seven commitments to Christ.

As I weeded my father's vegetables

My first memory of John is hearing him preach at a mission at Sydney University in 1980. I had been a Christian for about six months and what that did was to make me want to preach. It was as though he gave me permission to teach Biblical truth without jargon. His clarity, conviction and commitment to Christ made me realise that there was nothing greater I could do with my life than to declare the Word of God. Soon after that, I had been given six of John's sermons on tape. At the time I lived with my parents and I would take those tapes out to the farm and listen to them over and over again as I weeded my father's vegetables. From those tapes, John taught me predestination.

I loved the way John made you think that if you didn't agree with the Bible you were a nong. I regularly thank God for John's ministry to me personally and through his preaching.

Ray Galea
a catechist with the Department of Evangelism in 1990.

The following year saw John involved in evangelistic work on three university campuses. In March and September, (after again confiding his unease in doing so) he spoke at open air meetings at the University of Newcastle. For two weeks in July, John and Phillip Jensen combined once more as the speakers at a University of Sydney mission called "Future Failure". For the first two weeks in August, John spoke at the University of New South Wales outreach.

Sydney University—1981

Immediately after the 1980 Jubilee Mission at Sydney University, the staff at St Barnabas', Broadway, exhausted but exhilarated by the experience, determined that there should be another mission at the University the following year with the same two speakers, that it should be a joint venture of the four evangelical groups on campus following the successful and highly polished 1980 model and that Rosemary Pidgeon would, if necessary, be available again to act as full-time co-ordinator. The mission committee, chaired by Trevor Edwards, an ordained staff worker at St Barnabas', was quickly formed. The rationale for holding another mission in the succeeding year was that one-third of the student population would be new and a climate conducive to a greater degree of personal evangelism and discipleship would be created with the prompt return of two such competent, acceptable and well-known evangelists.

By the beginning of the 1980s, the general mood among undergraduates had

Mission sticker.

changed completely from that which had prevailed during the 1960s and 1970s. Students had become inward-looking. Their introspection caused them to be more concerned about their individual standing. The mission was entitled "FUTURE FAILURE". "It was decided to concentrate on the twin themes of the future and failure, which strike a chord in every student heart."[9]

The 1981 mission followed exactly the pattern of the 1980 mission. Each missioner prepared four talks, each of which was given twice, once in the Carslaw Lecture Theatres at lunchtime and once at the Women's College in the evening. The lunchtime meetings averaged 600 and the evening meetings 200. On occasions, the lunchtime crowd overflowed from the Carslaw Lecture Theatres onto the adjoining Victoria Park where the address was relayed by loudspeaker. About thirty people were converted and another fifty joined investigative Bible studies.

University of New South Wales—1981

John had no sooner finished the Sydney University mission than the 1981 August Outreach began at the University of New South Wales. It ran from 1–16 August. It was a two-week mission, beginning with a weekend houseparty for Christian members of the many Bible study groups on campus to encourage them in evangelism, and incorporating evangelistic services at St Matthias', Centennial Park, on Sunday 9 and Sunday 16 August. In preparation for the mission, students had been surveyed as to their attitudes about Christianity. "Fewer than 30% of the thousand students interviewed said they had read a Gospel. More than 70% had never really investigated the person of Jesus."[10] John spoke evangelistically at three meetings most days over the two weeks of the mission. The meetings ranged from

John and Phillip Jensen. Conference for Itinerant Evangelists, 1983.

large public meetings to small dialogue-type ones. At the end of the first week it was estimated that more than 1,000 students had been contacted through them. Each day people were converted and, following the pattern at Sydney University, many others enrolled in Bible study groups to further investigate the claims of Jesus.

Give us a demo!

I was talking to a young bloke after a uni meeting and he said that what he was going to do was to live it up until the end of his life–have a really great time–and then, just before he died, he would become a Christian.

I said to him, "How do you know you'll be able to become one at the end?"

He said, "I could become a Christian whenever I like".

I said, "You can only become one when God says".

He insisted he could do it, so I said, "Well, if it's as easy as that, why don't you give us a demo. Why don't you show me how you'll do it by becoming a Christian right now. If it's that easy," I said, "you'd be able to pull it off at any time, wouldn't you?"

"Yeah," he said, "but right now," he said, "I don't want to".

"Come on," I said, "you aren't trying very hard. If you really can do it, do it now. Should be a piece of cake." He started to get a bit touchy.

"I don't want to," he said evenly.

"Try a bit harder," I said, "*want to* want to".

"I don't want to," he said, gritting his teeth.

"Well," I said, "that's the problem, isn't it. What makes you think you'll *want to* at the end?"

John Chapman
demonstrating the truth of predestination.

Macquarie University—1982, 1983 and 1985 —and other activities

By the beginning of 1980, Paul Barnett had returned to Sydney from Adelaide, having been appointed the Master of Robert Menzies College at Macquarie University. He was naturally keen that a prominent place be given to gospelling. From 8–15 August 1982, John and Dr Barry Newman conducted a mission at Macquarie. It opened and concluded with evening meetings at the Macquarie University Church and lunchtime meetings were held on the intervening weekdays. While a great deal of hard work had been done by the organising committee, the numbers attending the meetings were not of the order that John had experienced at Sydney University and the University of New South Wales.

Almost immediately after the 1982 mission, John was again involved with undergraduates. He wrote:

In the last week of August I attended the Student Life "Spring Special". Student Life is the arm of Campus Crusade for Christ (Lay Institute for Evangelism) in Australia and students from the three Sydney Universities were present. I had met many of them during the missions at their universities. It was a good time but I was surprised at how critical they were of their local churches. I didn't ask any of them where they churched but I will pass on their criticisms so that "if the cap fits" we can take action on it. Most went like this:

In my local church no one taught me to read the Bible or pray. I knew I was supposed to do it but when I joined Student Life they taught me how to have a quiet time—what to do. The same goes for witnessing and evangelism. They taught me *how* to do it.

I don't know at what stage in the development of the members of the congregation you teach these things. Can I remind you of the "Teach Yourself to Use 2 Ways to Live" material which is available.[11]

Not good enough for God

On 27 September 1981, after an invitation from student friends at Robert Menzies College, I went to a Guest Service at Macquarie Uni Church. I had been several times before but my view was that I was not good enough for God. John Chapman was the speaker. As I listened for the first time, I was impressed with the truth of the gospel. Chappo showed me that the beauty of the message was that indeed I was not good enough but God still showed His love for me. It was my birthday and my friends had a party ready for me when I got back to the College. I was able to share with them that I had prayed the prayer at the end of the talk. There was much rejoicing!

The next year Chappo came to conduct a uni mission and not only was I keen for my friends to hear him but I was able to share with him in person my conversion story of the year before. He responded with great warmth.

Peter Rogers
Science teacher, Chatswood High School.

Encouraged by the 1982 Macquarie University mission, a mini mission was held at Robert Menzies College the following year from 24–26 May. In the Prayerletter for August–October 1983, John wrote "The meetings were well attended and it was a great thrill to see students bringing their unconverted friends under the sound of the gospel. We know that some were saved and for that we rejoice. Please pray for those whose responsibility it is to nurture these new Christians."

From 7–14 August 1983, John returned to the University of New England at Armidale. The university chaplain, Hugh Begbie, and the mission committee had arranged for the mission meetings to be held each evening after dinner in the various colleges as had been the pattern of the past. Paul Beringer of the Engadine Presbyterian Church assisted in the work. While John said that "I felt the sustaining of the Spirit of God during the mission" he was concerned that only about five percent of the student population seemed to have been reached through the meetings.

In 1985, John again ministered at Robert Menzies College at the invitation of the staff of the College with Ian Powell as his co-missioner. Ian Powell was then a Moore College student and working as a catechist with the Department of Evangelism.

The mission ran from 5–8 and on 11 August, with lunchtime meetings on campus and evening meetings at the College. A guest service was held on the final Sunday night.

Hard and soft

My wife and I have many fond memories of John, especially concerning his ministry to uni students. John always had plenty of time for uni students, and they for him. I remember one instance in particular that bears this out—it was in July of 1989. About seventy students from Sydney University and Macquarie University had gathered at Gerringong for a few days during the mid-year break for Bible study and spiritual refreshment. John was our main speaker.

Early one morning, after a particularly late night of activities and socialising, John was teaching from the Bible about the importance of gospel ministry and Bible study. Some of the group were extremely tired and a few heads started to drop a little. A few minutes later another head dropped and I could see that John had noticed. What would he do? Ignore it and plough on? No, not John. He paused, looked around the room and fairly shouted, "Wake up! Wake up! This is serious business! God's Word is not for sleepy soft-heads! Bible study is hard work! Gospel ministry is hard work! Now let's pay attention and be serious about learning God's Word. He's speaking to us through it right now!" Well, every head in that place not only picked up but every student was on the edge of his seat and we had one of the best Bible studies I'll ever remember—about being "hard-headed" and "soft-hearted" for the sake of the gospel.

Steve and Christy Sandvig
recalling John's involvement in a Student Life Conference.

Through mission after mission and despite the obvious blessing of God on these endeavours, John's sense of unease had never left him. Vestiges of anxiety and apprehension continued to accompany him on each occasion. It was not that John was ever unsure whether God would perform His rescue work, simply whether he would be effective as God's messenger.

Cambridge and Oxford—assurance at last

In December 1988, John made his tenth visit to the United Kingdom. He ministered at the Iwerne Students' Conference and in some parishes in and around London, including St Helen's, Bishopsgate, and the parishes of Wimbledon, Lowestoft, New Malden and Sevenoaks. He had also accepted an invitation from the Cambridge Inter-Collegiate Christian Union to preach at a mission for the colleges of the University of Cambridge from 12–19 February 1989. In association with this mission he preached at the Round Church, Cambridge, and at Holy Trinity, Cambridge.

John has always enjoyed his times abroad. He seems to have found a particular acceptance among the English although his almost extravagant zest for life in every facet must deeply challenge their reserve. Perhaps they enjoy in John the element of novelty. Perhaps they are less used to clergy as outspokenly enthusiastic as he about the wonder of God's Word and find his focus refreshing. Perhaps, again, there is a reflection of the truth that "a prophet has no honour in his own country" (John 4:44).

Once, when asked whether he felt he was better accepted as an evangelist at places beyond the Diocese of Sydney, he replied:

> Yes! Although it's hard to tell. You know what Australians are like and the tall poppy syndrome. I am often given more encouragement by friends overseas than at home. I think in the Diocese I'm just Chappo—"You can hear him anytime". And if asked, they probably think I'm quite good, but they wouldn't put me in world class. But I think they would be like that with everyone. I remember when I told Don Robbie (*Donald Robinson, the Archbishop of Sydney*) that I was going to mission at the CICCU at Cambridge. His look (and I stress look) was of **surprise** and **joy**.

Cambridge University, one of the two great historical universities of England, operates in conjunction with a group of colleges and collegiate institutions that are self-governing and distinct from the University. The function of the colleges is to provide lodging, corporate life and personal tuition for students, while the University arranges general lectures, conducts examinations and awards degrees. It is necessary to be a member of a college to be enrolled as a student of the University and a person cannot continue as a member of a college without being enrolled as a student of the University.

Billy Graham had conducted a mission at Cambridge University. He, too, had experienced uncertainty. In his first talks he had endeavoured to emulate the style of John Stott before he had been able, more confidently, to find his own voice.

Each college has its own Christian Union and, for the purposes of the CICCU mission, each CU appointed two of its residents as assistant missioners. They had the responsibility of speaking at meetings organised by the college CU as well as encouraging students to come to the central meetings that were open to the whole student body. John described the mission to the supporters of his work as follows:

> The Cambridge Inter-Collegiate Christian Union (CICCU) mission was a great thrill. The University is a residential one. Each college had two assistant missioners (making a total of 52) who spoke at many meetings at the colleges during the week. Each evening during the week we held public meetings in the Guildhall.

John spoke at these meetings on passages from the Gospel of Luke under the title "This is Jesus". Everyone who came was given a copy of the Gospel and encouraged to read it.

> We had attendances which ranged from 750 to over 1,000. I suppose overall we would have averaged about 850 a night. I thought that this was a wonderful effort on behalf of the CICCU members. We know of many people who came to Christ and there will be others who have been stimulated to investigate the claims of the Lord Jesus as well as many Christians who have taken heart to tell the gospel to their friends.
> The mission was brilliantly organised by a student committee under the chairmanship of Richard Coomb, a theology student from Ridley Hall.
> It is not possible to tell in detail of the joy of working with so many talented assistant missioners as well as the leaders of the CICCU. It was

a wonderful answer to your prayers. Please continue to pray for them as they press on with evangelism at this University.[12]

The fruit of the true vine

He stayed with us during the 1989 CICCU Mission in Cambridge, and our abiding memory of that time was of Chappo perched on a stool in the kitchen, doing his delicate needlepoint, and chatting to Fiona as she cooked. Every time we tried to shoo him upstairs to do some preparation for his next mission address, he would reappear within twenty minutes for some more conversation, saying that he had it all in hand.

During the Mission, we tape-recorded for him the old Henry Fonda film of "The Grapes of Wrath". We used to watch a bit of this gloomy story each night. And we discovered as the week went on that the more dismal and depressing "The Grapes of Wrath" became, the better Chappo seemed to preach each night to the Cambridge students. There seemed to be a connection between John Steinbeck's ever more dreary story and Chappo's vivacity and zeal in preaching Christ to Cambridge!

Mark Ashton

Rector of the Round Church at St Andrew the Great, who, with his wife, Fiona, and their children Chris, Clare and Nicholas, consider John one of their favourite house guests.

Five years later, in the first week of February 1994, John conducted a mission at Oxford University on behalf of the Oxford Inter-Collegiate Christian Union. No other Australian, it seems, had conducted a CICCU mission or an OICCU mission. John did both.[13] As with the earlier Cambridge mission, it was a mission planned on a large scale. The responsibility for its organisation lay with a mission committee headed by Dr Peter Harwood, a student at Wycliffe College.

Oxford and Cambridge Universities both have the same basis of organisation, being linked with a group of residential colleges. Each of the Oxford colleges had its own CU. At the time of the mission, the membership of the CUs varied from 8 to 150, with a total membership of about 350. The arrangements for the mission mirrored those for the Cambridge mission. Each college had appointed two assistant missioners with particular leadership, teaching and organisational responsibilities.

The mission began in a novel way, well-designed to capture the attention of the student population, with a cheese and wine tasting in the Town Hall. During each day of the mission, there were three rounds of meetings. In the morning, John spoke to the sixty or so assistant missioners. His talks were motivational Bible studies on Colossians in which he used material from the commentary of Dr Peter O'Brien. These meetings were considered to be as outstanding and as valuable as any he conducted during the week. At lunchtime, open meetings were held for students with specialist topics relating to their various areas of study, such as "Christianity and Science" and "Christianity and Ethics". In the evenings, the main meetings were held for the whole student body. Beginning at 8.30 pm and lasting no more than an hour, they followed the simple format of a brief drama, a testimony and then evangelistic preaching by John from Luke's Gospel. Again, everyone who attended was given a copy of that book of the Bible. Attendances ranged from 350–700. After these meetings, the OICCU members invited their friends home for refreshments and further discussions took place. It was an exhilarating time. Every night, people were converted and counselled.

Oxford University, established during the twelfth century, has traditionally held the highest reputation for scholarship and instruction in fields including the classics and theology. It might have been expected that John would have been more apprehensive about ministering at this institution of learning with its ancient and distinguished history than at any other university he had visited. However, just a few weeks before the meetings, two carol services had been held at Cambridge by the CICCU with an aggregate attendance of 1,000. A number of people had come to John then and told him of their conversion following his 1989 mission. This was gracious and generous reassurance from God. It reinforced John's faith in the power of the gospel to bring salvation. It reminded him that God's strength is made perfect in our weakness. It calmed him. It was the first time ever that he had approached a university mission without unease and a sense of fear. He spoke with a forthrightness, a directness, a boldness and a peace that he had not known before in such a setting. He enjoyed the experience immensely.

John at Oxford

When John took the Oxford OICCU Mission he stayed with us. He was a delightful guest. He obviously enjoyed the mission: we would be hearing his jokes right up to the moment we left the house to go to the meeting. He was a little conscious that he had not a great tertiary education, and he marvelled at how well the Oxford students listened. His Australianisms, his use of his age and his practical reasonableness, together with his obvious devotion to Jesus, won through.

David Fletcher
Rector of St Ebbe's Church, Oxford.

At Oxford, the main evening meetings were held in the Sheldonian Theatre, the octagonal, three-tiered lecture theatre designed in 1662 by Sir Christopher Wren. A gift to the University by Bishop Sheldon of London, the design of the theatre was inspired by the ancient Theatre of Marcellus in Rome. At no point did this setting bear any resemblance to the place on the opposite side of the world where, more than forty years earlier, John had held his first mission—the crudely built shearing shed on "Derra Derra" sheep station at Bingara. But no place is better than another for proclaiming the gospel. The message had not changed. And its power to save was as evident then as it had been all those years before.

In July 1994, Paul Barnett, holder of the Licentiate in Theology and Scholar in Theology awards from the Australian College of Theology, Bachelor of Divinity degree from the University of London, Master of Arts from the University of

Sydney and a Doctor of Philosophy from the University of London (and now a bishop), published his seventh book—*The Truth about Jesus: The challenge of evidence*. He dedicated the book to a man rather lacking in formal academic achievements, the repentant evangelist, John Chapman.

A footnote

At the end of November 1994, John was in England at Newcastle-upon-Tyne. He was again ministering to students, this time, the students of Newcastle University. The venue distinctly did not resemble the Guildhall at Cambridge or the Sheldonian at Oxford. It was "The Boat", a vessel moored under the bridge in Newcastle that is of the same design as the Sydney Harbour Bridge.

In a letter to the staff of the Department of Evangelism dated 1 December 1994, John wrote:

> Monday night saw me on "The Boat". It is a student watering hole and the university students hired the disco place (it has a revolving dance floor) from 7–10.30 pm. 300 kids were there and the music was so loud that no conversation could be heard! It was classic. Lights were flashing in every direction and dry ice steam was coming out of vents under the dance floor so it looked as if it was like Isaiah 6! When I got up to speak there was good listening. A couple of kids who were drunk started to muck up but Christian kids "bounced" them. I hated it. The Christian kids were ecstatic! I think I like the sort of evangelism where I am completely in control and don't have to trust God at all. He, in His infinite kindness, keeps pushing me into new and scary places.

---

1   Letter from SUEU President Larry Hand to EU members dated 29 May 1976.

2   Interview at Ridley College 12 December 1994.

3   The tape recording of that address in Adrian Lane's possession is very revealing!

4   BDM Prayerletter August 1977.

5   Prince, *Out of the Tower*, pp 65,66.

6   Rosemary Waugh produced detailed reports of the SUEU missions of 1977, 1980 and 1981. The report of the 1977 mission has been catalogued ISBN 0 9595622 0 6 by the National Library of Australia.

7   Anthony Brammall also recalls that as the mission went on, the mission's detractors became more personal in their ridicule. Signs started to appear saying "John Chapman tucks his singlet into his underpants".

8   *Sydney Morning Herald*, Thursday 3 July 1980, p 11.

9   Report of the Sydney University Mission 1981, p 2.

10 Chapman, *A Fresh Start*, pp 91,92. More detailed statistics of the results of the survey were given in the Prayerletter No. 4 1981.

11 Department of Evangelism Prayerletter No 3 1982.

12 Department of Evangelism Prayerletter May—July 1989.

13 T C Hammond led a mission at Oxford in 1947 or 1948 "although without marked success". See Warren Nelson, *T C Hammond: Irish Christian—His Life and Legacy in Ireland and Australia*, The Banner of Truth Trust, 1994, p 121.

John, 1980s.

REGIONAL MISSIONS

Billy Graham Crusade—1979

In 1976, the Archbishop of Sydney, Marcus Loane, decided to invite Billy Graham back to Sydney for another crusade in 1979 to mark the twentieth anniversary of the momentous crusade of 1959. A letter arrived on John Chapman's desk from the Archbishop informing him of his decision and asking John to be present with him, to give moral support, at a meeting of the heads of denominations at which the Archbishop would announce his decision and seek their participation. John's initial reactions to a 1979 crusade were negative. He says:

> I was very unsure as to whether we ought to put our effort into another crusade. The "climate" was very different from 1959. We had seen how hard it was to reach the non-churchgoer in our dialogue evangelism work. There was a massive gap between getting non-churchgoers to dialogue meetings and trying to get them to guest services on the following Sunday—very few fronted.

It also seemed that any plans that John and the Department of Evangelism had for evangelistic initiatives through the late 1970s and early 1980s would have to be deferred. A Graham Crusade was a major event. It would consume everyone's energies for two or three years because, apart from the Crusade itself, there would be a long period of preparation as well as a period of follow-up. John felt that "I needed a Graham Crusade like I needed a hole in the head".

In his frustration, John spoke with Phillip Jensen and outlined his misgivings. Phillip gave a pragmatic, hard-headed response. As John recalls:

He said something like, "You will be mad to oppose it. You won't stop it. And you can use it to do everything you have ever wanted to do and do it under the umbrella of 'Getting ready for Billy Graham!'"—which we did. I decided that I would not do anything by way of preparation that was not worth doing anyway. My test was—Suppose Billy Graham never gets here, would you still be doing this? If the answer was "Yes", I did it. If "No", I didn't. We ran courses on every conceivable thing. As the Billy Graham machine started to roll, we plugged the whole work of the Department into it. We had a great time getting ready. We had a great time during it. Once again I was wrong in my judgment of what would and wouldn't work.

In December 1976, the Archbishop called a meeting at The King's School, Parramatta, of clergy and full-time lay workers to sound out some ideas for a preparation programme for the 1979 Crusade. There was a very large attendance and those present showed an obvious and heartening enthusiasm.

The Diocesan Synod, through its Standing Committee, had appointed a Billy Graham Preparation Committee under the chairmanship of Bishop Ken Short of which John and the Department's Assistant Missioner, John Webb, were both members.[1] Through this Committee, the Archbishop held four regional meetings during Lent in 1977 at Parramatta, Wollongong, Lindfield and Sans Souci to encourage Anglicans to a renewed zeal for prayer and evangelism. The Preparation Committee also ran courses and conferences on a wide range of topics, including Neighbourhood Visitation, Personal Evangelism and Apologetics, Evangelistic Writing, Home Visitation Evangelism, Training Trainers for the Setting-Up of Nurture Groups, Letter Box Drops, Evangelism and Ethnic Groups, Evangelism in Flats and High Rise, Evangelism and the High School Student, and Evangelism in Your Shopping Plaza.

The inter-denominational Crusade Committee under the chairmanship of Bishop Jack Dain appointed John chairman of the Follow-up Committee. The Follow-up Committee had responsibility for looking after all those who went forward in response to the appeals made at the Crusade meetings. Its first task was to assess the material to be used for counselling and for following up new believers. In John's view, and in the view of his fellow committee members, much of it needed to be rewritten. It had a particular weakness. The Billy Graham organisation had long used a verse from the Book of Revelation as part of its evangelistic strategy, Revelation 3:20. The verse says "Here I am! I stand at the door and knock. If anyone hears my voice and opens the door, I will come in and eat with him, and he with me." The words are those of Jesus. The use of the verse in the context of a crusade carries the implication that each person is free to choose whether or not to invite the Lord Jesus into their life. It is entirely a matter of individual choice. It puts the individual sinner at the centre of the universe and suggests that he or she is able to hold God at arm's length. A respectful, unimposing and powerless God stands politely and patiently knocking on the door of an unbeliever's heart awaiting his or her response. If the unbeliever is prepared to open the door of his or her heart, to ask Jesus into his or her life, then Jesus can accept the invitation and enter as a guest and fellowship between them can take place.

Despite the place of this verse in the history of Billy Graham crusades, John had a number of proper objections to its use in evangelism. Revelation 3:20 occurs in a passage addressed to the angel of the church at Laodicea, so it is addressed to believers rather than to unbelievers. A believer, having been brought to life in Christ, is capable of making the response suggested in the verse, whereas an unbeliever, because he or she is dead through sinfulness and has all the characteristics of death, is totally incapable of making it. The response of repentance and faith that is the appropriate response to the gospel and an indication of a person's conversion does not necessarily occur through the process of "asking Jesus into your heart". Furthermore, if it is exclusively the right of the human will to choose God, there can be no basis of assurance for salvation because a person who can choose God one moment is free to reject Him the next. The Billy Graham view of Revelation 3:20, a view widely held by others, clearly embodied a thoroughly anthropocentric view of salvation.

Through the work of the Scripture Union's Owen Shelley, all the children's material, including the references to Revelation 3:20, was rewritten. The material also required revision because it was old-fashioned, sentimental and did not sound at all Australian. The revision of the adults' material had not progressed sufficiently before the Billy Graham organisation's Charlie Riggs arrived in Sydney in 1978 and stopped the project. While John and his committee fought hard to continue their work, at no stage were they able to convince Charlie Riggs or other representatives, such as Tom Phillips, of the changes they wanted. John says:

> They seemed genuinely surprised by our attitude on the appropriateness of Revelation 3:20 and said, "But, John, God has often used this verse in the past. He has used it all over the world." I pointed out that God had often used it in the past because it was the only verse in the Bible they had used so God was "forced" to use it. This didn't go down well! The Billy Graham organisation is so big it just rolls everything before it. What is strange is that they think they are co-operating with you but, in fact, they see the locals as the workers who will implement their decisions. Don't misunderstand me, they do have a massive amount of accumulated wisdom, but they often don't understand the local scene and they basically assume that they know better than the locals, which I found irritating in the extreme.

The Follow-up Committee produced material directed to four areas—personal Bible study, parish study groups, links with Christians at work and regional Bible studies. John wrote, "We are anxious to provide maximum help to new converts without trying to over-organise them".[2]

The Crusade ran at Randwick Racecourse from 20 April to 20 May 1979. "It turned out," John says, "a million times better than I thought. A significant number of people came to Christ." The clergy of the Diocese, in particular, made a valiant effort to get people to the meetings. In John's view, "The way the clergy responded was an indication of their deep love and respect for Marcus. I don't know if he ever really understood that." The Crusade was attended by 491,000 people, an average of 24,575 each night. The total number of inquirers was 21,331, which was 4.34% of those who attended the Crusade. Of these inquirers, the telephone surveys of the Follow-up Committee showed that 89% began attending church and 70% joined a nurture group. In reporting to the Department, John wrote:

> I am sure you will also be interested to know that this was about half the number of people who attended the 1959 and 1968 Crusades. I have not been able to obtain accurate figures on these but I understand the average was about 40,000 who attended each night and the response rate was 5.6%.
>
> What this means in terms of mass evangelism I am not sure. There are several factors I think which bear on it:
>
> (a) the logistics on the first day;
> (b) the week of rain that followed;
> (c) the difficulty of access in having to drive around the city.
>
> Whether or not these reasons sufficiently account for the decline is a matter of conjecture. I guess Bruce Wilson would say, "It isn't really appropriately Australian".[3]

Regionalism—the Sutherland Crusade

John concluded his report on the 1979 Billy Graham Crusade by saying:

> I think it would be true to say that we ought to try and encourage further mass evangelism efforts like this one on a regional basis in the future. I have discussed this matter with several clergymen and will report to you further if anything comes to light.

One of the clergymen John had spoken with was Peter Watson, then the rector of St Luke's, Miranda. Peter Watson and his congregation had supported the Crusade to the hilt but had found it difficult to get real outsiders to come. Peter felt confident that if a crusade were to be run on a regional basis at a neutral, non-church venue such as the Sutherland Civic Centre they would have greater success. The difficulty in using church buildings was that unbelievers, who did not frequent them, felt like uncomfortable intruders because Christians tended, almost automatically and unthinkingly, to make meetings in that setting resemble church services with all their arcane practices. An inter-denominational crusade would also necessitate the use of a neutral venue.

Peter Watson was also convinced that "Australians have got to hear the gospel in their own accent". In the Referral Room for the Crusade one night after a meeting, he spoke to John. Peter was sure in his own mind that if there were to be a regional crusade, John should be the evangelist. He suggested it to him.

Dudley Foord shared the view as to the potential of regional missions. Then the rector of Christ Church, St Ives, he began planning a two-week crusade, North Side Reachout, at the St Ives Showground for the middle of 1982.

At the beginning of 1980, John spent three months as a staff member at St Helen's, Bishopsgate, in London. It was his second three-month period of service at the church, the first having been at the beginning of 1976. As a consequence of that visit, the rector of St Helen's, Dick Lucas, was invited to work in Sydney during July and August 1982. John had not forgotten the matter of regional crusades or his discussions with Peter Watson. He did not feel, however, that he was an appropriate person to conduct a public ministry of that kind. He simply lacked the confidence to believe he could do it. He also questioned whether, because he carried no particular public notoriety or appeal, anyone would be sufficiently

Diocese of Sydney.

interested to come and hear him speak. John was aware that Dick Lucas was experienced in missioning on larger platforms. Dick had spoken at a mission conducted by the Cambridge Inter-Collegiate Christian Union at Cambridge University. His talks were from Mark's Gospel. John had also seen Dick Lucas doing what Dick described as "teaching evangelism" at St Helen's week by week as he expounded the Bible. John pressed Dick Lucas to undertake the task. When Dick came to Sydney, one of the appointments on his itinerary was the Sutherland Crusade. Mark's Gospel was to be his theme.

A few weeks before Dick Lucas' arrival, Paul Barnett, now the Master of Robert Menzies College at Macquarie University, had written to John. His letter read, in part:

I hope your Board won't mind me writing to them about the following ideas for evangelism in the Diocese. It is written after some thought and also as you know after some discussion with you. This is what I would like to say to them.

Could I, with respect, suggest that consideration be given to an ongoing programme of week(?) long regional suburban "crusades" conducted by John Chapman and an appropriate team, utilizing strategically located Town Halls or similar. My reasons for suggesting this are as follows:

1. Having now heard Leighton Ford (extensively in both Adelaide and Sydney) and also Luis Palau I believe John Chapman has as much or more

to commend him as an evangelist. He is clearer theologically than Mr Palau and at least Mr Ford's equal. His capacity as a public speaker is very considerable and the evidence is that God has used him significantly as an evangelist. He has the confidence of his fellow Anglican clergy as well as many of other denominations. Above all he is Australian. In no way do I detract from the faithfulness of Mr Ford or Mr Palau.

2. I am frankly concerned that John Chapman's health may not be able to be sustained in the present style of ministry. How thankful we are that he is as prepared to speak to small groups as to large and to inaccessible places as well as in Sydney. But how long can it continue? He is not only our best

evangelist (in my opinion) he is, in fact, our only evangelist. He is simply too valuable a resource to be burnt out in the present style of ministry.[4]

Paul advanced some further reasons and set out, in reasonable detail, a format in which regional evangelism might be undertaken. As a consequence of his letter, Paul Barnett was invited to

In mid-August 1982, Dick Lucas also spoke at Wollongong. Dick, Harry Goodhew and John.

address the members of the Board of the Department at their meeting in June where a full discussion of his proposal took place. One of the Board's members, Jim Ramsay of St Luke's, Liverpool, promptly offered to pilot the concept in the Liverpool area.

The Sutherland Crusade, entitled "Lifestyle '82", was an inter-denominational crusade. It was held in the Sutherland Civic Centre each night from 3–11 July 1982. It drew good numbers. The average evening attendances exceeded 700. On the youth night, when every scrap of space was occupied, the organisers lost count at over 1,400. Associated functions comprising a men's dinner and a morning women's meeting were also well attended. John says, "It was a good time. As I watched Dick night by night I decided that I could easily do it."

The gift of interpretation

John is very quick in sizing up a situation. One of the meetings at which Dick Lucas spoke during the Sutherland Crusade was attended by about 800 women. They were really packed in. Some of them had babies with them. There was a lot of noise. John knew that Dick would be distracted by it. Just before the meeting began, John jumped to his feet and said something like "Ladies, ladies, ladies! I can hear what your children are saying. I have the gift of interpreting tongues. What they are crying out is 'Mummy, Mummy! Please get me away from this boring man!'" John's appeal had the desired effect. He has the knack of knowing how far he can go.

Peter Watson
recalling the Sutherland Crusade of 1982.

Liverpool—South West Outreach

Arrangements were quickly made for John to speak at two regional missions during 1984. The first was at Liverpool in April and the second at Hurstville in September.

Lifestyle '82 logo.

A year of intensive planning and preparation went into South West Outreach, the Liverpool mission. It was an inter-denominational mission in which eleven churches in the area were involved. The local organising committee was chaired by Jim Ramsay. In order that John might become known to the members of the participating churches before the mission was conducted, and to increase their acceptance of him as an evangelist, he spoke at thirty-five meetings and in all but three of the churches during the three months before the mission commenced. The workload was heavy and intense.

In association with the discussions that had taken place within the Board of the Department concerning the directions for John's future work, there had been discussions concerning staffing. Throughout the 1970s, the Department's staff had generally consisted of John, as Director, an Assistant Missioner (if there were sufficient funds to employ one) and an office secretary. The role of the Assistant Missioner was to share the Director's workload and to carry the overflow. A change occurred in this role to some extent in March 1978 when Donald Howard replaced

John Webb. Part of Don Howard's role was to develop ministries among the business community of the city along the lines John had seen at St Helen's in London. In February 1980, the Department's work expanded in an entirely new direction. Luciano Ricci, then a layman, was appointed as an evangelist to Italians. During the course of 1982, Don Howard indicated his intention of returning to parish work. He left at the end of June 1983 to accept appointment to the parish of St Stephen's, Lugarno.

Don and Nan Howard's wedding.

Throughout the second half of 1982, the Board, having been given generous notice of Don's intentions, had considered a number of possibilities for his replacement. The options were another Assistant Missioner, a person to concentrate exclusively on Sydney's business community, a worker to nurture evangelism in the western and south-western areas of the Diocese, a crusade administrator or a high school evangelist. The Board had been actively pursuing the possibility of employing Neil Flower to pioneer a work from a base in the expanding and under-resourced western area of the Diocese. By the time these negotiations ended unsuccessfully, the amount of preparatory work required to successfully launch the two projected regional missions was becoming a major concern. On 28 November 1983, Howard Peterson, a layman and a parishioner of St Barnabas', Broadway, joined the staff of the Department as Outreach Projects Officer.

CHAPTER EIGHT

At the beginning of 1984, another change occurred in the Department's staffing. David Short, a third year Moore College student, was appointed as the Department's first catechist. He was immediately pressed into service to speak at many of the coffee shops and other youth meetings associated with the lead-up to the Liverpool mission. Over the next few years as other catechists worked with the Department, part of their training was gained in a similar way.

South West Outreach
Left to right: Luciano Ricci, John, Law Min Yaw,
Howard Peterson

South West Outreach ran in the E G Whitlam Recreation Centre at Liverpool for two weeks from 1–15 April 1984. The average attendance each night was 450. Because of the ethnic composition of the area, there were simultaneous translations into Italian, Mandarin Chinese, Cantonese Chinese, Vietnamese and Spanish. John had taped all his talks beforehand so that the translators could familiarise themselves with them.

John prepared fourteen evangelistic sermons from passages in Luke's Gospel, a remarkable accomplishment.[5] The major thrust of the programme was the reading and preaching of the gospel. Everything else was to serve it. All who came were given a copy of Luke's Gospel. They were encouraged to have it open before them during the meeting and to take it away and read it afterwards. This practice, as much as any other, reflected the clearly understood theological basis of the programme. It was this. In his letter to the Christians in Rome, the apostle Paul wrote of "the gospel of God—the gospel... regarding his Son" (Romans 1:3). God's gospel is all to do with His Son. It is not basically about humankind and human needs. It is about the Lord Jesus Christ. It tells who He is and what He has done. It was assumed that most Australians of the time knew nothing about Jesus. So, as they arrived, they were given a Gospel in modern English. The address was taken from that Gospel. Both the speaker and the audience were therefore focused on the person of Jesus. Together they examined the work of Jesus as revealed in the Scriptures that lay open before them.

The outline of the programme was:

1. Appropriate background music as people arrived.
2. Chairman's welcome.
3. A song from a vocalist.
4. A Christian testimony, drama or a book review.
5. Bible reading.
6. Talk.
7. A song from a vocalist.
8. Explanation of the response card.
9. Chairman's "goodnight".

Testimonies were included because John wanted people to see that the truth of what he was claiming was clearly demonstrated in the lives of ordinary, unexceptional men and women. Unlike, say, at the Billy Graham Crusades, no collection was ever taken up. The programme ideally lasted sixty minutes and never more than seventy minutes.

John has always determined in his evangelistic preaching that there must be nothing about himself or his setting that might give unnecessary offence to the unbeliever. Like Paul, he desired "to become all things to all men so that by all possible means I might save some" (1 Corinthians 9:22). Any offence was to come solely from the message of the gospel. The gospel's challenge to the pathetic desire of men and women for independence from God whose only Son Jesus has been given sole authority to rule the whole created order and every person in it—that was to be the real offence, that was to be the confronting focus—not the thoughtlessness or insensitivity of the preacher. "I tried to make the unbeliever feel at home," John says. "I wanted our events to be user-friendly." The care that was taken at every point to destroy any vestige of "churchiness" and to ensure that no-one would be alienated by anything that took place during the meeting is illustrated in John's instructions to the chairman concerning the Bible reading. They were as follows:

Wherever possible, we have encouraged the local clergy to read the Bible. When it can be seen that they are taking a high profile, there can be no doubt about their support for what is happening.

It would be helpful to remind them to take care about the way they introduce the reading of the Bible. The Gospel that people have in their hand is called "The Good News by Luke". They should be encouraged not to call it "Luke's Gospel".

I would suggest something like this: "When you came in tonight, you were handed a blue-coloured book called 'The Good News by Luke'. It is part of the Bible. I am going to read some of it and you can follow it by turning to page 55. You will see almost at the bottom of the page the heading 'The Lost Son' and under it the number 11. 'Jesus went on to say, 'There was once a man who had two sons...'".

The "in-group" words are "gospel", "chapter" and "verse". The non-churchgoer doesn't know what we are talking about. Please ask them to resist giving a sermonette about the reading. When the reading is finished, ask them to sit down without comment. No statement like "This is the Word of the Lord" or "May God bless to us the reading and hearing of His Word", etc. should be made.

South West Outreach had its successes and its failures. Many people were converted in the lead-up meetings, during the mission proper and over the weeks that followed. John delighted in telling of one woman's experience:

At one meeting, I met an elderly lady who was so far "down the tracks" that it wasn't an impertinence to ask her age, to which she laughed and said, "It depends on what you mean! Three weeks to be exact." (She was in fact 85.) She had only that month come into a new relationship with Christ.[6]

Part of Luciano Ricci's work among Italians involved establishing an Italian church in the Liverpool area. Its members had originally met at St John's Park before moving to the more central location of St Luke's, Liverpool. A special campaign of advertising in Italian was undertaken in connection with South West Outreach, including the distribution of 6,000 Italian invitations. Despite the publicity, not one non-Christian Italian attended the meetings.

John wrote to his supporters, "I found this work much harder (in terms of emotional strain) than anything I have done and am very thankful that God used your prayers to strengthen and sustain me."[7]

On the evening of Saturday 30 June 1984, a South West Praise night was held at the Cabramatta High School in thankfulness to God for His blessing through the mission. Many new Christians were present. There was much high-spirited singing and music-making. "Rather than evangelism, this time the Christian life was the accent. Chappo spoke brilliantly as usual, but this time to the Christians, on Matthew 20:20–28 on how success in the Christian life was the complete antithesis of success in the world; that it meant giving our lives away in service to each other in order to be a 'great one' allowing God and our brethren to serve as we serve them. It was a great night all round."[8]

Hurstville—Goodspeak '84

The regional mission "Goodspeak '84" was also an inter-denominational mission. It involved thirty-three churches and was held between 13–23 September 1984 in the Hurstville Civic Centre.

Over a four-month period in the lead-up to the mission, John spoke at forty-eight meetings, including guest services, prayer breakfasts, men's breakfasts and

John at Goodspeak '84.

dinners and women's coffee mornings and luncheons. Again, it was a deliberate strategy that many of the meetings were held at non-church venues, such as the St George League's Club and the St George Sailing Club. People without a church association felt more at home there. Christians felt more confident about inviting them. The strategy was successful. These meetings enjoyed large and enthusiastic attendances and, through them, people came to know the Lord.

Nearly 7,000 people attended the eleven Goodspeak meetings and more than 200 filled in response cards indicating either their acceptance of Jesus as Lord and Saviour or their desire for further information about the Christian faith. It was estimated that 45% of those attending each night had not previously attended a meeting. It was a time for reaping. John wrote in the Prayerletter:

> I was especially aware of your prayers. I was in bed with a flu virus for most of the time but was able to get to the meetings and speak. This physical disability was matched by fierce attacks from the Evil One in the form of terrible doubts. The details are not important but it was a strong reminder to me that our warfare is spiritual and it needs to be fought with spiritual agencies. Your prayers did it. Please don't let up in standing in prayer. Your partnership in this way does more than you will ever know.[9]

Goodspeak '84

Just a personal note to give you some feedback of a type that you may not get very often.

Back in 1984 I was pastor of Carlton Baptist Church when you spoke at a St George combined churches mission which was held at Hurstville Civic Centre (Goodspeak '84).

At that stage the church was struggling, it did have a good sized youth group but only one of them was a Christian. During the mission four girls (15–16 years old) responded to the gospel.

I worked very hard to disciple them and they blossomed into radiant young Christians. Over the next twelve months in ones and twos most of the youth group were converted. The rest of the church got very excited and instead of feeling defeated they had a strong belief that God would act and that He would use them.

I moved to Broken Hill back in 1986 but the church has gone from strength to strength. It all started during that Goodspeak Mission in 1984. Those four girls are still going on with the Lord.

I hope you find that encouraging.

A letter received by John and quoted in the Department's Prayerletter for August—October 1993.

At Liverpool and Hurstville, there was congregational singing, but this was dispensed with after those missions as it was found that many non-churchgoers, because of their unfamiliarity with church music, could not join in. With time, other changes were made. Regional missions became less and less like the special event crusades of the past and less and less like traditional church services. They developed a distinctive character of their own.

The Archbishop, Donald Robinson, came to both the Liverpool and Hurstville missions. On the occasions he came, he gave the Bible reading. He saw the public reading of God's Word at these events to be of great importance.[10] He later inquired of John why John had stopped inviting him to do it but no conscious decision to that effect was ever made.

One remarkable feature of the period covering the preparation for and conduct of the first two regional missions was that John did not forgo completely work of the kind he regularly undertook before those missions made their extraordinary demands. He continued to do some parish work, he spoke at various conferences, he took his share of the regular series of Bible studies in the city and he published his second book *A Fresh Start*. His workload was excessive. It is a wonder he survived. Indeed, immediately after Goodspeak '84, John wrote to his Board graphically describing the pressure of his circumstances. He put forward a number of suggestions as to how his range of tasks might be reduced. One suggestion was for additional staffing.

The later missions

By the end of Goodspeak '84, John had been booked to conduct regional missions until the end of 1988. In fact, over the six-year period from 1985 to 1990, twelve regional missions were conducted in almost every part of the Diocese of Sydney. The form of a mission was flexible. Each was adapted to suit the particular region having regard to its composition, its needs and peculiarities, the best strategies for getting people together and the extent of the desire for co-operation on the part of the participating churches.

Connection '85 logo and publicity drawing of John.

Connection '85 was based on the Warringah peninsula. Because of the geography of the area, one week's missioning took place at the Collaroy Classic, a cinema, and the other, during almost constant rain, at the Allambie Heights Community Centre. Consequently, the mission comprised two independent mini-crusades.

One of the difficulties in conducting regional missions was that, while some of the local clergy were keen to evangelise in this way, others were not. Yet those who were not so keen were reluctant to express their indifference. Indifference could easily have been construed as opposition to work that lies at the centre of the Christian life. Almost all Christians agree that evangelism is good in principle even if they find it hard to evangelise in practice. Another difficulty was that the lead-up time for a regional mission could be so extensive that the minister who was its real driving force might have moved to an appointment outside the region before the mission took place. The loss of such a visionary's catalytic effect could be significant. At Warringah, the support of the local clergy was erratic. The planning meetings were, on occasion, poorly attended. Some clergy had not adopted suggestions made to them concerning the preparation required. For example, more than half the guest services at which John spoke, despite his briefing, took the form of the Holy Communion. John's view was that:

> I think it would be true to say that this crusade has been the most difficult one we have done.
>
> On the negative side, many Christian people in the area did not avail themselves of the excellent opportunities to bring their friends to hear the gospel. This is always sad for them.

On the positive side, of those who have made the effort, many have seen their friends come to Christ. One minister told me last night that he was following up thirty people who had responded in one way or another. Rejoice with us over the people who have been converted.[11]

Despite all difficulties, nearly 5,000 people attended the mission and over 200 made responses.

John again expressed the strain caused to him by regional missions. "I know this is like a cracked record," he wrote, "but we do need to make our staffing needs an urgent matter of prayer. We need another evangelist to help with this work".[12]

The pattern of regional missions was temporarily interrupted in the second half of 1985. This was to enable the Department's staff to contribute their efforts to the Leighton Ford Crusade "Celebration '85" held in the Sydney Entertainment Centre in the last two weeks of September and two other events conducted at the time of the Crusade. These were a conference on local church evangelism and the first conference ever to be held specifically for Australian evangelists. The Australian evangelists' conference was organised through the United Evangelistic Crusade Council.

From 6–20 April 1986 at the recently refurbished Ashfield Town Hall, John was engaged in preaching the gospel to the churches of the inner western suburbs of Sydney through "Come Alive '86". The Ashfield Presbyterian Church was a significant contributor to the mission. On different nights, there was simultaneous translation of John's talks into Korean, Mandarin Chinese, Cantonese Chinese, Italian, Greek, Spanish and Arabic. There was an average attendance of 250 over the thirteen meetings. It was a good result considering the smallness of many inner-city

Come Alive '86 logo.

congregations. Following this mission, Howard Peterson's appointment came to an end and his place was taken by the Department's office secretary, Janet Kearsley, who had first joined the staff of the Department in September 1980.

The regional missions that followed were:

"A Fresh Start"	Wollongong Town Hall	14–28 September 1986
"Straight Talk '87"	Hawkesbury/Nepean	
	Kurrajong	8–15 February 1987
	Pitt Town	1–8 March 1987
	Riverstone	22–29 March 1987
	Windsor	5–12 April 1987
	Penrith and St Marys	21–29 May 1988
"A Fresh Start" Lower Blue Mountains		
	Springwood Civic Centre	1–8 November 1987
"A Fresh Start" Upper Blue Mountains		
	Lithgow	21–28 February 1988
	Katoomba	6–20 March 1988
"The Chapman Event"	Upper North Shore	15–30 October 1988

153

"South West Outreach"	Liverpool	12 February–7 May 1989
"Fit for Life with Christ"	Eastern Suburbs	6 August–17 September 1989
"A Fresh Start"	Kiama/Jamberoo/Gerringong	5–12 November 1989
"Make a Fresh Start"	Engadine	11 February–8 April 1990
"A Fresh Start"	Blacktown	11 May–3 June 1990
"A Fresh Start"	Chatswood/Mowbray	19–28 October 1990

The Chapman Event logo.

Fit for Life with Christ logo.

The western area missions in the Hawkesbury and Nepean area that ran through 1987 and into 1988 were an initiative of Bishop Ken Short, then the bishop in Parramatta. He sought to stimulate the people of his region in evangelism as one of a number of special projects associated with the celebration of Australia's Bi-Centenary in 1988. Because the region comprised a number of distinct communities, it was not appropriate to seek a single location. The same was true of the mission held in the Upper Blue Mountains where separate meetings were held in Lithgow and Katoomba and the mission on the South Coast involving Kiama, Jamberoo and Gerringong. In the case of the Eastern Suburbs mission, two combined public meetings were conducted only after all the individual meetings had been held in the participating churches.

In January 1988, Ian Powell joined the Department's staff. He had been its second catechist in 1985 and was now ordained. It was perhaps ironic that a basic team of the kind required to conduct missions of the scope and complexity of regional missions—comprising an evangelist, an assistant evangelist, a trainee minister and an administrator—was only assembled in 1988 at a point more than half way through their currency.

Regional missions were a clear sign throughout the decade of the 1980s of the grace and mercy of God and the power of the gospel to raise the dead to life in Christ. The ears of people were opened to hear the very voice of God as He was pleased to add to those whom He was saving. His gift to many was blessing for eternity.

Regional missions eventually gave way to the more traditional parish missions which were far less taxing in their organisational demands.

A Fresh Start: Mission Solent

John's involvement in regional missions was not limited to the Diocese of Sydney. Mission Solent, an inter-denominational organisation, had held a successful crusade with Leighton Ford in 1984 throughout the area comprising Hampshire and the Isle of Wight. As a follow-up, it invited John to conduct a mission under the title "A Fresh Start" during the whole of November 1986. John, by way of preparation, met with local clergy and spoke evangelistically at meetings at Winchester and Southhampton during his visit to England in May 1985.

This mission was one of the most extensive in which John took part as the principal evangelist. He wrote this report concerning it:

Mission Solent map.

What a time November 1986 was. Thank you for your prayers. They were wonderfully answered. The publicity for this series of meetings was probably the best I have seen. The organisers adopted as their theme, "Whatever you think... John Chapman is worth listening to". Everytime I looked around, I saw my picture with its slogan on it. I was on the back of buses, on posters in shop windows and, in most towns I looked like a new aggressive estate agent because of the signs on people's lawns advertising the Crusade.

During the month I spoke at fifty-two meetings. These ranged from preaching in Winchester Cathedral to coffee mornings in small villages. It's always difficult to quantify evangelism so I'll give you some statistics and you can draw what conclusions you will. The total attendance at all meetings was just over 19,000. 850 people filled in cards and asked for help. About 5,000 copies of Luke's Gospel were taken. About the same number of A Fresh Start books were sold. We heard of many people who were converted. Thank you for praying. I was wonderfully sustained.

The road to life. Mission Solent street sign.

Three meetings stand out in my mind. At Basingstoke, I spoke at a business persons' lunch at the Rugby Club. There were 150 present of whom 80% were outsiders which means each Christian brought four friends!! At a small village out from Winchester called Arlesford the women from a coffee morning group (eighteen in all) held a meeting to which 140 came. A little village called Whitchurch (population 4,000) had 400 at a meeting in the school hall.[13]

The passage—not the preacher

I had taken a friend of mine to church at St Barnabas', Broadway. My friend, although warmly disposed towards the gospel, had not at that stage been in the habit of church going for quite a number of years. John was the preacher and, as I remember, expounded Romans 6. It was a fine sermon, characterised by all the usual Chapman traits. It would have been easy to respond to the sermon by being fascinated by the power and personality of the preacher. Instead, my friend turned to me at the conclusion of the sermon and said, "What a great passage that is". I thought that nothing could illustrate better the essence of a fine preacher. It was not that the personality of the preacher had been hidden or down-played; it was rather that his personality had become the servant of the passage that he was expounding and in the end the hearer was focused on the Word of God, not on the servant through whom the Word came.

When someone has so strong and interesting a personality as John, it would be easy to turn Christian ministry into a personality cult and create disciples. John has managed to combine his strengths with service in such a way that he points to the true Master rather than to himself. For this we thank the Lord our God.

Peter Jensen,
Principal of Moore Theological College.

The message

When John first began his public preaching, he followed the styles he had observed others use. It was then common to preach on a text. A sermon was often constructed from a single verse of the Bible. Sometimes the texts chosen were very obscure. The preacher's ingenuity and breadth of scholarship could be well demonstrated in the exposition of a verse such as "Og's bed was made of iron and was more than thirteen feet long and six feet wide" (Deuteronomy 3:11). Another approach was to locate, from a concordance, all the references in the Bible to a single word and to preach on that word from those references. It was also common to treat the Bible as a book of allegory. There was nothing novel in that approach. Allegorical interpretation has a long tradition. As an example, the Book of Proverbs contains these verses:

There are three things that are too amazing for me,
four that I do not understand:
the way of an eagle in the sky,
the way of a snake on a rock,
the way of a ship on the high seas,
and the way of a man with a maiden (Proverbs 30:18,19).

Ambrose, the fourth century bishop of Milan, is said to have offered the following highly allegorical commentary concerning them:

The *way of the eagle* he understands to be the ascension of Christ, flying back as an eagle to his Father, carrying man plucked from the jaws of the enemy as his prey with him!... *The way of the serpent on the rock* shadowed the assaults of Satan upon Christ–on whom, as *on a rock* (unlike the first man, who was earth and dust) he could leave no mark, no footsteps of his malice... *The way of the ship in the sea* is the way of God's church through the sea of persecution. This ship cannot miscarry, because Christ is lifted up in the mast of it—that is—on the cross... Or—Christ is the ship, into which the souls of all true believers do go up; which, that it may be carried more strongly in the midst of the waves, is made of wood, and fastened with iron: this is Christ in the flesh. And who can tell the way of this ship, either into the womb of the Virgin, or the heart of believers? *The way of a man in his youth...* illustrates the ways of our Saviour Christ in his youth upon the earth![14]

Another practice was to use a Bible passage as a springboard for teaching a biblical truth that really lay outside the chosen passage. The preacher would not necessarily expound the nominated text. John gives an example of this in the Appendix to *Know and Tell the Gospel* entitled "Preaching Evangelistic Sermons":

I once heard an evangelistic sermon which began by declaring Jesus to be the One who was able to "raise" men and women from the death of sin to a new life of righteousness. "He is able" we were told, "to give a new beginning." Three parts of the Bible were used to show this—the raising to life of Jairus' daughter (Mark 5:35–43), the raising to life of the widow's son of Nain (Luke 7:11–15) and finally the raising of Lazarus from the dead (John 11:38–44).

Briefly the sermon went like this: "Firstly, age and sex are no barrier to being raised from the death of sin. Jesus is able to do so. He raised a small child, a young man and an old man. He can do it to you. Secondly, when Jesus raised Jairus' daughter He instructed that she should be given something to eat. When a person is made new by Jesus, the person should immediately take in spiritual food—for strengthening. The Bible is the spiritual food and should be read to strengthen us in the spiritual life. Thirdly, the widow's son at Nain was given back to his mother, into a social setting. This shows that people who have been raised from the death of sin to the new life should not isolate themselves from other Christians but meet with them and fellowship with them. Fourthly, when Jesus called Lazarus back from the dead, He gave immediate instruction to untie him because his feet and hands were tied up with the linen grave clothes. This signifies that the new Christian is to have nothing to do with the things which belonged to 'death'. There is to be a clean break from everything sinful." The sermon concluded with a strong appeal to all who were "dead" to call upon Jesus to bring them to new life. The logical problem of the "dead" speaking was not covered but it did occur to me as strange.

Everything in that outline is both true and biblical, but none of the statements is a true exposition of its text. The sermon is not in fact about Mark 5:35–43, Luke 7:11–15 or John 11:38–44. It is a sermon on

Ephesians 2:4,5–"But because of his great love for us, God, who is rich in mercy, made us alive with Christ even when we were dead in transgressions—it is by grace you have been saved." The question that kept nagging at me was, "Why didn't he preach on Ephesians 2:4,5?" What he wished to say is clearly stated there.[15]

John has readily and unashamedly admitted to having appropriated the best of other people's work. He has drawn from it and adapted and modified it to suit himself. He has made it his own. His approach to evangelistic preaching is a synthesis of several influences. John Stott of All Souls, Langham Place, in London had visited Australia to take the Bible studies at the CMS Summer School in 1958. He spoke from 2 Corinthians. John says:

> I heard only one of those Bible studies but I was so taken by the way he stuck to the text and stayed with it. He could show you the logic of the argument in the Scriptures. Prior to that, I had tended to get an idea from a passage and to leap all over the Bible supporting the idea from other parts so that the people I taught knew the "idea" but not the passage from which it came or how that passage fitted into some overall argument from the Scriptures. It is to John Stott I owe what ability I have to expound the Bible. He provided a model for expository preaching that I could copy and make my own. I needed time to practise.

The immediate result was that John's preaching tended to become longer and meticulously expositing. After John had listened to Dick Lucas, he was given a vision to do evangelism by teaching from Bible passages, particularly the Gospels. The Lucas model was a tighter one and less complex. It deliberately contained fewer ideas.

The form of evangelistic address that John has developed contains two elements. Firstly, the gospel focuses on Jesus as Lord and Saviour (as King and Redeemer) (Romans 1:1–5). Secondly, its purpose is to bring people to repentance and faith in Him (Acts 20:21). Consequently, John chooses Bible passages that will enable him to show Jesus as Lord and Jesus as Saviour through His death and resurrection. He says:

> As Jesus is shown to be Lord, so people should respond in repentance because they have sought to exercise independence of His authority. Independence demonstrates the fact and reality of sin. As Jesus is shown to be the Saviour, the only one who can save us from the punishment for sin, so faith is expressed as a response to the reality and effectiveness of His rescue work on the cross.

Following the address, the most obvious thing to do, John believes, given the content of his preaching, is to finish with a prayer for people to express their repentance and to put their trust in Jesus as Lord and Saviour. Accordingly, his practice has been to explain that he was about to pray a prayer of response. He would read out the text of the prayer first.

> Heavenly Father,
>> I haven't been serving you as my God.
>> I am sorry about that.

Please change me.

Lord Jesus, thank you for dying for me.

Please forgive me and take over the running of my life.

He would then tell those present that he was going to pray the prayer sentence by sentence and that, if anyone wanted to do so, they could pray it to God themself echoing it silently in their head. The prayer was then read, leaving an appropriate interval after each sentence. "However," John adds, "I must also say that such is the nature of the spiritual warfare that I have never *felt* that it was right to do it and, contrary to *all* evidence, I am still tempted to believe that nothing will happen. It is one of the reasons I *always* do pray as I have stated."

As to the appropriateness of making an appeal, John says:

All of us have suffered in the past by emotional and disturbing appeals that have made us wary, to say the least, about making any appeal at the end of evangelistic preaching. I remember once attending an evangelistic meeting where, at the end of the talk, we were all invited to stand. Then the Christians were all invited to sit down. Who is now left standing? The preacher then invited people who wanted to become Christians to sit! There was a 100% response. It is hard to get people to believe you love them when you treat them like that.[16]

John believes that "standing up to be counted" is not a part of repentance. Sooner or later, a person who has become a Christian must make a personal declaration of their faith but this should not necessarily be done at the moment of conversion. However, the benefits of calling for an indication of a person's response to the proclamation of the gospel are that some people will want to do something— to take some step—to show that a change has taken place in their life. Some will be given an opportunity to disclose a misunderstanding that can be corrected through subsequent pastoring. Others will want to take the next step as a consequence of their conversion and be linked into a regular programme where they can be nurtured and grow.

The question of response

I first met John in the early days of his visits to teach "Dialogue Evangelism" at St Helen's, Bishopsgate, when I was doing a curacy in South London suburbia. That approach to evangelism, with its mature theology of human response, was for me foundational in my approach to evangelism ever since. It was particularly John's cutting of the Gordian knot between the appeal and the visible public response, on the grounds that what should be the happiest day of their lives for a great many converted people became (by the evangelist's insistence on immediate public response) a guilt-filled day, when those converted did not have the courage to walk down the front as they knew they ought to. John's zeal to see people converted, with his reformed theological approach to how visible or invisible that will be, is salutary.

Mark Ashton
The Round Church at St Andrew the Great, Cambridge.

At all regional missions as well as on other occasions when John has preached evangelistically, at some stage before or during the meeting, a card, an envelope and a pencil were handed to each person. This enabled them to indicate on the card, if they desired, their response to the message they had heard. They could

disclose whether they had prayed the prayer, whether they had not but wanted some more information about the Christian faith or they could make some other comment. Everyone was encouraged to write something so that those who wanted help would not be embarrassed that they were seen to be the only ones doing any writing. The card was then placed in the envelope to preserve confidentiality. Following "Connection '85" John commented, "The card method will soon be so well

A Fresh Start—Upper Blue Mountains, 1988.

established in the Diocese that no one will be able to evangelise without a card, envelope and pencil!"

And the messenger

Whenever John rose to speak publicly, his audience would be conscious of a person of energy. His movement to the lectern was always purposeful and direct, as if he could not wait to get there. He began talking from the moment he arrived, if not sooner. Depending on the circumstances, there might be some loud asides or some banter with the chairman as he made his way to the place from which he was to speak. He had a strong sense of purpose. He gave the distinct impression that his part in the proceedings was infinitely more important than any other. Everything else taking place around him was peripheral and subordinate to the preaching of the Word of God.

John was always meticulously prepared. It would be tempting to presume that everything came to John easily because of his remarkable giftedness, that he somehow found the performance of his ministry effortless in a way that others do not find theirs. John has commented that it is extremely rare for anything to be good if it is totally spontaneous. The best is always thoroughly prepared. What his audience does not see are the hours of preparation spent at his desk. They have not witnessed the sheer hard work and application that have gone into ensuring the end result is of the highest standard. What is presented with such apparent facility is the result of much hard labour. The processes for John are no different than for any other. Care and thoroughness in preparation reflect his view of duty and obedience. They are marks of his piety.

Before speaking, John had generally rehearsed, in his bedroom or in his car, the things he was going to say, particularly the main lines of his speech. He appeared not to speak from notes, although he had an outline with him, no more than a dozen lines on a page, as points, not even as sentences. It was important that he be able to look at every member of his audience as often as possible. When he spoke, he never stared into space or at the floor. His eyes constantly met those of his audience. And as he spoke, he needed to have his hands free. His speech was accompanied with quick, forceful and symmetrical arm movements, often with arms aloft.

Clay feet bringing Good News

In the late 1970s, John ventured to the Eastern Suburbs Crusaders' Saturday Night Meeting on several occasions. Most of the young teenagers had no church contact and many came from broken homes. They were a rowdy bunch of boys. John wasn't sure if he was up to it.

When Chappo pulled up in his car, I couldn't understand a word he was saying. He was speaking with a weird echo—every word being repeated even before it was finished. No, not signs and wonders! He was speaking along with his talk which was being played back on the cassette player, memorising it. I was surprised that the "great one" had to be so thoroughly prepared—just like the rest of us!

During his talk on a parable of Jesus, one kid in particular kept mucking around and making funny noises. John used all the old techniques. He paused several times (waiting) but to no effect. Then he paused and looked in the kid's direction. No change. Then he paused and eye-balled the kid. Still no result. They were only separated by a body length. Finally, in total exasperation, John stopped, glared at the boy and said "You really are a right little pain in the neck. Sit still and be quiet!"

It was so effective that everyone froze for the remainder of the talk, including the leaders! It was a powerful message in more ways than one.

PS That boy never mucked around again *and* he kept coming! I don't remember whether he turned to Jesus but, over time, lots of the boys did and some are following in John's footsteps. Good one, Chappo!

Geoffrey Ellerton
recalling John's subtle approach to evangelism.

John always explained at the outset that God is a God who speaks to us and that the way He almost always does this is through the Bible. He would tell his audience that he was going to pray that God would speak to them now. He would then pray that prayer. He always expounded a passage of Scripture, usually from one of the Gospels. Everyone would have a copy of the passage in front of them and would be encouraged to refer to it and to check for themselves whether or not what he was saying was true. He spoke quickly, although his delivery became slower with increasing age and some of the dazzling verbal gymnastics of his earlier years all but disappeared. His voice was not a cultured voice, but it was strong and clear. It was unmistakably an Australian voice.

John stands in the line of born preachers who were not afraid to risk the charge of vulgarising their message by the use of colloquial language, the language of the vernacular. John Calvin's preaching, for example, adopted familiar and popular speech.

> Often he indulges in quite dramatic passages, making the characters with whom he is dealing express themselves in racy soliloquy or dialogue. Instead of making Moses, on receiving the order to ascend the mountain, point out how fatiguing and dangerous that would be for one of his years, Calvin pictures him as exclaiming, "That's all very fine! And I'm to go and break my legs climbing up there, am I? Of all the things in the world! That's a fine prospect!"[17]

"The most famous preacher in the sixteenth century was Hugh Latimer. He spoke with the same voice whether at court or at Paul's Cross or in the country. He was plain, bold, and shrewd, with a touch of racy humour, and a flair for homely illustration, and a colloquial dash that gave his words the power of instant penetration."[18] George Whitefield was accused of using "market language" and of speaking "John Bunyan's English".

Chappo cracking a funny at A Fresh Start—Lower Blue Mountains, 1987.

Charles Haddon Spurgeon was idiomatic, often abrupt, blunt and direct. These were preachers who wanted to use words that would be readily understood by everyone. They wanted to communicate. They wanted to make the complex simple, to make the truth sound plainly in people's ears. John spoke with a total lack of pretension. His speech was stripped of difficult or obscure ecclesiastical language. It contained no words like 'sanctification', 'propitiation', 'absolution', 'oblation' or 'justification'. Nor did John affect an ecclesiastical reserve. He opposed aloofness and pomposity. His aim was naturalness. His speech was leavened with innocent humour.

On the place of humour, John says:

> I don't think humour can be learned. You can either use it or you can't. If you can and you are really funny, you need to take great care. It can be a good servant but a hopeless master. Whatever happens, the gospel must not appear to be flippant.[19]

John has always had good illustrations, taken from everywhere, but particularly from the commonplace. As was said of Spurgeon, "...he could vivify his sermons by all manner of telling and homely, sometimes perhaps too homely, illustrations".[20] John was so clever in his use of an appropriate illustration that he could recast and embellish someone else's story and make his version of it far more interesting than theirs. Trevor Edwards, John's minister for a time at St Aidan's, Hurstville Grove, recalls:

I quickly learned that there were some things John did not need to know. In particular, new or unused stories or jokes needed to be guarded jealously. I once shared a new non-golfing joke with him after morning church only for it to be broadcast to half of Oatley at an open air anniversary service that same afternoon as he warmed up the local crowd.

John has always been a brilliant story teller, well-rehearsed and often extremely funny.

John would become enormously frustrated if anything happened about him that might distract his hearers from what he was saying. He was conscious that the Evil One is constantly seeking to snatch away the Word of Truth. The room had to be comfortable. The sound system had to be faultless. There must be no crying children. He had a number of verbal devices for getting attention quickly back to him if any distraction arose. All his strategies were aimed to give absolute centrality and supremacy to the preaching of the Word. Nothing was to impede it. Nothing was to take attention away from it. It was to be taught and heard in the most ideal of circumstances for to come under the sound of the Word of God was the most important thing that any person could do. Each occasion was to be as personal for each hearer as he could make it. Each occasion was to be potentially climactic.

John rarely spoke for more than half an hour and it often seemed less. There are very few people who, having heard him preach, cannot remember something he has said. John says, "When I'm preaching, I try to do what is best for the person who hardly ever goes to church, to help that person feel at ease and able to concentrate on the message".

Although the apostle Paul may have written these words to address a different circumstance, John is equally entitled to say:

When I came to you, brothers, I did not come with eloquence or superior wisdom as I proclaimed to you the testimony about God. For I resolved to know nothing while I was with you except Jesus Christ and him crucified. I came to you in weakness and fear, and with much trembling. My message and my preaching were not with wise and persuasive words, but with a demonstration of the Spirit's power, so that your faith might not rest on men's wisdom, but on God's power (1 Corinthians 2:1–5).

Plain knitting (and purl)

Soon after I "married into the Department", John invited us to his unit and I admired the cable-knit sweater he was wearing. He had knitted it himself after learning the art from books borrowed from the library.

When I expressed amazement, he said, "There is really nothing to it. There are only two basic stiches, purl and plain. So I selected a style and followed the pattern."

Isn't that Chappo? He has amazing ability to simplify the complicated with remarkable results.

Nan Howard
whose husband, Donald, worked with the Department of Evangelism from 1978–83.

CHAPTER EIGHT

1   John Webb had joined the staff of the Department at the beginning of 1976 and continued until his appointment to the New Housing District of Georges Hall on 23 November 1977.

2   Prayerletter No. 3, 1978.

3   Bruce Wilson, a sociologist, then the rector of St George's, Paddington and later the Bishop of Bathurst, had expressed certain views about the nature of Australian Christianity. These views later appeared in his book *Can God Survive in Australia?* Albatross Books, 1983.

4   Letter from Paul Barnett to John Chapman dated 22 April 1982.

5   John has commented on this statement, "It is not all that remarkable. You may be interested to know that over the years the 14 has grown to 27! Each time I use the series, I add a couple more."

6   Prayerletter No. 2, 1984.

7   Prayerletter No. 2, 1984.

8   Howard Peterson writing in Prayerletter No 3, 1984.

9   Prayerletter No. 4, 1984.

10 Perhaps the Archbishop had 1 Timothy 4:13 in mind.

11 Prayerletter No. 2, 1985.

12 Connection '85 Report in the records of the Department of Evangelism.

13 Prayerletter No. 1 (February—April) 1987.

14 Quoted in Charles Bridges, *A Commentary on Proverbs*, The Banner of Truth Trust, 1979, p 607.

15 John C Chapman, *Know and Tell the Gospel*, pp 167,168.

16 John's notes for Lecture 5 on Evangelistic Preaching in the *Communicating Christ* series.

17 "Life of Calvin", A Mitchell Hunter, quoted in W Y Fullerton, *Charles H Spurgeon: London's Most Popular Preacher*, Moody Press, 1966, p 103.

18 Marcus Loane, Presidential Address to Synod, 1976, Year Book of the Diocese of Sydney, 1977, pp 227,228.

19 John's notes for Lecture 4 in the *Communicating Christ* series.

20 The (English) Daily Telegraph 14 January 1888, quoted in Fullerton, *Charles H Spurgeon*, p 85.

Hear ye! Hear ye!
Town Crier and Evangelist.

KNOWING AND TELLING

The early theological influences

It would not be accurate to describe John Chapman as merely a simple proclaimer of the gospel. He is also a theologian. His desire to serve God with the wholeness of his being has caused him to spend much time in reading and reflecting in God's Word. His increasing knowledge has enabled him to contribute significantly to our understanding of the theology of the gospel and of evangelism.

John's own formal theological education was scant. Such formal education as he had was acquired haphazardly.

After his conversion, John's early theological influences had come almost exclusively from reading. He began to teach himself from books such as J C Ryle's "Knots Untied" and "Holiness", Griffith Thomas' "The Thirty-Nine Articles" and "The Catholic Faith" and Calvin's massive and monumental "Institutes of the Christian Religion". He had sat under a biblical ministry for only two of the six years between leaving Sydney as a twenty-one-year-old manual arts teacher at the end of 1951 and his ordination at the end of 1957. During 1956, he had attended St Paul's, Oatley, where he was probably preaching more times than he was listening, and in the following year, he had studied a single subject as a student at Moore College. When John commenced his ordained ministry in the Diocese of Armidale, he resolved that he would teach himself theology beyond the influences he had received to that point. It was not until then that he began to acquire what he thought to be a proper theological understanding.

While in Armidale, John had four main sources of stimulation. Firstly, he spoke regularly at the weekly meetings of the undergraduate members of the Evangelical Union. Secondly, he met regularly with the Graduates' Fellowship of the Australian Fellowship of Evangelical Students. The occasional talks he gave to its members at their monthly meetings on Sunday afternoons involved him in much earnest and careful preparation. The Graduates' Fellowship introduced him to the writings of Leon Morris and to numerous Inter-Varsity Press publications. The standard of the contributions offered by the other members was high and John also learned a great deal from them. Thirdly, he drew on the friends who were closest at hand. Peter Chiswell and Ray Smith had received a fuller and rather more balanced theological education than John. He found their companionship to be of great assistance. Fourthly, as time went by, other Moore College graduates made regular visits to stay with John and John made occasional visits to Sydney. On one occasion, he spoke at a houseparty organised by the Parish of Lindfield. At it, he made the acquaintance of Paul and Anita Barnett. They became friends and Paul Barnett was a considerable stimulus to John's theological thinking. Later, when Paul was on the teaching staff at Moore College, the Barnetts sometimes spent their holidays in Armidale with John.

In the dust of Quirindi, circa 1966

Anita and I had a holiday with John in Armidale and we travelled around the Diocese with him. I will never forget going with him to the primary school at Quirindi. No classroom was free so John taught these very small children squatting down in the dust under a peppercorn tree. To this day I can still see him cupping his hands like the begging Bartimaeus and the children cupping their hands too. What a gifted communicator he is.

Paul Barnett.

From his tiny period of structured teaching at Moore College, from his discussions with Moore College graduates and from his other contacts, John's thinking was influenced, in particular, by two members of the Moore College staff—Broughton Knox and Donald Robinson. Outstanding men, they gave him the surest foundation for his future work. From them, John acquired a desire to be biblical and to go wherever the Bible led him. They taught him to have such a care for the text as would cause him to let it say what it says rather than to make it say what he wanted it to say. In 1965, Broughton Knox took a series at the CMS Summer School at Port Macquarie on the Nature of God. John says, "These really informed me (or sharpened me) on how the gospel fitted in to the whole overall picture. He did a mini-theology course. His topics were—Sovereignty of God, Holiness of God, Righteousness of God, Kingdom of God, Purpose of God and Love of God. (I later turned them into a series of talks that were an even greater blessing to me.)"

Over a period of more than twenty years, the period that embraced the ten years of his ministry in Armidale and the first twelve years after his return to Sydney, John kept working to increase his biblical understanding and to fill the gaps in his education. In particular, he worked to develop a comprehensive and reformed theology of evangelism. He says, "Everything I read on evangelism left me cold. That is why I had to carve out a theology. Walter Chantry's book *Today's Gospel—Authentic or Synthetic?* was the first thing by a thoroughly reformed person I had read who had written anything on evangelism." John grappled with a whole range of issues. What is the essence of the gospel? Are there two different gospels, that of Paul and that of Jesus? What is the role of the minister in evangelism? What is the role of the church in evangelism? Is there a special gift of "evangelist"? What is the relationship between God's work and our work in evangelism? Why does God choose some and not others? Why is evangelism so hard? Of these, there were two issues that required particular reflection.

Donald Robinson had written several articles on the nature of the evangelist.[1] In them, he had commented on the passage in Ephesians 4 that lists several spiritual gifts. Verses 11 and 12 say:

It was he (the ascended Christ) who gave some to be apostles, some to be prophets, some to be evangelists, and some to be pastors and teachers, to prepare God's people for works of service...

Robinson had concluded that there was a gift of the "evangelist". The gift was not given to all believers, but only to some. Consequently, as not everyone was given the gift of evangelist, not everyone had to do evangelism. The only ones who had to do it were those who had the gift.

The charismatic movement that had swept through and preoccupied much of the Australian church in the late 1960s and during the 1970s also placed great emphasis on the gifts of the Spirit. Many Christians searched the evidence of their lives against the varying lists in Romans 12, 1 Corinthians 12 and Ephesians 4 as if those lists comprised an exhaustive catalogue of the gifts in order to try and pinpoint the gift that was peculiarly theirs. A common approach was to seek to identify your gift from what you felt you were good at, what it was you enjoyed, what it was you could do without difficulty. If you spoke in tongues (or what was thought to be tongues), your gift was obvious. Billy Graham's gift was obvious. He was clearly an evangelist. But if you found evangelism to be hard and struggled to do it, then the natural conclusion was that it could not be your gift. As John often remarked, not many were quick to claim the gift (in Romans 12:8) of generous giving!

Through Broughton Knox, John had understood that the minister's role was principally that of the pastor, or teacher. It was a role that consisted of teaching God's Word to God's people. This was to be done when God's people gathered. Consequently, the minister's role was performed through the diligent teaching and explanation of the Scriptures, Sunday by Sunday, to the flock whom God had entrusted to the minister's care. This marked something of a departure from the understanding and general practice of the previous generation. In a very broad sense, the ministers of the previous generation were basically evangelists at heart. They saw their principal responsibility as being towards the harvest field comprised of people of nominal church membership. They tended to proclaim the gospel in public worship on Sunday in order to evangelise this group while they studied the Bible privately with the faithful in a Bible class during the week. Broughton Knox's students, on the other hand, tended to be teachers first and evangelists next. They saw their principal responsibility not as being to the nominal membership but to the people of God. They were to teach the congregation. Although Knox may never have said it, John understood, at least by implication, that, while the minister might also have a role in proclaiming the good news of Jesus Christ, that was not part of the minister's role as pastor/teacher.

Following ordination, John accepted that his role was to be that of a pastor/teacher. However, because his immediate experience was of congregations comprised of many people who were either unconverted or at best very badly taught, his role in practice was very much that of the evangelist. At the time, he did not recognise that to be his role. He certainly did not think to claim the title of evangelist for himself.

John sought to contend with these issues biblically. "They were," he says, "hard ideas to counter. I had to hammer out a 'new' view of how evangelism fitted into the whole of church life." In 1981, he published the summation of his work in his book *Know and Tell the Gospel*. *Know and Tell the Gospel* is John's distinctive contribution to the theology and practice of evangelism.

Developing the theology

One vehicle John used to develop his views was the Bible study he and John Reid conducted in the Chapter House. The Bible study was held weekly throughout the year, except for the period from mid-December to the end of January. It generally took the form of a six-week series that worked progressively through a particular book. Because it met during the lunch hour, it consisted of the teacher speaking for half an hour with no opportunity for interchange with those who attended. The on-going and systematic approach was a good discipline for both speaker and hearers. Initially, John's participation in this form of ministry was probably an expression of his thinking that his principal role was to be that of the pastor/teacher. But it was also to serve another purpose. John says, "I wanted to use it to develop an on-going theology of evangelism and to show that evangelism was respectable for Christians (theologically). Not that I thought this hadn't been done. It was just what I wanted to do."

From the time of his arrival at the BDM/Department of Evangelism, John continued the practice of previous missioners of producing a periodic prayerletter. The Prayerletter generally appeared quarterly. John introduced the practice of prefacing each edition with a brief exposition of Scripture. It is possible to trace something of the growth in his understanding of the theology of evangelism through these introductions. For example, in the Prayerletter for October 1974, there is a four-point explanation of Romans 1:1–6 in almost identical terms to that which would appear seven years later in Chapter 2 of *Know and Tell the Gospel*.

In March 1975, the Prayerletter was prefaced with these words:

2 Thessalonians 3:1

Finally, brethren, pray for us that the Word of the Lord may spread rapidly and be glorified, just as it did also with you.

The New Testament seems to pulsate with the wonder of the spread of the gospel throughout the world—indeed with its triumph. We should reflect in our lives this same spirit. We should be those who long more and more to see the Word of the Lord spread rapidly. A strange fashion has crept into our thinking of late which I believe has not helped us. People have drawn our attention rightly to the fact that one of the gifts which the Spirit gives is that of the evangelist (Ephesians 4:11). However the conclusion which many have drawn from this fact seems strange. They reason that since all people do not have this gift then only those who have this gift are obliged to engage in evangelism. It has had a devastating result! Suddenly **everyone** has decided they don't have the gift and are therefore absolved from engaging in the spread of the gospel!!!

May I draw your attention to:

1. We don't know what the "evangelist" (Eph 4:11) really did or what the evangelist's gift is. There are only three references in the New Testament; Philip was one (Acts 21:8), Timothy is told to do the work of one (2 Tim 4:5) and among the gifts which the ascended Christ gives is the evangelist (Eph 4:11).

2. In the light of this scant information, I believe we should be fairly cautious in identifying this gift as that which we would call "personal evangelism".

3. All people find it difficult to engage in evangelism and we all need support from others. We should not conclude we do not have the gift because we find it difficult (Eph 6:19). However in 2 Thess 3:1 Paul requests these Christians to pray for the rapid spread of the gospel and for the Word of the Lord to be glorified.

   Will you do this and will you also pray that you will be made "bold" to preach the gospel to your friends (Acts 4:29).

By the time of the book's publication, John was even more definite. "In spite of the specific gift to the church of the evangelist, and the command of the Great Commission given to the apostles, the Bible teaches that **all** Christians are to directly engage in evangelism."[2] He drew this conclusion from the authority of verses such as 1 Peter 2:9,10 where God's people are described not only as a special people but as a people who are given a special task, that of declaring the praises of God. "All Christians belong to the people whose purpose is to 'declare the mighty deeds of God'."[3] As it had been since Old Testament times, God's chosen people were to mediate God to the nations of the world.

Give thanks to the LORD, call on His name;
make known among the nations what He has done,
and proclaim that His name is exalted.
Sing to the LORD, for He has done glorious things;
let this be known to all the world (Isaiah 12:4,5).

Writing on New Year's Day 1981 for the Department's first Prayerletter for that year and just a few months before *Know and Tell the Gospel* was published, John gave this summary of the position he had reached as to the minister's role:

2 Timothy 4:1–2,5

In the presence of God and of Christ Jesus, who will judge the living and the dead, and in view of His appearing and His kingdom, I give you this charge: Preach the Word; be prepared in season and out of season; correct, rebuke and encourage with great patience and careful instruction... keep your head in all situations, endure hardship, do the work of an evangelist, discharge all the duties of your ministry.

THE MINISTER AS A TEACHER

These instructions to Timothy show clearly how important is the teaching office of the Christian leader. Paul reminds him that he exercises his ministry in "the presence of God and of Christ Jesus". He is reminded that he will give an account of his faithfulness on the day of judgment. He is reminded of the certainty of this event in unmistakable language "in view of His appearing and His kingdom" (v.1). He can be left in no doubt about the solemnity of this. He is to do it "in season and out of season". He is to do it negatively (correct, rebuke) and positively (encourage) and he is to stick at it (with great patience).

Pray that your minister will be faithful and work hard at his teaching.

THE MINISTER AS AN EVANGELIST

Because he is primarily a teacher of God's Word, he will also be an evangelist. To "discharge all the duties of his ministry" will require him to do the work of an evangelist (v.5). For too long we have driven a wedge between teaching and evangelism. I don't think the Bible does! Notice the way Paul describes the Colossians' response to the gospel: "...you heard it and understood God's grace in all its truth. You learned it from Epaphras" (Colossians 1:6–7). Epaphras taught them the gospel.

Pray that your minister will be faithful and work hard at evangelism.

THE MINISTER AS AN EXAMPLE

It is important that the minister do so because the minister is supposed to equip us for our ministry (Ephesians 4:11–12). The minister is meant to be an object lesson in godly living. The minister is meant to set an example for us to follow (see 1 Corinthians 11:1, 4:16; 1 Thessalonians 1:6; Philippians 3:17; Hebrews 13:7). If the minister is not a faithful teacher, the minister will encourage us to neglect the study of God's Word and we will begin to believe that obedience to God is a matter of indifference. If the minister is not a faithful evangelist, we will begin to think that the gospel is not urgent. We will begin to forget the peril our friends and loved ones are in. We may even begin to think that we are somehow relieved of doing evangelism ourselves.[4]

In 1980, John was given the opportunity to present the fruit of his labours. As part of his programme during a three-month visit to England at the beginning of that year to work as a staff member of St Helen's in London, he delivered a series of lectures at the Southampton School of Christian Studies on successive Friday nights. The School was under the chairmanship of Dr Peter May, described by John as "a medico, a member of General Synod, and a dynamic Christian leader".[5] It was just the occasion John needed to formalise his work.

On his return to Australia, John prepared a manuscript for publication.

Know and Tell the Gospel

Know and Tell the Gospel: The Why and How of Evangelism (later subtitled "Help for the Reluctant Evangelist") was published by Hodder & Stoughton (Australia) in July 1981. It carried the following dedication:

To Geoffrey Fletcher, evangelist and friend, who over the years has never tired in the work of the gospel. An inspiration and challenge to us all.

The book has two sections. The first section reflects the "know" part of the book's title and is headed "Knowing Why". It gives John's understanding as to what the Bible says about evangelism. It sets out the conclusions reached in his search for understanding and his resolution of conflicting points of view. In the book's preface, John wrote:

I argue in this book that the unit of evangelism is the individual Christian rather than the church—that the minister is to be both evangelist and trainer as part of his pastoral/teaching role—that the local church is to train and encourage the individual for an evangelistic task—and that the individual Christian is caught up in this work, which God initiates and controls and for which He provides all the strength needed to accomplish it.

Saviour and Lord: not one without the other

Jesus is able to save us from sin and death because of His overthrow and defeat of Satan. He is able to save because He is Lord. Consequently it is not possible to accept Jesus as Saviour and not as Lord since He saved by being Lord.

The Bible may separate these functions of Jesus to describe them but they are inseparable when applied to mankind. That is why the true response of a person to Christ is a genuine repentance which involves recognising Jesus as true King in God's world and thus seeking to live under His authority. Great damage has been done by encouraging people to invite Jesus into their lives as the One who will save them and forgive them without any real call to repent of an independent attitude towards Jesus' right to be Lord.

John Chapman

Know and Tell the Gospel, p 34.

The first section is like Paul's letter to the church in Rome with its wise theological insights and its cogent theological arguments. It is a strongly structured, logically argued and well-illustrated thesis. It gives a clear and thoroughly biblical perspective. It demonstrates one of John's great skills, that he can put the deepest truths into simple words. You do not have to be a theologian to understand what he has written.

John's insistence on the sovereignty of God and the responsibility of mankind as revealed in the Scriptures and the unique interaction between God and mankind is strongly stated in the chapters entitled "Who Does What?—God's Work and Ours" (Chapter 6) and "Why Doesn't God Choose Everyone?" (Chapter 7). They are models of a reformed theological understanding. John argues biblically that God initiates the gospel, God initiates evangelism and God also initiates human response. In acknowledging the encouragement and assistance of a number of people in the development of his arguments, John says, "I lived in the era of Broughton Knox, who was so grace oriented, and Paul Barnett and the Jensen brothers who were putting their minds to these issues and thinking about them all the time".

Four years after the book's publication, in speaking to a conference for Australian evangelists organised in connection with Leighton Ford's "Sydney Celebration" in September 1985, John gave a graphic illustration of his view of the role of the evangelist under the sovereignty of God.

> I said that we evangelists ought not to think too highly of ourselves. I said that I thought evangelists were like people who rushed around the orchard and gave the trees a bit of a shake. And if the fruit was ripe, it fell off. And if it wasn't ripe, it didn't matter how hard you shook, nothing happened. And when it really was ripe, well, if an old cow wandered into the orchard and bumped into a tree here and another one there, even it would knock the fruit off.

God works through His Word

Some people have expressed the idea that preaching is a waste of time unless God has regenerated the hearer, as if God did His work apart from His Word. No indeed! It is through His Word that he works (Genesis 1:3). How does He bring us to faith? The apostle Paul explains that "faith comes from hearing the message, and the message is heard through the Word of Christ" (Romans 10:17). Consequently we are not to be inactive, but eager to tell people the gospel. It is the powerful way God saves people.

John Chapman
Know and Tell the Gospel, pp 65,66.

The second section of the book is titled "Knowing How". It enlarges the "Tell" part of the book's title. It is a training manual—a handbook of ideas to equip—that sets out a variety of suggestions and methods for engaging in evangelism. This section is more like the letter of James with its practical Christian wisdom. Knowledge alone is never enough. "...faith by itself, if it is not accompanied by action, is dead" (James 2:17). Faith must result in deeds because true love always shows itself in action.

Many writers on evangelism offer only one means of approach as if a single technique will suit everyone. With John there was no such inflexibility. He documented a range of methods. This enabled people to choose the method most suited to them and the particular gifts God had given them. They could be themselves. It also enabled them to choose a method that might be more relevant to the needs of those whom they sought to evangelise. They could be truly personal.

In the first section of *Know and Tell the Gospel*, John addressed a theme he was to return to many times. It contrasts living with speaking, example with proclamation. Is the gospel somehow incarnate in the life of a Christian so that it can be discerned from a godly lifestyle? Or must the gospel be specifically announced? He had written:

> Godly living is a top priority of all Christians (Romans 8:29). However, the godly life is at best ambiguous. People will certainly recognise **that** a Christian is different if he lives the Christian life. They will not, however, be able to work out **why** he/she is different.[6]

On a later occasion:

> The work of Christ is applied to us through the gospel. Paul reminds the Ephesians that it was when they heard the gospel and believed it that they were included in Christ (Ephesians 1:13). Someone told it to them. There may be many things which will cause a person to want to listen to the gospel. It may be the kindness of a Christian friend, or the winsomeness of a life lived before them, but in the end it is the gospel which saves them. There is no way that I can live my life so that a person will understand that Christ has died and risen again for them. They may perceive that they are sinful and that the whole world is but they cannot perceive the remedy unless they are told.
>
> Pre-evangelism is important but it is not evangelism. Bridge building is for "crossing the gap". It is not an end in itself. It was when the Ephesians heard the gospel that they knew that there was "redemption through his blood" and they were able to know the forgiveness of sins by putting their trust in Christ.
>
> We are called to live for the praise of his glory. Part of that will be through speaking the gospel to our friends. **Evangelism is speaking.**[7]

In an interview published in "The Inside Scene Magazine" for "Church Scene" in October 1994, John was even more emphatic:

> Brothers and sisters, we cannot proclaim what God has done by the way we live. There is nobody alive who can live in such a way that somebody can perceive that Jesus died and rose so their sins could be forgiven. It is utterly impossible—and it is twaddle to go on as if the gospel can be spread simply by the way you live your life.
>
> Of course the gospel can be reinforced when people recognise that I'm taking it seriously—when I'm kind and gentle and loving, and when all of the fruits of the Spirit are seen in me. But nobody can understand the

gospel except that it is explained by words. How can I comprehend that "the Son of God loved me and gave himself for me" except you tell it to me? How can anyone in Australia perceive that they can be forgiven for their sins and be in right standing before God except we tell them about the work of Jesus? Do let's get that straight!

I'm not talking about how that's to be done—but about the fact that it is to be done. Within the framework of our circumstances and gifts we are all expected to do that.[8]

Accordingly, all the techniques suggested by John in the second section of the book reflect an understanding that evangelism consists of speaking.

While John's theology of evangelism has not changed since the book was written, his thinking about the practice of evangelism has continued to develop. For example, he has reconsidered the question of how to make an appeal at the end of an evangelistic sermon. *Know and Tell the Gospel* outlines a variety of methods, including asking people to signify their response by coming to the front of the church, asking them to wait in their seats while others leave and asking them to speak to him or to the minister at the end of the meeting. The card method subsequently developed in the context of regional missions has now become John's preferred method of recording response.

Within four months of publication, the book's first modest print run of 3,000 copies had sold out. In 1983, the book was published for the first time in Great Britain. In 1985, it was published in the United States of America by NavPress with the subtitle "A down-to-earth guide to sharing your faith". By July 1991, the tenth anniversary of its original publication, more than 40,000 copies had been sold, including 14,000 on the UK and USA markets. During those ten years, *Know and Tell the Gospel* had been reprinted at least once every year and twice in 1985 and 1987. In 1995, it is still in print.

In May 1979, the Department of Evangelism adopted a new logo. Based on Romans 10:14, it sought to convey the idea that one needs to speak of Jesus and another needs to hear.

The author's original concept

produced the first logo

and with further development, the current logo.

The book has been a source of help and encouragement to many. In a letter received by John in 1986, a correspondent wrote:

Before I left for holidays, my Bible study friends gave me a copy of *Know and Tell the Gospel* as a farewell present...It has really helped me tremendously with my poor old attempts to spread the gospel, and amongst my friends at Macquarie University it has become another text book for us (although it's a lot more practical than physics texts).[9]

When John was in the United Kingdom in May and June 1987, Derek Prime, the minister of the Charlotte Street Chapel in Edinburgh, invited him to speak at an evangelistic weekend in that city. John stayed with a couple there who had read *Know and Tell the Gospel* and, as a consequence, had begun using their home for evangelism. A clergyman has written about *Know and Tell the Gospel:*

> I have regularly read and re-read John's book over the past ten years. I find it always challenges my complacency, and helps me to face some real questions. It's good to have a friend who is brutally honest and John's book fulfils this role admirably.[10]

A Fresh Start

Within twelve months of the publication of *Know and Tell the Gospel*, John had written a second book. It was produced reasonably quickly in a concentrated spell of writing. This book was intended to serve a rather different purpose. Whereas *Know and Tell the Gospel* was a handbook on evangelism for believers to explain its theology, to challenge each Christian's commitment and to give practical encouragement through the presentation of a range of methods for gospelling, *A Fresh Start* was written for a different audience. In its preface, John wrote, "(This book) deals with how we can become friends with the living God. It is written for people who are prepared to look into Christianity. It sets out the fundamentals."

The Lord in His world

On one occasion after Jesus had been teaching from Peter's boat they set out to cross the sea of Galilee. It was evening and Jesus had fallen asleep in the back of the boat. A severe wind storm arose so that the disciples despaired of life itself, in spite of the fact that they were experienced fishermen who knew the lake and knew their boats. It was more than a breeze on Sydney Harbour. One of them shook Jesus with the rebuke, "Don't you care if we all perish?" Jesus stood up in the boat and commanded the winds and the waves: "Quiet! Be still!"

Here is Mark's description of what followed. "The wind died down and it was completely calm. He said to his disciples, "Why are you so afraid? Do you still have no faith?" They were terrified and asked each other—"Who is this? Even the wind and the waves obey him!" (Mark 4:35–41).

Jesus is shown to us as master in His world. Certainly no ordinary man can do what Jesus had just done. Any day you are tempted to think you are the master of the creation take a ferry trip from Circular Quay across to Manly, or across the Channel from Dover, and as you come to where the swell is greatest have a go! Command the waves to be still. (I would advise you to do it quietly out at the stern of the ship where no one can hear you.)

John Chapman
A Fresh Start, pp 106,107.

A Fresh Start is divided into four parts. Part 1 addresses the fact of mankind's rebellion against God's authority and the awful consequences for the whole of creation. It examines God's solution through the death and resurrection of Jesus Christ. Part 2 looks at the evidence for the existence of God, whether there is any reliable information about His nature and the relationship between God the Father and Jesus. Part 3 warns of "the seriousness of our danger if we continue to reject God's free offer of pardon and friendship"[11] and of the fateful consequences of that rejection. It warns of the futility of seeking God's acceptance on the basis of conventional goodness. Part 4 explains how, through repentance and faith, a person becomes a Christian and how such a person can be sure that he or she is a Christian. The cumulative effect of the four parts is to enable the reader to undertake a thorough examination of the Christian faith and to give simple guidance as to how he or she might make a fresh start.

The book was designed to be an evangelistic tool that Christians might give to their unconverted friends in order to introduce them to the gospel. It was to serve its purpose admirably.

A Fresh Start also utilised material John had worked with and had re-worked and refined over twenty years of evangelistic endeavour. In fact, it is largely an edited collection of his evangelistic sermons. For example, Chapter 3—Something is Terribly Wrong—began as an evangelistic sermon on Genesis 3 and the section in Chapter 4—What Has God Done About It?—headed "Many ways to describe it" (dealing with various descriptions of Jesus' death that help us to see its true significance) was an evangelistic sermon on Romans 3:23–25a.

By July 1982, the manuscript was in the hands of the publisher. The book was expected to be available before Christmas that year. As events transpired, it was not released until April 1984. The delay occurred partly because Paul Barnett, the book's editor, had thought that the book would be improved by making a number of changes and by the inclusion, in particular, of a section indicating that the life of a person who became a Christian "should be marked by goodness, especially in relationships with other people".[12] While John did not disagree with Paul's suggestions, he was frustrated that he had so little time for rewriting. Eventually, a three-and-a-half-page "PS" was included at the end of the book to deal with the nature of the transformed Christian life.

There is nothing abstract or obscure about John's writing style. It is free of theological technicalities. It is regularly punctuated with anecdotes. It is always full of interest. He writes with a vigorous directness which has, as he is fond of saying, "the subtlety of a train smash at ninety kilometres an hour".[13]

> In a totally pragmatic way he employs a "programmed learning" style that enables, for example, the second section of the book (on such questions as the existence of God, the deity of Jesus and the reliability of the Gospels) to be bypassed if they are not a problem to the reader. So too the third section on "What's the Alternative?" can be bypassed by the reader who wants to get down to the business of "What's to be Done?", the final section of the book.

The end result is a very useable tool in the hands of those enquiring about faith in Jesus Christ. In fact, it is perhaps without rival for its straightforward, Australian, "home-grown" approach.[14]

In reviewing the book on its publication in England, Richard Payn, John's fellow student from the Moore College class of 1957, wrote:

A Fresh Start rests upon a firm biblical base and, as the author seeks to persuade his reader to act upon the evidence he presents, he follows good apostolic tradition. "In the light of his (Jesus') claims," he urges, "you cannot say, "What an interesting person–do have another cup of coffee."[15]

Some fresh starts

I would just like to say thank you to you as a fellow believer in our Lord Jesus for your wonderful book "A Fresh Start". My husband and I in the past few months have been greatly blessed in seeing three of our friends come to accept the Lord Jesus as their personal Saviour through reading your book.

Prayerletter No. 3 August–October 1986

John preached at St Matthew's, Manly, on Easter Day 1985. During the service, a doctor from the congregation testified how she had been converted through reading "A Fresh Start". "How I rejoiced to hear this," John said.

Prayerletter No 2 May–July 1985

At the end of 1992, the impact of "A Fresh Start" was still being felt in the lives of its readers. A letter was received at the Department of Evangelism from a student worker in the country. She wrote:

One of our workers during a mission here spoke to a student K. and then sent him a copy of "A Fresh Start". Last night K. came to the Chapel for the first time and said for the last three days he had been reading this book and the New Testament and believes in Jesus now. During the open prayer time, he prayed and thanked God for creating us and sending us Jesus to pay for our sins. Isn't that wonderful!

Prayerletter November–January 1993

Three months after the release of A Fresh Start, John wrote to the recipients of the Department's Prayerletter:

This (the book's reception) has startled us all. Two editions have been sold and the third (not yet printed) is half sold in orders. We want you to rejoice with us. Not only because it is being used but because God has seen fit to use it in the way you prayed for. Two notes sent to us tell the story.

1. A phone message 2/5/84 for JCC. Phillip Jensen rang to say "We have seen a person converted by reading A Fresh Start."

2. A letter dated 22nd May.

"Having given my new copy of *A Fresh Start* to her, my much prayed-for friend wrote back shortly after—'The book you gave me by John Chapman answered a lot of questions I had been asking. The main point it cleared up for me was the problem I was feeling that there was some missing link that I had for becoming a Christian. I found my answer. It was my will. I've been waiting for some spiritual, mystical happening to occur. After reading *A Fresh Start,* I've learned that isn't what happens ...Anyway, I've taken my first step. I've asked God to help me see my sins and seek repentance.'"[16]

Within the first twelve months, 10,000 copies of *A Fresh Start* had been sold and the book was being republished. Two years after its Australian publication, it was published in Great Britain. By May 1991, it had sold 40,000 copies and its sales had caught up to *Know and Tell the Gospel.* Shirley Watkins, the Religious Editor of Hodder & Stoughton (Australia) said at the time, "They both have been excellent for those of us who need a trusty framework on which to build a verbal witness to the faith". Like its counterpart, it is still in print.

Many testimonies have been received as to the book's role in helping the lost return to their Heavenly Father.

Audio and video tapes

From his earliest days with the BDM/Department of Evangelism, it was a common practice for John's talks to be taped, particularly those given at the city Bible studies. Although he far preferred working with a live audience, he also produced some studio tapes. Many recordings on a wide variety of topics have been made over the years.

At South West Outreach at Liverpool in April 1984, the first video tapes were made of two of the talks John gave from Luke's Gospel. "People around the Cross" and "The Resurrection of Jesus" were available by the end of the year for purchase or hire. Towards the end of 1986, the Department arranged for Anglican TV to produce a series of video tapes for which John gave four talks called "Telling the Gospel's Truth". In September 1988, John and Ian Powell made four more video tapes at the Robert Menzies College Chapel before a live audience. The titles were "Birth of the Rescuer", "What's So Good about Good Friday?", "Will the Real Christian Please Stand Up" and "The Most Shocking Verse in the Bible". Ian Powell commented, "This experience was harrowing and fun. The roll up on a (Rugby League) grand final afternoon was pretty impressive."[17] By July 1991, another series was in preparation. In response to requests for training, five messages of forty-five minutes each were made to prepare people for personal evangelism. Called "Tips for Sharing the Faith", they featured John, Ian Powell and Dudley and Elizabeth Foord. The topics dealt with were personal godliness, gospel outlines, bridge building, tough questions and leading someone to Christ. The tapes were accompanied by a set of discussion questions.

A keen desire to evangelise and to equip others to evangelise had seen the production in John's hands of a range of resources that were able to be flexibly utilised in diverse circumstances. There is no doubt that they found their mark in helping to bring many to repentance and faith in the Lord Jesus Christ.

A satisfied customer

Reflecting on my two years at "X" caused me to realise how dependent was my ministry on that of the Department of Evangelism. Many people, under God's sovereign grace, have been encouraged, challenged and brought to faith via *A Fresh Start*, the Video and Audio Tapes, *What is a Christian?* (English, Greek and Italian) and through the Dialogue Evangelism strategy.

This is a superb ministry most worthy of our continued financial and prayer support.

An extract from a letter received at the Department of Evangelism in April 1989 and quoted in Prayerletter May—July 1989.

After the extract in the Prayerletter, John appended the footnote: "We agree with this!"

---

1   "The Theology of Evangelism", *Interchange 3*, 1971, pp 2–4; "The Doctrine of the Church and Its Implications for Evangelism", *Interchange 15*, 1974, pp 156–162; "The Church and Evangelism", *Interchange 21*, 1977, pp 62,63.

2   Chapman, *Know and Tell the Gospel*, p 16.

3   Chapman, *Know and Tell the Gospel*, p 43.

4   These thoughts are reflected in closely similar language on p 78 of *Know and Tell the Gospel*.

5   Prayerletter No. 4 (November—January 1987).

6   Chapman, *Know and Tell the Gospel*, p 43.

7   Prayerletter May–July 1988.

8   *Church Scene*, 21 October 1994.

9   Prayerletter No. 4 (November—January 1987).

10 Prayerletter November 1991—January 1992.

11 Chapman, *A Fresh Start*, p 131.

12 Chapman, *A Fresh Start*, p 196.

13 Chapman, *A Fresh Start*, p 30. This is a favourite expression of John's in describing his approach to biblical exposition and evangelism.

14 John McIntyre, lecturer in Christian ethics at Ridley College, Melbourne, reviewing the book in *On Being*, February 1985.

15 *CWN Series*, 29 November 1985, p 7.

16 Prayerletter No. 3 1984 (August—October).

17 Prayerletter November 88—January 89.

World traveller.

SINGLE ITINERANT EVANGELIST

Three strands

There are three prominent strands that have been inseparably woven together in John Chapman's life and ministry. There is principally, although not exclusively, that of the evangelist. John is an exceptional evangelist. It is not too extravagant a claim that he has been the outstanding Australian evangelist of his generation. John is, of course, not only an evangelist—he is also an able teacher of God's Word—but evangelism has been a major focus and at the forefront of his work from the outset. Another strand is singleness. John's ministry is a ministry that has in many ways been shaped by the fact that he has chosen not to marry. Singleness has given John great freedom to do his gospel work. It has caused him no division of his interests. It has also enabled him to have the ministry of an itinerant. That is the third strand. John's ministry has regularly taken him to every other State and Territory of Australia and to many other countries of the world.

These strands are not the only ones to be found at the core of his life; there are many other interwoven threads that make up the strong rope of John's extraordinary character. He has, for instance, a strong intellect. He has a deep and real concern for people, shown in many ways, and "especially to those who belong to the family of believers" (Galatians 6:10). He is inclusive, giving of himself. He is a fine host, a good cook, a witty conversationalist. His practised self-discipline leads to a well-organised life. He has an administrative ability that requires everything to be done properly, with timeliness and thoroughness. He has a lifelong love for tennis and for golf. This list is incomplete. The difficulty in enumerating the qualities of John's character is that there are so many.

From John's perspective he did not, at some decisive moment, seize upon evangelism, or singleness, or the work of an itinerant, but rather he grew into them.

Evangelist

I well remember the first time I was ever called an evangelist. It was on a visit to Hong Kong and I was introduced as—"My friend, John Chapman. He is an evangelist." My immediate reaction was to say something like—"Well, I'm not really one of them!" Later, I reflected as to why I was so negative to the title. It conjured up all the things I dislike about tele-evangelists and ranting preachers. Why I didn't immediately identify myself with the great evangelists of the past and present like George Whitefield and John Wesley, Billy Graham and Leighton Ford, I do not know. However, I should never be ashamed of the title because it is one which can rightly be given to God Himself.

The Scripture foresaw that God would justify the Gentiles by faith, and announced the gospel in advance to Abraham: "All nations will be blessed through you." So those who have faith are blessed along with Abraham, "the man of faith" (Galatians 3:8).

John Chapman
writing in the Department of Evangelism's Prayerletter, November–January 1991.

Evangelist

John began, unconsciously, to walk the path of the evangelist from the outset of his Christian life, although it would be more than twenty years before he came to accept that description for himself. The wonder and the sense of rightness that had come upon him with the gift of God's Spirit had caused him to want to tell others. It had been a great embarrassment when he had failed to meet his first challenge. At an early stage, Doug Abbott had introduced him to the Youth Department where Graham Delbridge had enlarged his vision and where he had learnt some simple outlines of the gospel. There followed opportunities to practise—at houseparties, at Bingara and in other youth work in the Diocese of Armidale. Later, as Youth Director and then Director of Christian Education for that Diocese, his work began to take its more distinctive shape as a significant ministry of evangelism. John says:

> While my time as a curate at Moree had shown me that if you taught the Bible correctly, people would be converted, it was during my time as Youth Director that I began to develop evangelistic skills. I was running Youth Leaders' Conferences and Sunday School Teachers' Conferences and at all of these I would take a session called "Spiritual Life of the Youth Leader", etc. These were straight evangelistic events as I gauged that most (well many) were not converted. Much of the work I did when I visited parishes on weekends was evangelistic.

182

Evangelism, at that time, almost invariably took the form of parish missions. That was the settled method, not only in Armidale but throughout the church. John's early missions were like mini Billy Graham Crusades. Bishop Moyes conducted them and John assisted him. John's principal functions were to run a children's mission in the afternoons and, in the evenings, to conduct the singing "like Cliff Barrows".

Parish missions eventually waned and gave way to dialogue evangelism, but still John did not regard himself as an evangelist. He says:

My view of ministry at that time reflected the current view of Moore College which I was absorbing from Peter Chiswell, Ray Smith, Paul Barnett and anybody I could talk to. I thought a ministry role was that of a pastor/teacher rather than an evangelist but the really odd thing was that I was doing evangelism most of the time.

I think I thought that most church people in Armidale were either unconverted (or at best were very badly taught). There had been no evangelical ministry to them ever! So, while likening my role to the pastor/teacher, I was doing the evangelist thing all the time. Geoff Fletcher says that I told him soon after I joined the staff of the Department that I wasn't an evangelist!! He never stops reminding me about it.

While John acknowledges the influences of others in providing models for his work, in the area of evangelism he was an innovator.

Graham Delbridge fixed me with a great vision for evangelism and evangelicalism. He, more than anyone, helped me to look beyond Sydney to Australia "outside". I think Broughton Knox and later Paul Barnett helped me to see that teaching the Bible was what ministry was about. John Stott provided a model to do expository preaching that I could copy and make my own. Dick Lucas gave me a vision to do evangelism by teaching from the Gospels and from other parts of Scripture.

With regard to evangelism, I think I ploughed that furrow on my own initiative—many of the staff and Board members of the Department of Evangelism stimulated my thinking but most of my work on evangelism was mine.

When we first started dialogue evangelism, I remember I adopted what I had seen others do. By the time I got to Sydney I had worked out my four areas to evaluate a good evangelistic opportunity, namely:

- Are there unbelievers present?
- Was the gospel presented?
- Was the gospel presented in categories people could understand?
- Was the atmosphere conducive to listening or not?

The greater part of John's evangelistic work has been carried out in Australia. While it is becoming increasingly difficult to identify clearly and emphatically the common elements of the typical Australian character, there are some features of it that may be seen as having relevance to the proclamation of the gospel. Australians

Katoomba Youth Convention, 1979.

speak straightly to each other. An outspoken honesty is preferred, even at the expense of another's feelings. Language is to be used to uncover feelings and ideas and not to shroud them. This enables the gospel to be spoken boldly. On the other hand, Australians have always been resistant to authority. Australians are an egalitarian people, or so they like to think. No Australian is another's servant. The total authority of a sovereign God can be an alien idea. Also, Australians, and Australian men in particular, rarely talk about anything that touches them personally or at depth. While John has tried to probe the Australian mind (as he says "if there is one!"), particularly to show where it scrapes against the gospel, he has not deliberately sought to be Australian or to Australianise the gospel. He says, "I am proud to be Australian and I try to use Australian illustrations (even in the UK where I have to explain most of them!). I think I try harder at communicating than at being Australian. So, if I do most of my work in Australia, the two will be the same I guess." Yet John would be described as a distinctly Australian evangelist.

When, on one occasion, John was asked the question "What makes a good evangelist?" he replied:

Whenever I take one of my unconverted friends to hear an evangelist what I want is—

a)   A good, clear presentation of the gospel.
b)   The implications of the gospel pressed home on the hearer.
c)   The evangelist to understand where the unbeliever is and the difficulties he or she has in moving from unbelief to belief.

Since this is what I am looking for in others, I guess it is what I think a good evangelist is! The evangelist needs to understand the gospel in its complexity so that when in its presentation it is simplified, no essential feature is omitted. The evangelist needs to be able to communicate clearly, winsomely and forcefully.

Each of the strands of evangelist, singleness and itinerant has its difficulties and dangers; each has its joys.

As an evangelist (and a Bible teacher), John's workload has been heavy and demanding. It has never slackened. He has regularly preached about six or seven times every week. Such a workload has made it impossible for him to prepare an entirely new sermon for every occasion. He has generally only been able to prepare two new pieces a week. Preparing new pieces has been seen by John to be essential in order to ensure that he does not stop thinking of new and imaginative ways to tell old truths. Staleness does not enliven hope. On the other side of the coin, and when coupled with the itinerant nature of his ministry, John has been able to use the same material over and over, improving it in the process.

It has also been necessary for John to read and study on a wide biblical front and not to narrow his focus to evangelism, as a specialist in another area might do. An evangelistic ministry cannot be sustained over the period of John's service from a limited or narrow theology. A small understanding would have sustained only a small work. His deepening and widening understanding has fed a life's work of rare quality.

Those who engage in public evangelism are constantly expected to deliver sermons of the highest standard. There is a pressure to see their work produce fruit. Many Christians have spent much time with their families and their friends, living the Christian life in front of them, speaking to them about the gospel and praying for them. There can be a sense of climax as they bring them to a place where they will hear the gospel proclaimed. For the sake of those they love, they want the evangelist not just to be good but to be very good. They long to see the seed fall into good soil and take root. John has always been aware of this. Then, if results do flow, there is a temptation for the evangelist to think that he or she is somehow special and should be given more credit than is deserved. John reminds himself of the hard work done by those who have gathered his hearers.

Fuel for thought

Who would believe it? During the petrol strike at the end of last year, two university students came to the Office to get a quantity of *What is a Christian?*. When I asked why they needed such a quantity, one of them replied in this way: "Where I live, there are very long petrol queues and people wait in them for hours. I thought I would go along and invite them to read something Christian while they wait." I understand between them, they distributed more than 100. (I wonder if their prayers prolonged the strike!!!) I was greatly moved by their zeal and resourcefulness and questioned as to why some people are "self-starters" in evangelism and others never do any. Please "pray the Lord of the harvest to thrust out more labourers".

John Chapman
writing in the March 1977 Prayerletter. (The two students were Geoffrey Ellerton and Michael Blake.)

The greatest danger for the evangelist is that he or she is regularly under attack from the Evil One. The evangelist is in the front line of a constant and terrible warfare fought by a powerful enemy "who leads the whole world astray ...who is filled with fury because he knows that his time is short ...who makes war against those who obey God's commandments and hold to the testimony of Jesus" (Revelation 12:9, 12 and 17). In John's case, the ever present temptation is fourfold. It is, as he describes it:

- to believe that people will think I am mad
- to believe that no-one will be impressed by the gospel
- to believe that no-one will be converted
- to believe that *now* is not a good time to challenge people to turn to Christ.

John says, "I minister the gospel (as in Romans 1:16 and 17) to myself and press on!" The ultimate joy for an evangelist is knowing that the work of the gospel is at the very heart of the work of the sovereign God.

Singleness

John had enjoyed the fellowship of mixed company during his early association with the Congregational Church and throughout his involvement with the Youth Department from 1948 to 1956. When he enrolled at Moore College in 1957 he purposely chose not to develop any close attachment because, as remarkable as it may now seem, it was not possible at that time for students who were married to live at College with their wives. Ray Wheeler, one of John's fellow students, was married. Ray Wheeler lived in at the College while his wife, Dorothy, and their children lived in the rectory at Wilberforce to the west of the Nepean River some 65 kilometres from Sydney.

Following ordination, there always seemed so much work to do that John simply drifted on in bachelorhood during the two years of his curacy at Moree. After that he found his work to be so exciting and so all-absorbing that he did nothing about marriage. In John and Dorothy Wheeler's view:

He was one of those people who were just too busy doing the Lord's work to devote the time needed to develop a relationship. Not that there were not a number of suitable girls quite willing to play their part. In those days, his early thirties, he probably could not consider it right to change his demanding lifestyle with its constant travel and frequent speaking engagements, so relationships with women necessarily took a peripheral role.[1]

John confirms that perception:

By the time I was thirty I think I had decided to stay single because by then I had carved out both a ministry and a way of life that were satisfactory. I had also seen in John Stott a model of the single minister who had a useful ministry and so I didn't worry so much, although my friends had urged me prior to this to get cracking before it was too late. In fact, my worst periods were between twenty-five and thirty-five. My friends used to take me for long walks around the park at night telling me how important it was that I should get married. Some of them even suggested my ministry would be adversely affected by not marrying. It would have been a great help if they'd read the Bible, wouldn't it?

The biblical picture is one in which men and women are created by God for fellowship. Men and women are to live in whole and satisfying relationships with Him and with one another in order to experience the fullness of what it is to be human. While the marriage of a man and a woman will fulfil the need for companionship and for the expression of sexuality, Jesus taught that marriage is a temporal, not an eternal, institution. In the fullness and reality of the Kingdom of God, there will be no marriage (Matthew 22:29,30). Meaningful and satisfying relationships are not found only in marriage. Singleness is entirely appropriate. It is not an inferior condition. Indeed, single people can be more singleminded about ministry. They are free to give their time to their King. God has made each person differently and each one is to find contentment in the gifts that he or she has been given. Service that furthers the gospel most is the best service. That service will involve a cost whether it is given as a single person or as a married person.

John's wholesome attitude, thoroughly instructed by biblical truth, is well-expressed in a sermon of his on singleness. It was preached in his home church, St Aidan's, Hurstville Grove. An edited transcript of part of it follows. In it, John's voice comes through clearly. He began by reading 1 Corinthians 7, with a running commentary, and then continued:

John, Dick Lucas and John Turner, London, 1983.

The dominant perspective

I think the question that Paul has been asked is "Is it good for a man to stay single?". And what Paul is saying is this. If you're married when you become a Christian, the matter is settled; you don't need to put your mind to it. If you're married now, it's not a question you ought to raise. But if you are single now, it's a very important question that you ought to raise and put your mind to. And therefore—because in any given congregation we've got loads of single people—we need to start thinking like God does and to at least raise the possibility with the singles that they will stay single for the sake of the gospel and for the spread of the gospel. Now if you ever think to raise that as a possibility, bully for you. If we don't ever raise it as a possibility, we're certainly not biblical from God's point of view—but whether we're single or whether we're married, the urgency for the spread of the gospel is the dominating thing of our life. Whether you're married, whether you're single, whether you're buying things, whatever you're doing, you'd be saying to yourself, "This is a temporary measure. This life here and now is a temporary measure. It is not where I'm ultimately heading." And that ought to colour the whole of our horizons so that, whatever I'm doing, that is the perspective I'm working from.

Now our Lord, himself, says something like this, doesn't he? Do you remember when they asked him the question about divorce? They say, "Is it all right to divorce a person for any reason at all?" He said, "The only reason is for marital unfaithfulness". And they say, "It would be better never to marry if that's the way, wouldn't it? You can't get divorced except that's the only basis? Well, we'd be better to stay single, wouldn't we? All stay single forever." And Jesus said, "Yes, you would, as a matter of fact— if you could receive that saying. Yes, but not everybody can receive it." So he goes on to say, "Some people are born eunuchs, some people are made eunuchs by men, and some do it for the sake of the Kingdom. If you can receive this saying, receive it." Now it sounds at that stage as if you're a bit superior, but Paul just cuts them all down later. He says, "No big deal if you can do it—it's a gift from God. No big deal if you can't do it—it's a gift from God. If you stay single—it's a gift from God. If you get married—it's a gift from God." So we don't want to misunderstand what he's saying at this point.

Reasons for singleness

Now, what are Paul's reasons for staying single? Why, so you can serve God better. You can do it with a single mind. "And" Paul said, "I just want you to be spared troubles". Now it would ill behove me to start making a list of the troubles which married people have from my vast experience of nothing—so I won't enter into it. But for those of us who are single, let me say—so you won't kick the cat in your bad moments—you ought to start to capitalise in your mind on the advantages you've got by being single. And Paul says, "The reason why I'm suggesting it to you is so you can give yourself to the things of the Lord and so you'll be spared many of the problems which married people have got". In Australia, one in three marriages ends in divorce. You can't divorce without an enormous amount of unhappiness. You're spared that. You're spared the unhappiness of seeing children grow up who don't turn out Christian. You're spared that, that terrible heartache. That's not your problem. That's not going to be your problem, either. Now I'm saying—because one of the problems about being single is to be given over to self-pity—and I just want to say this, too, because of those of you who are married—at least half of you will enter back into singleness again when your spouse dies—so one of the big temptations about living on your own is to think that you're hardly done by. And I say if you want to get over that, you need to think positively about the fact that you're *not* hardly done by. That's what the Bible says; you're not hardly done by at all. If you're lucky enough to have been married, well and good. If you're single again now, well start to enjoy it. That's a Bible perspective. Whatever state you're in now is the state God has called you to, so, in it, learn to function in it. I should think that one of the things we've got to be careful about is not to idealise either what our marriage was like when it was on or what other people's marriages might be like but we don't really know about. Paul says, "I want to spare you that pain". That's the reason, and the other reason is so you can give yourself to the things of the Lord.

Not an inferior state

Third thing. Paul has a positive view of marriage; he has a positive view of singleness. Neither is better than the other. They are just different in exactly the same way that a wife is different from a husband. They have different roles to play in the family. But if you say, "Which is the inferior?" "Which is the superior?" it is a non-Christian question. The Bible never addresses itself to this. The only time the Bible addresses itself to who is superior is who serves the others most. They are the great ones. If you're single, if you're married, you win either way.

The family of God

Let me say something now about what I'd like you to ponder with me on about this passage. Singleness and the family of God I want to talk about. It's interesting to me that Paul says to the unmarried—and so perhaps the marrieds might... No, you'll need to stay awake! I was going to say perhaps you marrieds could have a bit of a snooze now, but you'd better stay awake. In verse 9 of Chapter 7, he says, "If you cannot control yourself"—and he's talking about sexually—"if you cannot cope with that area, then you ought to get married". Now it's interesting to me that in Genesis Chapter 2 when marriage is ordained, it's not only ordained for sexual expression; it's actually ordained as a remedy for loneliness. God says, "It's not good for man to be alone". And so he gives him a wife, a helper for mutual companionship. Now it's interesting to me in this Corinthians' passage that that is not the reason Paul gives now. It's not loneliness or mutual companionship which will take you into the marriage state. No. I think he has got a different view of the family of God and he simply takes for granted that in the family of God there will be *no* lonely people because they will be subsumed into their new family. Now it's interesting. Remember when the people come and say to our Lord, "Your mother and your brothers are outside". He says, "Who is my mother and who are my brothers?" He said, "My mother and my brothers are those who hear the Word of God and keep it". So *that* family supersedes his biological family. You remember at one stage when the rich young ruler comes to Jesus and goes away very sad and Jesus says, "It's easier for rich people to go through the eye of a needle..."—I'm sorry—"It's easier for a camel to go through the eye of a needle than a rich man to enter the kingdom of Heaven"—got that completely botched—"It's easier for a camel to go through the eye of a needle than for a rich person to get into Heaven". And Peter then makes a very interesting statement and says, "Lord, we've given away everything to follow you". Then comes this statement. "There is no man who has left mother, father, husband, wife, brother, sister, children for my sake and the gospel's who will not receive a hundredfold in this world, mothers, fathers, brothers, sisters, wives, husbands—with persecutions—and, in the world to come, eternal life." Now it's in this area that we need to pay the greatest attention. I am not going to be anybody's grandfather—at least it will knock Abraham into a cocked hat if it does happen, I should think, but, I think generally speaking, we could assume that I'm not going to be anybody's grandfather—but in this family (*indicating the congregation*) I should expect lots of grandchildren. You may not be a grandmother, but in this family you ought to expect loads of grandchildren. And that is how you ought to view them and I ought to

Charlie Oates, Chappo and Suzette Oates Richmond, Virginia, 1986.

view you. You and I are bound together in a family that takes precedence against our biological family.

Now that's a hard saying, isn't it, because Australians at the present moment are worshipping their families and their children. That's got to be as close to worldliness as we can find anywhere. Everything has got to be done at the present moment for our children. But if we do that and we neglect our family in Christ, there will be a

terrible nemesis to pay for that at the end of the day. But that's another question for another day and you didn't ask me to speak on that—that's a gratuitous nothing on the side.

Or take the saying in Luke Chapter 14, "If any man comes after me and doesn't hate mother, father, brother, sister, etc., etc., he's none of mine". Now that's, I take it, a hyperbole in the saying that this family and following Jesus supersedes in importance a biological family. Now, am I right in that? You'd better go and check it back in the Bible. If I am right in it, let me ask you, "Do you think that's the way you think about this family rather than your own family?" And that is why I want to say we need to work very hard in this area so that when those of you who are married—at least half of you—become single, as it were, again, the terrible shock of that will be able to be softened by your membership in this big family. OK? That's where a great deal of attention needs to be paid I would've thought, wouldn't you? So that in this family we know who belongs. And that is how I view you.

A word for singles

Let me just say one or two things then about singles in the congregation. I think we all need to reflect God's attitude at this point and if you need to make mental adjustments at this point, then make them. OK?

It's not a big deal, so we shouldn't be leaning on our singles to believe that it is a big deal that they ought not to be single. OK? (*John describes the well-meaning but unhelpful advice he was given to marry.*) Now parents are likely to get edgy when their children are in the twenty-five years of age bracket and still single. You may not get so edgy if you leave a few advertisements lying around, real estate advertisements for a nice home unit or a flat somewhere. But I'm saying, "Don't you get edgy and lean on them". You should be encouraging the single people in the congregation to get on with the things of the Lord because they've got time to do it. And those of you who come back into that condition again, don't simply go on with the lifestyle you had before. A new lifestyle has come to you. You can devote yourselves to the things of the Lord. One of our problems in this area is that nobody gives too much thought to it as if it's never going to happen, so it takes us by surprise. I think you ought to plan for that like you plan for retirement, so that when that new condition comes, it doesn't take you by surprise. You say, "What am I going to do now?" Why, the very things of God and the spread of the gospel. You say, "Well, I've got more time to do it now. How can I do that?" I know that you won't go on indefinitely, because of your physical condition and such. You mightn't be able to do very much more than pray and you mightn't have enough physical stamina to do that for very long before you drop off. And I'm saying you need to plan for that.

Another thing, too, for the singles, just in passing... One of the things that has always been nice for me in this congregation as a single person is—I always get treated like a person. I don't know if you ever think about me as being single, but I never think about myself as being single and I don't ever think of you as being married. I mean, it has never occurred to me to sort of categorise people like that. I just think about you as you and that's how I want you to think about me as me, and don't think about me as me in transit to some other condition. I might be in transit (although I think I'm not) but there are some single people in this congregation who, I think, probably may be in transit and, if they are, think about them as they are right now.

Let me tell you the temptations of single people so that you can pray about them and help them. Their two biggest temptations are that of sexual fantasy and that of loneliness, and they are not too far removed from each other in my judgment. Can I just say to the singles, it might be the temptation of everybody for all I know, but it is specifically ours and it is unhelpful to dwell on either of them. But you ought to take action and not just mope around. OK? You can always turn your loneliness into something else by ringing somebody or by inviting them to your place. But take action, and take positive action in regard to that.

From left: Frank and Iris Elliott, Maxine Cook, Jan Lamb, Ray Wheeler, Tony Lamb, Dorothy Wheeler, John.

The advantages of the single

person—I'm going to state them again and then climb down from my perch—are these. You are flexible. You've got time to do things. You've got money with which to do them. And you do not need to be distracted in any way from service to God. Now let me say that and say it straightly, because in this area what will be worldly will be to dissipate our time and our efforts and energies in other than things of the gospel and take our norm from married people who don't have anything like the flexibility or time or money at their disposal that we've got—see the point I'm making there?—so that we are uncluttered in our service to God, if you don't mind me saying it like that. It's not meant to be a loaded term, but I'm saying we mustn't take our stand from people in different conditions to us. We've got to be saying, "Look to the spread of the gospel"—"Look to serving Christ"—and to do that with a will which we wouldn't be able to do if we had other responsibilities. **And be happy.** Be happy that you can do it, because that's what Paul is really saying in the end. He says, "I want you all to be happy in the service of Christ". If you get married, good. If you stay single, good. If you can't stay single, you're not inferior, there's nothing wrong with you. If you can, you're not a weirdo, it's good. See the line he's taking in the end? He wants everybody with a joyful heart to serve Christ. OK, let me conclude.

Wherever you are, be happy, OK? We need to explore what it means to be members of the family of God and make sure that we're looked after and not forgotten there and that people are able to be caught up into that family—so that we do not gear up our church towards our biological families in a way which excludes people, but we ought to be all inclusive in our family orientation—not that we gear towards families, but we gear towards this family. If people can stay single for the sake of the gospel, we ought to encourage them to do it. Now I haven't spoken about marriage, for which I know precious little. I could tell you what I think the Bible says. But that's what I think the Bible is saying about the single person, all right? The last thing you ought to do is to ever feel sorry for them and the next last thing you must never do is to tell them that you feel sorry for them. Because it is a total denial of what God has called them to.

It is a typical example of John's preaching. He has worked hard to understand what the Bible says. He has worked hard to communicate its wisdom to others. He has shown its practical application to demonstrate its relevance. He has, with frankness, shared himself and his experiences. He has spoken to singles, but he has shown those who are married that singleness may again be their condition so his teaching is also a word for them. He has shown his warm humanity. He has challenged his audience to read the Bible for themselves and come to their own views. He has laughed at his mistakes. He has used some stratagems to ensure his audience does not lose interest. But his sermon has not been included here to illustrate those points. It is here to show, in John's own words, the place and purpose of singleness.

John, of course, has known times of loneliness. There have been times when the companionship of conversation would have been dearly prized, because everything has gone well and the exuberance should be shared, or because all has shattered and fallen and the anguish is almost beyond the endurance of one man. He is rigorous in avoiding self-pity.

Well Chappo, how'd it go tonight?

When I've come home at night from a meeting that I've not been totally happy with and I'm going over in my head everything that's happened and I'm so hyped up I don't feel like going to bed, the temptation is to do something like to eat a tub of ice cream or to sit down in front of the tele until I fall asleep in my chair. I have often thought that I should make a video of myself that I could put on when I come in. I would put the video in the machine and on I'd come and I'd say to myself, "Well, Chappo, how'd it go tonight?" And I'd leave a pause on the video so that I could answer. And then on the video, I'd say, "What sort of an audience was it?" Another pause. "Did they seem to be paying attention?" Pause. "And did you preach the gospel?" Pause. "Well then, what are you worried about? Go to bed."

John Chapman
sharing some thoughts on how to unwind alone.

John also acknowledges the importance to him of the ongoing love of his Christian family. He has found his family wherever he has been. On two memorable occasions in the five years before his retirement from the Department of Evangelism, John reminded the members of this family of their importance to him when many of them met to join him in celebration. The first occasion was in 1990 on his sixtieth birthday. A party was held in Centennial Park in Sydney. It was an appropriate venue, central and of an adequate size to accommodate the crowd who came! The second was in September 1993 to mark his retirement from the position of Director of the Department after twenty-five years of outstanding service. A celebratory dinner was held in the dining room at Moore College. It was an exalted night of the greatest affection and goodwill, full of praise and thankfulness to God—an evening shared together over a meal, with humour, singing, tributes, storytelling and prayer—a foretaste of the kingdom of Heaven. John spoke with tears in his eyes of the value to him of the friendship of his brothers and sisters in Christ.

The Centennial Park birthday gathering, 1990.

CHAPTER TEN

John has taken his own teaching well. He is never maudlin and rarely sentimental. His life is full of friends, full of activity and full of fun.

John of Golf

I have only seen Chappo lost for words once in the twenty-five years I have known him.

We were golfing—about to hit off on the Ninth tee at Concord. The Ninth at Concord is a short par 3, but more importantly, it is the halfway hole where golfers join the course, so there is usually a queue waiting to play. This day the queue included the Club Patron and Club Captain, both of whom are responsible for maintaining the standards—members' dress, language, sportsmanship, etc. So we were on our best behaviour; socks pulled up, collars down, waiting to show off our best 5 iron to the green.

Chappo stepped up.

Now, to the left of the tee, over John's left shoulder, was the practice putting green where members were quietly (emphasis on quiet) practising the putt.

Chappo hit off. The ball designed to sail straight to the green lobbed over John's left shoulder, as though he'd used a wedge and not his 5 iron and plopped into the middle of the practice green.

Normally, after a good shot there is recognition—"good on ya", "yes" or applause; after a medium shot it's normally "bad luck", "keep your head down". However a shot like this—what can you say?—only stony silence. And Chappo's response? Stony silence. It was a delightful moment. I wasn't his partner that day, I'm glad to say.

David Cook

Chairman of the Katoomba Christian Convention and Principal of Sydney Missionary and Bible College.

As always, John could draw analogies with the Christian life. "Every hole is like a new day. No matter how badly you have just done, a new hole is a new opportunity."

John Wheeler

who was persuaded by John to join the Armidale Club.

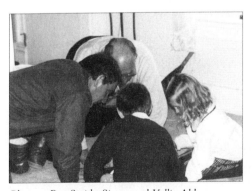

Chappo, Ray Smith, Simon and Kellie Abbott playing "Hungry Hippo".
Sewickley, Pittsburg, Christmas, 1989.

More fun and games, Christmas, 1989.

Itinerant—at home

When he began his ministry as a young newly ordained clergyman in the Parish of Moree in December 1957, John had thought he would be working indefinitely in the Diocese of Armidale. He and his fellow students at Moore Theological College, Peter Chiswell and Ray Smith, had thoughtfully surveyed the future and had agreed that their work there would need to be of long duration. From the time of his ordination, John had thought his ministry would be parish-based. Even when he was appointed Youth Director and later Director of Christian Education he had expected he would return to parish work. It had never occurred to him that he would spend his days as an itinerant. He says:

> I remember thinking when I was first appointed Youth Director that I would do this for a stint and then go back into parish work again. I was so convinced of this I had worked out that, in normal parish life, I would have to preach at least two times a week. So I made it a habit to prepare at least two sermons a week (even though, as an itinerant, you can use the same material over and over again) because I thought that if I ever got out of the habit I would never get back into it again. It's just that I'm so slow on the uptake that I've kept on doing it, even after thirty years! Although I must say it has been a terrific boon over that time.

Distance no deterrent

Bronwen and I remember with thankfulness to God John Chapman's care of us when we first came to Sydney in 1977. We had met John previously in Adelaide when he had spoken at our church. When we came to Sydney we were completely new to the Diocese. Soon after we arrived in the parish of Lalor Park, John invited us to his home in Penshurst for dinner to meet some other people in Sydney. From this contact, John has been a regular visitor to our home no matter where we were in the Diocese.

When he came to Lithgow once to preach at an evangelistic dinner, one of our children was rushed to hospital with acute appendicitis. John accused us of arranging this so that he could sleep in the vacant bed overnight! That night he saw our A A Milne animals and admired them. Every time he visited us afterwards, we gave him one more animal for his collection.

We were so glad that John was prepared to travel to the fringe of the Diocese to encourage and teach. He always encouraged those some distance from Sydney to keep on inviting him to visit them despite the distance.

Ian Cox
Rector and Senior Canon of St Michael's Provisional Cathedral, Wollongong.

John's singleness has enabled him to have his distinctive itinerant ministry. The way he developed his work has been suited to a person whose home was where he was. Armidale gave John a lot of practice for a lifetime as an itinerant. During his Armidale years he could be away for weeks on end travelling from parish to parish. A married man could not have done it. Lengthy absences like that would not have been conducive to building a good marriage and sound family life. In the Diocese of Sydney, John, for over thirty years, has travelled untiringly, constantly crossing and recrossing its territory, visiting parish after parish. Distance has never deterred the pursuit of any venture.

Particularly during the 1970s and the early 1980s, but also in later years, John on many occasions took the Bible studies at the annual CMS Summer Schools, Katoomba Conventions (both Summer and Easter) and Katoomba Youth Conventions. These were probably the largest stages regularly available to preachers in Australia at that time. John occupied them more often than any other person of his generation. From large stages like these and from small, he has taught the Bible to a whole generation of Christians from Sydney and beyond. It has been an outstanding contribution to the true life of the city and this nation.

Being an itinerant, too, has its advantages and disadvantages. Material can be recycled and refined. John has been able to work at his own pace. He has been spared much time-consuming and energy-consuming work dealing with pastoral problems. He has never, for instance, had to worry about whom he will or will not baptize or marry. He has probably enjoyed a longer and closer relationship with the Board of the Department than many rectors enjoy with their parish councils.

The hardest feature of being an itinerant is that of not being able to see the long-term effect of any work. Preaching one-off sermons to constantly differing groups has denied John the luxury of preaching over a long period of time to the same people. The wonder and beauty of changed lives cannot be seen when contact with people is brief. There is also the danger of neglecting membership of the local church by always being somewhere else. John has always had more opportunities than he could take—more invitations than he could accept. His work has, to some extent, taken from him the ability to have close fellowship with other Christians of the kind that occurs in a pastoral setting.

And beyond

Being an itinerant has also given John a greater freedom to travel throughout other parts of Australia and abroad. He says, "It is always good to be able to get away. It gives me time to reflect on the work we are doing and to see it against the background of other work." It has given him a wider variety of circumstances and ideas and the experiences he has gained have, in turn, enhanced his ministry at home.

Throughout the history of the Department of Evangelism, its missioners commonly embraced a vision of a missionfield that reached beyond the limits of the Diocese of Sydney—a missionfield that had no borders. There was uncertainty, however, as to the appropriateness of travelling beyond the diocesan limits and the frequency with which that might be done. This uncertainty was principled. It stemmed from the sense of obligation the evangelist had to those who were supporting him materially and in other ways. It reflected his understanding that he was largely employed and expected to do a particular job in a particular place.

Towards the end of 1977, after having been with the Department of

Evangelism for almost ten years, John produced a statement of his work for the preceding year. In summary, it was as follows:

Number of times as preacher   294
89% with Anglicans
11% with non-Anglicans

Evangelistic events   203 – 70% of total time
90% with Anglicans
10% with non-Anglicans

Non-Evangelistic events   91 – 30% of total time
87% with Anglicans
13% with non-Anglicans

Percentages of total time

Evangelistic work/Sydney Anglicans	56
Non-evangelistic work/Sydney Anglicans	25
Evangelistic work/Non-Sydney Anglicans	7
Non-evangelistic work/Non-Sydney Anglicans	2
Evangelistic work/Non-Anglicans	6
Non-evangelistic work/Non-Anglicans	4
	100

This caused the Board to reflect and to resolve that, as a working guideline, John should be at liberty to tithe his time. That is, a tenth of his time, about six weeks of each year, could be spent in work at places outside the Diocese. The tithe need not be to the minute. There would be no complaint if it were to be generous rather than niggardly. The Board could see that it would never be the loser if its resources could supply another's want. God would reward it as He had promised. If a good evangelistic opportunity presented itself, it could be taken. The Board could also see that John's judgment was to be trusted.

John first discovered the joys and stimulus of overseas travel in 1960 when, as the sole clerical representative of the Diocese of Armidale, he attended the Pan Anglican Congress at Toronto,

Ontario, 1963.

Canada. After the conference, he flew on to England and returned home via East Africa, India, Hong Kong and Malaysia, visiting and encouraging many friends. John was smitten by the experience. During the next thirty-five years, he would travel outside Australia more than twenty times, visiting many parts of the world.

Mission at St Andrew's School, Singapore, 1974.

John's travel has been widespread and the purposes for it numerous. He has been a principal speaker at conventions and conferences at Mt Tamborine and Townsville in Queensland, the Bible College of South Australia, Tumut in New South Wales, Belgrave Heights in Victoria, Perth in Western Australia, Canberra, Hong Kong, Aberystwyth in Wales and Pounawea in New Zealand. He has taken dialogue evangelism to Tasmania, to Christchurch and Auckland in New Zealand, to parts of the United States of America and Canada and to London. He has taught the Bible in the Riverina, the Eastern Highlands of New Guinea and South Africa. He has regularly revisited the Diocese of Armidale to preach and teach in many of its parishes and on many special occasions. He has conducted missions in Singapore, at the Melbourne Showground and Geelong in Victoria, in Rockhampton, in various parishes in the Australian Capital Territory, at Karachi and Murree in Pakistan, at Darwin in the Northern Territory and Anchorage in Alaska. He has conducted clergy schools in the Diocese of Willochra, in parts of England, in Vancouver, Toronto and Calgary in Canada and in Pittsburg, New York, Richmond, Boston and Seattle in the United States. In 1974, he attended the International Congress on World Evangelism at Lausanne in Switzerland and in 1983, the Billy Graham Conference for Itinerant Evangelists in Amsterdam, Holland. He has spoken to representative gatherings of various denominations–Lutherans, Presbyterians, Baptists and Seventh Day Adventists–and various Christian organisations, including the Gideons, the Church Missionary Society, the Australian Fellowship of Evangelical Students, the Church of England Boys' Society and the Evangelical Fellowship of Anglican Churches.

John has made many visits to the United Kingdom.

As he has travelled, John has always exercised a ministry of encouragement to expatriate Australians who are cut off from their culture. His visits with them are highly prized.

John in South Africa—1994

It was a thrill to greet John Chapman on African soil. He had come to give Bible studies and talks on Evangelism at the Synod and Clergy School and he won the hearts of CESA (The Church of England in South Africa). Most of our students travelled up for the occasion and Chappo gave them additional instruction during business sessions. The only question at the end was "When can you come back?" For Lorraine and myself it was a precious time to catch up with a friend who has helped us so much from the earliest days of my Christian life.

David Seccombe
Principal, George Whitefield College, Kalk Bay, South Africa.

The English connection

The most significant ministry John has exercised outside Australia has been in England, chiefly in and around London. It has been a strategic ministry sustained through regular visits over more than twenty years.

In 1974, Dick Lucas, the rector of St Helen's, Bishopsgate in London, was invited to speak at the Church Missionary Society's Summer School at Katoomba in the Blue Mountains. John was asked by John Turner, who was then the General Secretary of CMS, to collect Dick Lucas from Bishopscourt, the residence of the Archbishop of Sydney, where he was then staying and to transport him to the conference centre. The event was memorable for two reasons—the brilliance of Dick's Bible teaching and the awfulness of the weather; it rained without a break.

Later that year the two men were able to renew their acquaintance in London. Before going to Lausanne for the International Congress on World Evangelism, John attended a conference in England conducted by John Poulton. He called in at St Helen's where he was warmly greeted. Dick Lucas arranged for John to speak to the staff.

In 1975, there followed an invitation to John to work as a staff member at St Helen's for three months in 1976. The circumstances of the invitation were redolent of the grace of God. Part of Dick Lucas' letter read:

My dear John,

I write with good news about our weekend away with the Church Council and other Christians at the heart of the work here at St Helen's.

During one of the planning sessions I mentioned to them your very kind offer to give us three months in 1976, but I also made it very plain to them that the financial responsibilities would be ours and therefore didn't paint too rosy a picture of the whole situation.

To my joy, the meeting really seemed to come alight to the possibility of having you and indeed as far as I remember there was no dissenting opinion of any kind.

Directly after the conference we had a telephone call from the Treasurer to say that somebody had contacted him to offer the return fare from Australia in full so this was a rather marvellous confirmation from our end that we should go ahead with the plan.

I am writing, therefore, to invite you very warmly to spend three months attached to St Helen's in 1976 in order to pioneer and lead training of men in evangelism in their own homes.

I take it that this would still be the main priority for your energies but obviously there would be plenty of other opportunities such as preaching on Tuesdays, evangelistic opportunities amongst students and such other visits as you yourself would like to fit in, when you are in this country.

The 1976 visit began a pattern of travel to England that would continue for the rest of John's working life.

Chappo's back!

We can't wait to see again this well-known and well-loved figure emerging from the customs at London Airport, full of presents for friends as well as unbelievable stories about the antics of the Diocese of wherever he has just come from in his world adventures.

John's visits over here have become legendary. When rumours about a return visit begin to circulate, I am deluged with requests. I think he'd better come over for a year soon and finally clear up this enormous backlog which weighs upon me, as I keep replying "no", "wait" and "one day, perhaps" to all who want a visit.

Dick Lucas
St Helen's, Bishopsgate, writing in 1993.

Within 12 hours of his arrival at Heathrow, John is on the phone ringing up all his friends, greeting them with his typical "Chapman here".

Jonathan Fletcher
Emmanuel Church, Wimbledon.

For me, the outstanding characteristic of John is his warmth, sociability, sensitivity and affability mixed with courage and bluntness and a sharp edge to his theology which is always a challenge, an exhortation, and an encouragement. He is very dear to us indeed and we have seen so many over here blessed in so many different ways by his ministry. He is, as everyone will testify, enormously in demand over here. The moment the whisper goes round that he is returning to the UK, all sorts of feelers are put out from all over the country to see whether it will be possible to bring him to our own "necks of the wood".

Mark Ashton
The Round Church at St Andrew the Great.

English evangelicals had been increasing steadily in number since the Second World War. There was some degree of polarisation among them which became acute in the 1960s, the Free Church reformed communities looking to Dr Martyn Lloyd-Jones for inspiration and guidance, the Anglicans organising their growing strength under the leadership of the revered John Stott.

From 1950 to 1979, Lloyd-Jones was the chairman of the annual Puritan and Reformed Studies Conference (later the Westminster Conference). He was a Calvinistic Protestant who embraced reformed theology. He was an articulate man of firm convictions and a man whose opinions could not be ignored. The branch of English evangelicalism that looked to him was unsure as to the place in ministry of evangelism, particularly public evangelism. This had been brought about to some extent by various areas in the practice of evangelism that "the Doctor" had criticised. Dr James Packer has written of him:

> Conventional 20th-century evangelism, to the Doctor's mind, had three
> great weaknesses: its manipulative emotionalism, displacing intellectual
> persuasion, was a kind of brainwashing that encouraged false conversions;

the standard form of appeal ('now I give you an opportunity to respond... I want you to get up out of your seat and come forward...'), in which the preacher acts as if he were the Holy Spirit has the same tendency; and the constant failure to insist on radical and thorough repentance in conversion sentences true converts to shallow and stunted growth thereafter.[2]

In particular, Lloyd-Jones questioned the value of big crusades.

He challenged the low level of spiritual life in the churches. He was saddened that orthodoxy was often dead, activist but not alive; saddened, for example, that many saw big crusades as the answer to this lack of spiritual life. He simply stood off from the Billy Graham crusades from 1954 onwards and was roundly criticised as being against evangelism.[3]

Dr Martyn Lloyd-Jones said, "I have always believed that nothing but a revival—a visitation of the Holy Spirit, in distinction from an evangelistic campaign—can deal with the situation of the church and of the world".[4] He is also on record as disparaging apologetics. "Nothing has so caused us to forget God... as our concern for apologetics," he told the 1971 conference of ministers in Wales.[5]

The arrival of the charismatic movement in the 1960s was to have profound consequences, especially among Anglican evangelicals. Fine men, like the late David Watson, a gifted evangelist, became widely admired leaders of the "Renewal" movement. But among the less happy results of this period were a disturbing distrust of doctrinal and historical evangelicalism and a reversion to an untheological Arminianism in evangelism.

The late 1970s, the period co-inciding with John's first working visits to London, was a particularly productive period in John's ministry. He had developed and refined dialogue evangelism into a sophisticated evangelistic tool. He had worked out the place in evangelism for apologetics. He was regularly engaging in public evangelism on the main university campuses in Sydney. He was seeing the development of aids to personal evangelism, for example, in the form of "2 Ways to Live", that placed their focus on the sovereignty of God rather than on the significance of human response and of the introductory Bible studies for inquirers and new converts called "Just for Starters". He was immersed in the 1979 Billy Graham Crusade, particularly in his capacity as chairman of the Follow-up Committee. He was turning his mind to the appropriateness of the appeal in evangelistic meetings and the form that it might take. He was working to complete a comprehensive expression of his theology of the gospel. He was developing and formalising his thoughts on evangelistic preaching.

Dick Lucas and John on holiday at Interlaken, Switzerland, 1986.

201

John and Jonathan Fletcher.

Jesus Christ can turn your life upside down!

Consequentially, when John, another Calvinistic Protestant, arrived in London, he brought with him the fruits of all these endeavours. His ministry was one of ripening maturity. He came with a clear, strong and thoroughly reformed theology of the gospel. He could argue well for his position from the Scriptures. His approach was rational, not emotional. He coupled this with some practical means of evangelising that were easily taught and could readily be used. He appeared to his English brethren to embrace a comprehensive, codified approach to gospelling. Dick Lucas recalls, "When he first came to us he did a series on God and His sovereignty, and so on. I remember then being amazed at the theological nous of this man. After all, he'd come across to do evangelism and we weren't used to a travelling evangelist quite like this!"

John demonstrated to British evangelicals that they could continue with their evangelism and be thoroughly reformed in their doctrine. Jonathan Fletcher, the rector of Emmanuel Church, Wimbledon, comments:

We didn't need to be encouraged in evangelism—we've always been flat out at that. We needed to be rescued for reformed theology. I think Chappo has been more influential in the second group than in the first. Interestingly, therefore, his **theological** input has been more important than his **evangelistic** input.[6]

John also brought a different attitude. Unlike the English who tended to have too great a respect for the sensibilities of others, he did not pull back at the point of commitment, but contended for the gospel with determination, almost amounting to a ruthlessness. John and other Australians are seen by people in the United Kingdom and North America to be blunt and outspoken. This is sometimes misunderstood as rudeness. But it is an Australian characteristic to question and to argue. John was more confronting in his presentation of the gospel than his English counterparts and, out of nothing more than a Christ-like love for those to whom his message was directed, he pressed for their response.

Accompanying this was John's insistence that the truth of the gospel message was reinforced by the way the believer lived his or her life. Consistently right conduct in every area of life was a demonstration of its authenticity.

For John's part, he says:

> It was Dick and the people at St Helen's who made me feel as if I was "better-than-average". I don't think I had ever thought about my ability as an evangelist or as anyone who even knew much about the subject. The Board was very supportive of me and my work yet somehow I never thought of myself as anyone who was special. The London people did— and put me onto a very large platform (and often). I got enormous confidence from them.
>
> To have been invited to mission at both Oxford and Cambridge would never have come my way except through the St Helen's connections.
>
> The more I went overseas the more I realised that we were not behind in our thinking about evangelism. In fact, to the contrary. We had a contribution to make.

Faithfulness and friendliness

I grew up in a Christian home with a faithful Christian heritage, for which I am most grateful to God. However, if I'm honest, I think that I assumed that, as I have gone through many doors as my parents' daughter, so too would I get into heaven on their coat-tails. It was on a rock one afternoon of a houseparty at Rathane in 1969 that the penny dropped: John told me, and I really heard for the first time, that the Lord wanted a relationship with me, standing on my own two feet. I know that, in heaven, John will have many bright stars in his crown—this is one small one who is everlastingly grateful for his faithfulness and forthrightness.

When John came to visit us in England in the early '80s, on one occasion he took my sister-in-law, Jane Robinson, and me to the National Art Gallery where he gave us a guided tour more interesting and informative than any official one. However, it's the journey home on the tube that really sticks in my mind. By the time we got off at Bow Road, the typically British, silent carriage of people had become one of best friends—laughing, joking, swapping phone numbers—all due to John! He had begun by telling those nearest us what we'd done that day—and then he'd systematically pulled from his bag all he'd bought. He showed his souvenirs round the whole carriage, asking people if they thought he'd chosen well, whether the prices he'd been charged were reasonable and what they thought Australians would think of his purchases! At first, people looked sideways, then they smiled, then laughed, then chatted— first to him, to Jane and to me, then to each other. It was remarkable. John managed to relax the entire atmosphere of the carriage—and Jane and I were very proud to be with him!

Kathy Manchester
recalling two occasions with John.

There is a vestige of colonialism in this assessment that seems a common factor in a number of people of John's generation. There is no particular reason

Richard Bewes, Rector of All Souls Church, Langham Place, John and Cliff Richard, January, 1992. The photographer and other member of the foursome was Cliff Richard's manager, Bill Latham.

now why Australians should look generally to England or to North America for Christian example or for Christian leadership. There is also an intimation that John was unable to hear or to accept the approbation of his Sydney friends. Why should he? They were his friends. Their function and, if they were members of the Board of the Department of Evangelism, their duty, was to give him every encouragement. How could their judgments be objective? They were doubtless overstated out of the bias of their friendship. So, he did not hear or was dismissive of their praise.

There is no question that John found acceptance in England and that it was an acceptance an Englishman could not expect. His difference was that he was classless. He could not be fitted into any pigeonhole. As well, his ready inclusiveness, his genuine interest in people, his gregariousness and his ever-present, self-deprecating and totally disarming humour made him irresistible.

1   Letter to the author dated 20 December 1994.

2   Essay by Dr J I Packer entitled "A Kind of Puritan" in Christopher Catherwood ed., *Martyn Lloyd-Jones: Chosen by God*, Highland Books, 1988, pp 52,53.

3   Essay by Robert M Horn entitled "His Place in Evangelicalism" in Catherwood, *Martyn Lloyd-Jones*, pp 20,21.

4   Interview with Dr Carl Henry in Catherwood, *Martyn Lloyd-Jones*, p 100.

5   Essay by Robert M Horn in Catherwood, *Martyn Lloyd-Jones*, p 21.

6   Letter to the author dated 16 March 1995.

Guardian of the gospel.

LEADERSHIP

Who are the leaders?

Leadership is not necessarily or exclusively the function of an occupant of high office. In some cases, it will come from a person who has undertaken the responsibilities of a significant position within an established organisation because that person has been seen to be someone who will match the opportunities offered by the position with his or her capacities for giving guidance and direction. But that is not its sole source. Leadership is also given by others. True leadership comes through what is contributed. It comes through the ability to discern and articulate the truth, to give clear focus, direction and vision, to motivate, encourage and persuade, to confront error and reinforce what is right. A leader has the courage to uphold the truth. A leader has the ability to take initiative, to break new ground and bring challenge. Leadership is shown in the capacity to inspire, to turn pessimism into optimism, to turn despair into hope.

Leadership in ministry is no different. It may come from any source. It is not necessarily or exclusively the function of the holder of a particular ecclesiastical office. John comments:

> I have contended that the Diocese of Sydney has hardly ever been run exclusively by the designated leader. He is so busy with diocesan affairs that the visionary leadership is often supplied by others. Take, for instance, the leadership vision of Broughton Knox. He changed the face

of the Diocese in twenty-five years by the vision he offered of the parish minister. Others modified it as time went on, but basically it remained the same. Dudley Foord offered leadership during his Moore College days and specially when he was the rector of St Ives. He was responsible for starting the School of Theology that went for a long time at Moore College and the College of Preachers. It was like an informal clergy conference where we read papers to each other. It was a rallying place where people got inspiration (particularly in the late '60s and early '70s). I think as a bishop or as archbishop you have limited time for ministry. You do not spend the major part of your time teaching the Bible which is what I think ministry is all about.

Throughout his Christian life, John is another who has given leadership in ministry to the church. Leaving Sydney at the end of 1957 for the years of service in the Diocese of Armidale was an important step in this development. John says:

Being away from Sydney made me take initiative in leadership. I'm sure that had I "grown up" as an ordained man in Sydney, I would never have taken the leadership role I did because there were established leaders already up and running. In Armidale, I knew that no-one else was going to do it, so I did it. I think this gave me great confidence that I might not, or I might, have had in Sydney.

John's leadership has been shown in a number of distinctive ways. It has been shown through his unrelenting focus on the gospel, in his thorough commitment to evangelism. It has been shown through the breadth and quality of his Bible teaching. Through his deep and constantly developing knowledge of the Bible and of biblical theology, he has presented a model for theological reflection about the world and everything in the world. He has encouraged confidence in the sufficiency of Scripture. The answers to the questions that confront mankind can be found in its principles. There is no aspect of life that need be faced with fear. John's leadership has been shown in his standards of personal holiness. He has given leadership through the constancy and diversity of his activity, with steadfastness and with irresistible energy. He has formally taught and instructed many as well as giving them example.

The absolute primacy of the gospel

Perhaps the most outstanding area of John's leadership has been his insistence on the absolute primacy in ministry of the gospel. The gospel has certainly had this place in his own ministry. John has gospelled untiringly. He has studied and articulated the theology of evangelism. His audiences have not merely been exhorted to evangelise but have been shown how to do it. He has presented clear examples of evangelistic preaching to his own and to the following generation. He says, "I tried in my sermons to present a model for clergy to follow. I wanted them to say 'I could do that' and do it." He has supplemented practical example in evangelistic preaching with classroom teaching. Through his books, tracts, tapes and videos, he has provided a diversity of readily useable evangelistic tools. He has not allowed himself to be sidetracked into spending the major part of his time in the areas of pre-evangelism or post-evangelism. He has not, as some have, confused those areas with evangelism itself.

Preach the Word

One thing I valued most with John was that one could always rely on him to use the opportunities to preach the Word and not pussyfoot around as so many do when one has them in their pulpit. I believe that every possible opportunity must be taken, and John never let me down.

Frank Elliott.

John's intellect and his sharply analytical mind have been nurtured and stimulated in the remarkable environment that is Sydney evangelicalism. He describes it in this way:

Sydney Anglican evangelicalism is a unique phenomenon in the world. It is marked by a fierce insistence that the Bible and only the Bible is to direct our thinking about all matters Christian. Australians are utterly opposed to anything that smacks of show or hypocrisy and so have very little time for showy piety either formally at church or informally in their life privately. This is often seen by others as a lack of piety, but piety is seen in Bible reading habits, prayer and godly behaviour (or ought). However, because of their high view of the Bible, the Christians with whom I have grown up have a passion for truth and this is often seen as lacking in love. I have never been able to understand this. Often sentimentality is mistaken for love, but in the end it is useless.

Like any good analyst and strategist, John has been able, from time to time, to step back from the many insistent demands of the moment to look at the overall scope of his work and its setting and context. Following a period of long service leave at the end of 1982 that had been spent visiting friends in the USA, Canada, England, Scotland and Hong Kong, John wrote:

Being away for three months enabled me to reflect on our work, the gospel, and what is happening in different parts of the world. As I see it, the work of evangelism is always under threat from inside organised Christianity and from outside. I noticed as I moved around that, when people had lost their confidence in the Bible as the Word of God, several inevitable consequences followed:

a) they were uncertain about the content of the gospel;

b) they were uneasy about the urgency of the gospel;

c) because of (a) and (b), they now believed that people of other religions would probably go to heaven and so had no ground left to do evangelism;

d) the idea of God's judgment on sinful mankind disappears.

However, even among those who believed the Bible to be the Word of God, evangelism did not seem to be in its rightful place. Some seemed to spend so much time and energy on defending minor issues that they had little left to do any active evangelism.

Evangelism is hard work

I have thought for a long time that for many Christians they would be active in evangelism if they could find an easy way to do it. Rejection is so hard to bear, and the thought of it is nearly as bad. I don't think that there is an easy way any more than there was an easy way for our Lord. I think that it is worldly to wait for it to become easy. Such an attitude needs to be repented of and not allowed to stay unchecked. All the Christians I know who are active in any piece of evangelism tell me that it is hard work, and I certainly have found it to be so.

John Chapman

Department of Evangelism Prayerletter, February–April 1988.

It seems to be a characteristic of the evangelist to present issues, not simplistically, but simply. The evangelist has the ability to go to the very root and foundation of things. The colours of the evangelist are black and white; there are no tints. It is part of this characteristic that enables the evangelist to be sharp-eyed in perceiving assaults on the gospel and the necessity for its ongoing proclamation. John reflects:

The sinfulness of humankind is such that it is easy to let the gospel slip through your fingers like sand, to forget vital aspects of it and to distort others so that it has little resemblance to the original. I have been struck by how easily the early churches slipped away from the gospel (for example, Colosse, Galatia and Corinth). They did it while being convinced that they were either orthodox or the logical progression of the gospel! If they, who had heard the gospel preached by the apostles, could so easily become mistaken, then so can we. The gospel must not only be preached, but also guarded (1 Timothy 6:20; Jude 3).

John is a vigilant guardian and defender of the gospel. He has spoken out frequently against numerous views that have sought to modify or displace it. These have included such things as easy sanctification and holiness movements, the charismatic movement, the socio-political movement and liberalism.

On the charismatic movement and the Keswick movement, John has expressed this opinion:

Anything that challenges the Bible as the Word of God is bad news in the long run because the gospel gets forgotten. The charismatic movement, of which John Wimber is the latest exponent, appears to have swept all before it. It is a movement that appears to give short term gains. Yet, basically, it is not a biblical movement. It does not rely on the Bible as its guide or as its final authority even though many of its adherents claim they do. Some make the claim because:

a) formerly they were evangelicals and so brought it with them, and/or

b) they need it to gain some respectability.

However, it is the Spirit who communicates directly with them who is their authority. The real difficulty comes in being able to recognise the difference between the voice of the Spirit and the voice of my spirit (or my gut reaction). I think they have not taken to heart how the "heart of man is desperately wicked". We will talk ourselves into believing anything we like given this "direct message" method.

In the end, their "experiences" (of the Spirit) become their authority. As I have said, this doesn't always seem to be the case as many charismatics have been former evangelicals and retain strong biblical ideas, but their authority base has moved. (Having said this, I hasten to say that to speak of the charismatic movement as if it is uniform in its belief is not an accurate way to think of it. In fact, by its very nature, it isn't all that doctrinally oriented so it will never be uniform in what it believes.)

Charismatics are a threat to good evangelism because they have blurred the gospel by making the work of the Spirit an essential element of the spoken gospel. To speak of Jesus and His work is insufficient (although not for the Father—see Romans 1:1–5!) and their experience is what they both preach and seek for in their converts rather than informed minds and hearts that respond in repentance and faith. My opposition to this movement has earned me the criticism that my preaching is cerebral and academic in outlook and coldly logical. I am surprised by this as it isn't the way I think about my work.

I think another thing about charismatics is that their "second" blessing theology is a total misunderstanding of justification by faith and so diminishes the work of Christ (not that they mean to!). It is very like the Keswick Movement of my early Christian days. It promised so much but was unable to deliver. Because of a wrong view of Romans 6 and being "dead unto sin", I was led to believe that I could know "continuous victory over sin" in my life by exercising faith in the fact that I have died to sin! The result was devastating indeed. I rocketed into sin faster than ever because I was not resisting, fleeing or fighting as I should have been. So many of the promises made in the healing ministry come into this category. They cannot be delivered. People get hurt and often become so hard to reach for the gospel and the "healers" don't realise this because the people have left them and gone elsewhere.

Another challenge to the gospel has been the movement to socio-political action as part of evangelism.

It is the evangelical equivalent to the social gospel of the liberals. This came to evangelical circles via the Lausanne Conference in July 1974 and so notable evangelical leaders gave it legitimacy. It suggested that social action and evangelism both sprang from the gospel and, to use their illustration, were twin arms of a pair of scissors. One was of no value without the other. This seemed to me to be an assault on the primacy of evangelism (which is gospelling). What is the gospel except it is told. It cannot be abstracted as if it exists without being proclaimed. Our Department is heavily criticised in other denominations because of our stand here. We are pictured as those who are **only** interested in proclamation and have no concern for "the poor".

The relationship between the gospel and social involvement was the subject of John's attention in two Prayerletters in the first half of 1983. The issue had been a contentious one between evangelicals for a decade. It had been taken up by Archbishop Loane in his Presidential Address to the Sydney Synod in October 1976 when he had announced that Billy Graham was "willing to mark the twentieth anniversary of the great 1959 Crusade by a return visit to Sydney for a three week Crusade in 1979".[1] In addressing the relationships between the gospel and social concern and the gospel and proclamation, the Archbishop had expressed the view that "the social concern that springs from true Christian compassion must not be seen as an alternative to the primary and all-compelling duty of the church to engage in continuing proclamation of the gospel. Each new generation needs to hear the message of Jesus Christ and Him crucified as though it had never been heard before."[2]

In the first Prayerletter for 1983, John wrote:

Among evangelical Christians, there is still a great deal of confusion over the relationship between evangelism and social concern for people. In its extreme form, it results in people saying they are doing evangelism when they are meeting people's needs physically, socially and emotionally. This idea is not new, but is it new for evangelicals to be saying it? However, in its less extreme forms, it still represents a problem for us to know the relationship between the idea of "doing good to all people" and that "God commands all people everywhere to repent".

Notwithstanding every good work done by the Lausanne Continuation Committee, I am myself still convinced that gospelling is the more important of these activities. The need to be saved does not just take its place on a list with other needs people have. People's need to be reconciled to God is of paramount importance. Social welfare work is much easier to do than evangelism. You see results for your work, the recipients are usually grateful and the world at large approves the work. Evangelism, on the other hand, has none of these benefits. My fear is that when we think that evangelism and social welfare work are **equally** important, then in due course the easier will take more of our time and money.

Given that this life is all there is, then relieving the lot of our fellow human beings is the most important. Given that eternity is true, then evangelism is of the highest importance. I believe this can be clearly seen in the ministry of the Lord Jesus and it must be so with us. (See Luke 4:42–44; Luke 5:15–16; Mark 1:32–39.) I do not think that people's needs are unimportant, but the priority of the way Jesus met the needs of the man in Luke 5:17–26 should be ours.

The publication of this view prompted a critical response from some readers. John pursued the issue in the following Prayerletter:

Some of you were kind enough to take up with me the statements I made in the last Prayerletter on the matter of evangelism and social concern.

Firstly, let me say that my statement about the Lausanne Continuation Committee should have read, "Confusion exists among evangelicals notwithstanding the good work of the Lausanne Continuation Committee". They have given a great deal of time to clarify for us the balance between these issues...

I am uneasy about making socio-political involvement part of discipleship. On one hand, it seems so right, yet the lack of New Testament teaching or even a model causes me concern. If it is so important, why is the New Testament silent? Why doesn't Jesus speak out about these matters? There were plenty of oppressed people—"The poor you always have with you," He said. He didn't fail to recognise that fact. When asked the question, "Is it lawful to give tribute to Caesar?" He seems to be at pains **not** to make a political comment at all. The apostles likewise seem preoccupied on other issues, namely the godliness of Christians and the spread of the gospel. We should be preoccupied with this also. I am aware that some Christians argue that the explanation for the silence in the New Testament is that in their political climate they had no opportunity to take political action as we have in our democracy. That might be the reason—but it might not. I find it hard to urge on Christians, as part of their discipleship, that which isn't clearly taught in Scripture.

Further to my note in the last Prayerletter, I need to say that I did not mean to imply that those people whose occupation involves them in social work were doing an inferior work and should leave it for full time evangelistic work.

I do wish to reiterate what seems to me to be crystal clear from Scripture, namely that evangelism is to have top priority in our thinking, doing and giving. There is no doubt that this was so in the life of the Lord Jesus and the apostles. (See Luke 4:42–44; 5:15–16; Mark 1:32–39.) People's needs **are** important and meeting them with love and concern is an obligation on all Christians, but the priority set out in Luke 5:17–26 must be kept clearly in our minds.[3]

John adds:

It has been difficult to maintain this position and not be misunderstood as a person who is disinterested in the physical/social plight of the underprivileged, difficult especially since I have leaned to socialism in my politics (which is so different from most of my Anglican peers!) However, I have, and I still staunchly maintain that **no action** I can take can cause a person to understand that Christ died for them except I explain it by **words**. I also believe that "I am to do good to all people and specially to the household of faith".

On liberal theology:

The real trouble with liberal theology is that it is worldly. It states what the spirit of the age believes, only it gives it a religious face and so seems to give legitimacy to its views. When we wave goodbye to our biblical moorings we will drift into sentimentality and will call it "love".

On sentimentality, the forerunner to liberalism, John prefaced his first Prayerletter for 1983 with these words:

SENTIMENTALITY AND REALISM

Luke 11:27–28

As Jesus was saying these things, a woman in the crowd called out, "Blessed is the mother who gave you birth and nursed you". He replied, "Blessed rather are those who hear the Word of God and obey it".

It seems in religion that sentimentality is never very far away, diverting people away from reality.

The way of sentimentality

Jesus had been accused of casting out demons by Beelzebub, the prince of demons. In the ensuing verbal encounter, Jesus claims that the much longed for kingdom of God had arrived in His person. To add further weight to the seriousness of His claim, He says, "He who is not with me is against me, and he who does not gather with me, scatters". It is an urgent call for decisive commitment. A woman in the crowd says, "What a fortunate mother yours is to have a son like you!" There is no denying the truth of the statement but it allows the full force of the need to acknowledge her allegiance to Jesus to move out of focus.

Several years ago at a dialogue evangelism meeting, having poured out my heart in a gospel presentation, I was slightly shaken when a man said, "Thank you for that. I've always believed good people go to heaven!" I could hardly believe my ears. Such sentimentality is never far below the surface. It comes to light in times of crisis, as when a loved one dies. People speak in non-factual terms about the goodness of the person and seek to be reassured that they are in heaven. I remember discussing the gospel with a man who told me of his grandmother who had spent her life in raising money for the Red Cross. "You're not asking me to believe that she ended up in the same place as Hitler, are you?"

Jesus does not want warm feelings but solid commitment to Himself as Lord in the kingdom of God.

The way of reality

Jesus does not deny that the woman's statement is correct. Indeed, it was exactly those terms that the archangel Gabriel used to address His mother (Luke 1:28). However, it was not a good enough response to the challenge He had made so He brings the crowd back to reality. "Blessed rather are those who hear the Word of God and obey it." Nothing is more important than that and nothing must divert us away from doing obedience to God's Word.

It is nice to believe somehow that all people are secure. The Bible tells us that "all have sinned". It's comforting to believe that all the dead (at least all the ones we know) are in heaven. The Word of God says, "God commands all people everywhere to repent because He has fixed a day when He will judge the world in righteousness".

We need to live in the world of reality. Our nice, kind, thoughtful, gentle, generous friends are going to hell unless they repent. We need to be ruthless with ourselves in this matter. We must not become sentimental and allow the urgency of the gospel to slip away from us.

As we begin a new year, will you recommit yourself to be a "hearer and a doer of God's Word"? Will you recommit yourself to the great task of leading people to Christ?[4]

The experience of parish ministry has demonstrated, over and over, that if the principal focus of the work of the parish is on the proclamation of the gospel—if evangelism is the driving force—then everything else seems naturally to fall into place. This does not happen if the primary focus is elsewhere, if it is on, say, nurture, pastoral care, visitation or good church services. If the gospel does not come first, the church falls into the comfortable inactivity of mere maintenance. There ceases to be the dynamism and vitality of growth that brings excitement and encourages confidence in God, that issues in praise to Him and confidence in Him and that, in the process, forces a proper ordering of priorities and a proper allocation of resources.

The ministry of encouragement

John has exercised a remarkable ministry of personal encouragement to many people throughout his Christian life. He has the ability, in a totally non-judgmental way, to encourage men and women to want a closer and more intimate relationship with the living God, to persist in and strengthen the daily disciplines of prayer and the reading of God's Word, to take the things of God more seriously, to grow in every good way into maturity in the Lord Jesus Christ. It is a reflection of his obedience to the command "Be holy because I, the Lord your God, am holy" (Leviticus 19:2). Many people testify to numerous acts of kindness, acts that show a particular understanding of them and a sensitivity to their needs–the giving of some small but particularly appropriate gift, an act of practical assistance or an item of thoughtful and timely correspondence.

When the ageing Bishop Moyes asked John if he were free one Sunday evening and whether he would like to accompany him to that evening's engagement, John sensed, although Moyes would never have admitted it, that Moyes was beginning to doubt his ability to drive at night. John set aside his own plans so that he might be Moyes' driver. Service of that kind wins the trust and confidence of those to whom it is given. John's care for Bishop Moyes and others engaged in ministry in the Diocese of Armidale was an important factor in facilitating the change of direction in that Diocese. Harry Goodhew gives another example:

There was an occasion which meant a great deal to Pam and myself. We were almost devoid of funds when we finished College and were preparing to marry. The generous element in John's character prompted a gift to us of some £25, which was a large sum of money in those days and went a long way to enable us to put down a deposit on a bedroom suite.[5]

An encourager of younger ministers

John has always been a great encouragement to us Pipers and to me in particular. When at Lalor Park, I well remember a conversation in which he imprinted upon my mind that justification meant not only being forgiven but also being declared right. When at Hurstville Grove, he used to sit with the five others at the 10 am service and take notes furiously as I preached. When at Kiama, he visited us for evangelistic occasions and wrote a very kind and courageous letter correcting my attitude when preaching at a CMS Summer School. When at Adelaide, he constantly encouraged us by phone calls, letters, cards and visits. He is great fun and a great favourite with all the family. He has kindly encouraged Dorothy in her partnership with me in the gospel and has with good humour encouraged Katy, Matthew and Elizabeth to grow up in Christ. He has even volunteered to write to Elizabeth's headmistress about her school projects.

A highlight of our trip to England was John's lightning conducted tour of the National Gallery, his knowledgeable discourse on the Hay Wain and his taking us to the Angus Steak House. A highlight of our ministry at Holy Trinity, Adelaide, was the week-long mission. John preached at this on his sixtieth birthday.

John has been such a good, faithful and praying friend to our family and we love him dearly in Christ.

When I was invited to Adelaide, I had it in my heart that I came on behalf of three men to preach and explain the apostolic gospel–one of them was John. We count it a high honour that he is a special friend.

Reg Piper
a member of the Board of the Department of Evangelism since 1993.

The most powerful reason compelling me to say something is to acknowledge the extraordinary capacity John has as an encourager of younger ministers. When I was at Lalor Park and Miranda, he often exercised that ministry to me. In particular, I recall his willingness to be the speaker at our second houseparty at St Luke's, Miranda. The early years there had their difficulties but John's splendid addresses over that weekend seemed to be a watershed and a breakthrough. We never looked back after that and everybody seemed to be on-side for the gospel. It marked a real change of tone for St Luke's.

There is so much one can say about John Chapman by way of admiration and interest but what I want to say, above everything else, is I thank God for him.

Peter Watson
a member of the Board of the Department of Evangelism from 1978 to 1991.

Service given with such apparent naturalness and often with enthusiasm is infectious. John's appetite for life has generated enthusiasm in others.

John has exercised a wonderful ministry of encouragement among the children of his friends and is universally regarded with great fondness by them.

In the ministry of prayer, John has, in Prayerletter after Prayerletter, thanked those who have been in intercession for his work, always sharing the blessings of its fruit, always reminding them that through their prayers they are fully caught up with him as his fellow workers in the gospel and always exhorting them to keep praying.

The indefatigable correspondent

A few weeks ago, I called John on the phone. I had been going through my old correspondence files and had come across several of his epistles written over the years. A card here, an aerogramme there, a few letters of a page or two, but what struck me about them was his role as an encourager. There was no real reason he had to write. He was simply motivated by the love of God shed abroad in his heart by the Holy Spirit.

Donald Howard
writing in July 1993.

Of all the periods when John helped me, the period when he was the most helpful was when I went to the States (to study at Gordon-Conwell Theological Seminary). I was in the States for four and a half years. During that time, he wrote to me every week. Two people did that. My mother wrote to me every week and Chappo wrote to me every week. Now, that really helped me through some very tough times as a student in a foreign land. It kept me in touch with Australia, but more than that, it was just someone who was committed to me, who prayed for me, who loved me and who cared for me, despite the incredible demands made on his time. And I would say it was that pastoral care, the writing of those letters, that is the main thing for which I am grateful to Chappo.

Adrian Lane
a member of the Board of the Department of Evangelism from 1977 to 1985.

The Board of the Department of Evangelism

In the brief history of the Department of Evangelism, a history of less than seventy years, John has been its longest serving evangelist. For twenty-seven years, this organisation has been the base from which he has carried out his work. During that time, its staff has grown from a single evangelist with some secretarial assistance into an organisation with, at its peak, five full-time and four part-time staff members. John recalls:

When I joined the Board, money came from the three sources it does now—individual donations, parish donations and Synod grants. We were always scraping the barrel. Had Geoff Fletcher not left when he did in early 1969, we would never have survived financially into 1970. In those early days, there was just about enough money for $1^2/_3$ staff members. When Brian Telfer left, we didn't appoint Phil Jensen for another twelve months to save money. We did this with every subsequent appointment until Don Howard came. As his appointment continued, we just had to lift our game. I remember I spoke in Synod once about how, since the Synod had set up the Department, it should meet our budget totally.

Broughton Knox subsequently pointed out to me the value of having to appeal to the parishes and to individual Christians because if we lost their support then we couldn't function. It was a discipline for them and for us too. It helped to keep us sound. I have come to agree with him in this.

Having regard to the strength of his view of the importance of evangelism, it is not remarkable that John should express the opinion that "I was constantly disappointed that the amount of money allocated to the Department of Evangelism by the Synod was scandalously small by comparison with that 'wasted' on other projects that I thought of less importance".

Service on the Board

Student ministers from Moore College regard "getting the nod" to work with the Department of Evangelism a great privilege and opportunity to grow in ministry skills. For me it has been the same to work with John on the Board of the Department. It is not only that the work of the Department is so vital but the meetings themselves were so stimulating. This I attribute to John's vision for gospel ministry, his commitment to it, his ability to analyse issues so clearly and his enthusiasm. He is not only a great preacher of the gospel. He is also a great defender of it with a nose to sniff out error and with a heart and lips to expose it.

Any contribution we made as members of the Board was eclipsed by the benefit received. I have always come away from our meetings excited by the gospel, encouraged to be faithful to my ministry in the parish and stimulated to think of ways that we as a Department and I as an individual could further this work that is so close to God's heart.

I am equally convinced that the articles and expositions John wrote for the Prayer Diary served the same purpose on a wider scale and became for many the basis of Sunday sermons and Parish Bulletin articles.

And what a bonus to enjoy hospitality at John's table over many of these meetings, and to often leave with the "leftovers" lest they "clutter up the fridge" not to mention the arteries!

Brian Telfer
a member of the Board of the Department of Evangelism since 1976.

John attracted to membership of the Board of the Department many people he had encountered in his constant travelling within the Diocese of Sydney who showed a similar keenness for the great cause he served. Many of them had demonstrated in their own work and witness a desire to proclaim the gospel and an inventiveness in doing it. They were people who shared his priorities. It seemed axiomatic that they were, or very quickly became, his friends. The Board members and the Department's staff were, in a sense, the members of John's immediate family. The Board was a place for sharing ideas, for giving mutual support and encouragement. It was a sounding board. It acted as the "ginger group" on evangelism, seeking to discover, to develop and to disseminate good ideas and good habits for evangelism. It was zealous for the advance of the work. John has said, "There are few committees that I go to which I enjoy as much as the Board meetings and where we are so unified in our purpose. I appreciate this fellowship very much indeed."[6]

The government of the Church

John has been an active member of several organisations of the church. He says, "I tried not to spend a lot of time on committees because it is secondary to real ministry but not unimportant. I think that one effect of my role on committees in the Diocese was that it raised the profile of the Department of Evangelism."

The good Archbishop

It was the first of our annual lunches at the Archbishop's residence for our Post Ordination Training. They're always a time for the unusual, like being prompt and dressing clerically. However, when it came lunch time, there was nothing unusual. While Dan Willis and I were making our way from the bathroom, our friends ensured that the only two places left at the dining table were on either side of the Archbishop (Donald Robinson).

I felt like one of the Zebedee boys. I was beginning to wonder if my mother had been to see him. Remember Rick, when it comes to the table setting, you eat from the outside in. Oops, keep your elbows off the table. What else had mum told me?

Things were not going well and, to make things worse, Dan had entered into conversation with one of our friends. Yes, you're right, I was now alone with the Archbishop. A silence existed for a few moments, he asked me a few questions, and I answered like any good Anglican clergy—carefully. Finally I mustered up the courage to ask him a question. "Tell me, Archbishop, what do you think makes a good archbishop?" I will never forget his answer. He said, "You worked with John Chapman, didn't you?" "Yes," I replied. With a wry smile the Archbishop responded, "You should ask him. He's always telling me what makes a good archbishop."

Well, how does one respond to that? I kept eating.

Rick Lewers
a catechist with the Department of Evangelism in 1987.

John became a member of the Synod of the Diocese of Sydney very shortly after his return from Armidale and quickly established his reputation as a lively, forthright and frequent contributor on many issues. He enjoyed vigorous debate. For twenty-five years he was one of its most influential orators. He had often prepared a speech but he was also able to think quickly while on his feet. He was clever in his ignorance of the Standing Orders. He would invariably throw himself on the President's mercy while explaining without a shadow of a doubt the result he sought to achieve so that his point would be made while some expert found a way for him to make it. He says:

I thought that the Sydney Synod was a great forum because you had so many able people who were all trying like mad to be Christian while grappling with very complex issues. Unlike Parliament, where they rarely grappled with the issues, Synod tried to do that. Some of the best debates I witnessed took place there. I was specially impressed by the two electoral Synods where debate was of the highest standard.

As an agent to bring about change, Synod was almost useless. It is far too big and far too conservative. Change needs to take place at the grass roots first—we need to see that it can be done at the grass roots in such a way as to commend it—and then it can be formalised as a last step in Synod.

John was a key participant in the electoral Synod that resulted in the election on 1 April 1982 of Donald Robinson as Archbishop of Sydney. He had been one of Donald Robinson's strongest advocates. He had moved the final motion for his election, speaking when moving the motion as well as in reply at the close of the debate.

John's last appearance in Synod was on 1 April 1993, the final evening of the electoral Synod that resulted in the election of Harry Goodhew as Archbishop of Sydney. It was an enthralling evening. At its commencement, there were two outstanding candidates remaining, Harry Goodhew and Paul Barnett. The final round of speeches for and against the candidates had concluded the previous evening, John having moved the motion "That Paul Barnett be invited to be Archbishop of Sydney". Following the pattern set eleven years before, he was the last to speak on behalf of the candidate he was proposing. All the speeches were over. The final evening was the moment for the members to cast their votes. In the interval during which the votes were counted, the Synod granted leave for two motions to be moved without notice. The second of these was a motion to thank Bishop Donald Cameron for his chairmanship of the proceedings. He had acted throughout with great skill and graciousness. His judgments and directions at all times had been clear and fair. It had been an exemplary performance. It had won the admiration of all. The motion thanking Bishop Cameron had been immediately preceded by another motion. It was in the following terms:

That, in prospect of the ending of his membership, this Synod gives thanks to God for the unique and utterly outstanding contribution made to the life of the Church through this and previous Synods by Canon John Chapman and records its appreciation for all his wise counsel, his godly example and the wit and warmth of his friendship.[7]

John had had no warning that the motion was to be moved. After the speeches of the mover and seconder, he was invited to respond. He did so in an engaging and moving speech that began, typically, while he gathered his thoughts, with the recounting of his latest humorous anecdote. John told a story of a friend's young grandson, Murray, who had recently begun attending a pre-school centre where all-day care was provided. The children were required to have an afternoon nap. If they were unable to sleep, they were told just to lie quietly on their beds. The superintendent suggested to the boys and girls that they might take the opportunity during these times to pray to God. When Murray later related these events to his mother, she was intrigued to know how he had responded. "Did you pray?" she asked him. "No," he said, "I don't know how to pray. I've never done it." "Well," she said, "what did you

Members of Standing Committee of the Sydney Synod, 1981.

do then?" "I told God a joke," Murray replied. It was vintage Chappo. John then spoke of the high regard he had for the Synod as one of the great forums of the Church, of his enjoyment of its debates and of the deep affection he had for all its members. He said how he would miss it. When he had finished speaking, the motion was not formally put. There was no need to. It carried with a standing ovation of considerable duration.

John was elected to the Standing Committee of the Synod in May 1975. He resigned in 1983 as he believed that parish clergy were under-represented and that his departure would create a vacancy to which a parish clergyman might be appointed. However, the Standing Committee replaced John with a non-parish clergyman and so, as he says, "I gave up and returned at the first opportunity". He was re-elected in 1985 and served a further period until 1993.

Out of darkness

Since the completion of the construction of St Andrew's House in 1976, meetings of the Standing Committee of Synod have been held in the Cowper Room, generally once a month on a Monday evening. The Cowper Room is a large inner room with no natural lighting. The meetings start at 6.00 pm and usually finish somewhere around 10 pm. The lights in the building are on a time switch and go off automatically. One night the Standing Committee was working through a particularly solid agenda when the room was suddenly plunged into total darkness. For a few seconds there was complete silence until a voice that was unmistakably Chappo's said from somewhere in the inky blackness, "I've gone blind!"

Warren Gotley
the Diocesan Secretary.

For twenty years from 1973, John served as a Sydney representative on General Synod. He has been a member of the Moore College Council since 1970. In 1975, he was elected by Synod a Canon of St Andrew's Cathedral.

On the question of church politics, John says:

A brace of canon, Williamsburg.

I have tried as hard as I could all the time to fight against the tendency for power in the Diocese to be centralised. My view is that all bishops in time try to centralise power because they can exercise power more efficiently by this method. They are not sinister in this, just efficient. However, when power is in the hands of *few* people and when that power affects the preaching of the gospel, we are in a dangerous situation because, if we make a mistake in the few we pick or appoint, the preaching of the gospel is under threat. Power must be in the hands of the laity. Then the clergy cannot neglect to teach them. Synodical power must not be by-passed. If it were, there would be a terrible price to pay. All power, and particularly the power to appoint people to key positions must have checks and balances. I have complained often about the way I have had to proceed to get someone appointed to the staff of the Department of Evangelism—Board approval and Archbishop's approval. Yet I have come to see that there is great wisdom in this. We are **all** less likely to make a mistake. But suppose I had power absolutely to make appointments, then gospelling is in danger.

A strong character subdued by a strong doctrine

In giving leadership, John has exhibited characteristics that have marked his nature out from others.

John has the most extraordinary common sense. He shows an unusual wisdom. It is a remarkable and rare quality.

As well, John is a man of compassion. He is genuinely interested in people. He has a real concern for others. His nature reflects the kindness shown by his parents for neighbours like Fred Davis and his family, and Mrs O'Connell, but it is a quality that has been refined in a Christian way. He has a strong sense of individual justice.

Without being ostentatious about it, John is a person of prayer. This is a fundamental quality for any leader, particularly for a leader in evangelism because all evangelism must be done within an atmosphere of prayer and against the background of a godly life.

John is a natural and consummate politician. He is a politician to his fingertips. He has played his full part in the forums of the church. He has not been disinterested. He has never been one to sit in silence. Whether it has been in supporting a point, questioning a point or turning a point aside, he has sought to guide the Christian family with the utmost care and concern. His commitment, while it may not have appeared the case, has often been costly. There have been differences of opinion with close friends. There have been nights of little sleep. But unlike many politicians, John has never been devious. Whether he has supported another's point of view or opposed it, his stand has been open. It has been principled, it has been reasoned and it has been explained. Those with whom he has contended have known exactly where he stood. And through the process he has never withdrawn his friendship.

There is a competitive side to John's nature. It is the kind of competitiveness found in the best of sportsmen—the tenacity, the unyielding spirit, the will to succeed despite the opposition. In the light of the sporting abilities of both John's parents, there is the possibility that this, too, is a characteristic inherited from them. But if it is, it, too, has been remoulded in a Christian way. John shows it, for example, in his evangelism. It is a quality that has kept him at the forefront of the great battle. It has enabled him to do the "hard work".

> It's like his tennis. The thing you ask yourself is—How does John win against younger, more athletic people? And the answer is this intense competitiveness. I think it is one of the keys to the whole of his life and character. He never lets a point go. It must be one of the reasons for his energy, his refusal to let a thing go, whether it is an injustice or a misunderstanding or a blockage in evangelism. He keeps at it.[8]

Some have found in John an abrasive and confronting quality. There can be a tendency to state a point of view too strongly. Where this is so, it has arisen from John's intense conviction of what is right and where truth lies.

The sovereignty of God is the most comforting doctrine. It is the ground for hope. It is the constant and dominating focus of John's faith. It is his understanding of this doctrine that has enabled him to come to terms with his own overwhelming personality and not be deflected by his human following. Had this man's character with all its extraordinary qualities not been subdued by a stronger God, had he not been transformed by God's extravagant love, had God's hand for blessing not been upon him, who knows where he might have led us? Instead, he has guided us in paths of righteousness for the sake of the name of the Lord Jesus Christ.

---

1   Year Book of the Diocese of Sydney, 1977, p 229.

2   Year Book of the Diocese of Sydney, 1977, p 227.

3   Prayerletter No. 2 1983 (May—July).

4   Prayerletter No. 1 1983 (February—April).

5   Letter to the author dated 15 March 1995.

6   Prayerletter, December 1971.

7   The motion was moved by the author and seconded by Phillip Jensen.

8   Dick Lucas in a conversation with the author.

John and Ian Powell.

PASSING ON THE TORCH

Paul and Timothy

There are differing ways in which a great legacy of wisdom and experience in evangelism might be handed on to a succeeding generation. It might be shown by constant and widespread example. It might be set down in writing. It might be taught at large. Or it might be imparted more directly through close personal teaching and on-the-job training in a way that explains clearly and applies individually the knowledge that has been acquired and the lessons that have been learnt.

The ministry of the apostle Paul constitutes a biblical model for the application of each of these ways. Paul gave example. In writing to "all the saints in Christ Jesus at Philippi" he said, "Join with others in following my example, brothers, and take note of those who live according to the pattern we gave you" (Philippians 1:1 and 3:17). Paul committed his instruction to writing. Under the inspiration of the Spirit of God, he produced the most remarkable collection of letters that any man was ever to write. Paul gave general teaching. "Whatever you have learned or received or heard from me—put it into practice" (Philippians 4:9). And in his ministry, there is a model for personal instruction, for the training and equipping of a younger man by an elder of the church. For over fifteen years, Timothy served an apprenticeship with Paul. He travelled with him. He heard him teach. From the closest quarters he observed his example. Timothy had been given

223

the responsibility for some special missions as Paul's delegate. In different ways, Paul trained him. "Timothy," Paul eventually was able to declare, "has proved himself, because as a son with his father he has served with me in the work of the gospel" (Philippians 2:22).

Like Paul, John has given enduring example to all. He has modelled the Christ-like life. He has committed his theology of the gospel as well as some practical means of gospelling to writing. And, in two particular ways, he has shown a consciousness of the need to prepare the succeeding generation for the great work of carrying on the ministry of the gospel.

Catechists

In April 1982, Paul Barnett, aware of the insight and long experience of his friend and of the fact that his years of restless activity could not continue with the same intensity for ever, wrote to the Board of the Department of Evangelism in the following terms:

His (John's) present style of ministry is quite counterproductive in the training of younger and gifted evangelists whom we will one day need. John's present ministry is almost all solo effort. There is no Timothy, no apprentice, nor will there be unless the pattern changes.

Paul's comments were made in the same letter that had raised for consideration the possibility of regional crusades. He saw that those crusades might provide the environment in which the evangelistic preaching of a suitable protege could be nurtured and developed. A trainee would be able, at first hand, to watch John in action and might be given opportunities to speak evangelistically at some of the events that formed part of a crusade.

At the time Paul Barnett's letter was written, John was fifty-one years of age.

The Board of the Department did not immediately appoint a second and younger evangelist as it had done previously with Brian Telfer, Phillip Jensen and John Webb. It opted, rather, for the appointment of a crusade administrator. But a seed had been sown nevertheless. In John's fertile mind, the seed was quickly to take root. The pattern was to change.

In 1983, in a report to the Board, John wrote:

I took up the matter of the appointment of a catechist with Bishop Reid (representing the Archbishop's Examining Chaplain) who gave us the green light. Consequently, I invited David Short to join us for 1984. David is married to Bronwyn and is in Second Year at Moore College. (By the time he commenced work with the Department, he had entered Third Year.) He has worked with Terry Dein (in the parish of Yagoona) for the last two years. He will begin in February. His pattern of work will be:

1. Twice a month he will go to his local congregation.
2. All other services he will come with me where I am preaching.
3. Once a month he will preach evangelistically (where I can observe him).

4. We will meet weekly to discuss the Sunday activity (either his or mine), talk about evangelism in general and pray.
5. He and I will discuss together what invitations will be accepted.

His stipend will be according to the diocesan scale. As you can see, it is designed to be a learning time as well as for ministry.

The decision was taken that, because a catechist would receive a highly specialised training with the Department, an appointment should not be made for more than one year.

David Short's appointment was experimental. It was an experiment that succeeded. He proved himself a worthy evangelist. Later, he remarked lightheartedly that, as the Department's first catechist, he was both "the pioneer and perfecter".

David Short's appointment became the first of an unbroken pattern of annual appointments. For the first three years, a single catechist was trained each year, for the next four years, as the staff of the Department increased, the number was increased to two catechists each year and subsequently there were not less than three catechists each year. Catechists were chosen, almost without exception, from theological students who had approached the Department and indicated their desire to work in this capacity under the supervision of its staff.

Catechists 1984–1994

1984	David Short	1991	Robert Smith
1985	Ian Powell		Philip Wheeler
1986	Stuart Robinson		Nick Foord
1987	Alan Stewart	1992	Zac Veron
	Rick Lewers		Bill Salier
1988	Gordon Cheng		Andrew Heard
	Ed Vaughan	1993	Lyn Yap
1989	Graham Bannister		Peter Smith
	David McDonald		Shaun Potts
1990	Matthew Pickering	1994	Richard Chin
	Ray Galea		Mark Leach
			Richard Shumack
			Graham Stanton

The criteria for selection were that a potential catechist needed to demonstrate a keen desire to be involved in evangelism and needed to have already developed a better than average ability at public speaking. This was an important quality because a new appointee would almost immediately be involved in public speaking, sometimes at large gatherings, and commonly to audiences that included unbelievers who had been brought to hear the gospel through the loving concern and hopeful anticipation of their friends. Consequently, before they undertook their first engagements, because they had had no opportunity to practise, they needed to already possess a reasonable level of competence.

CHAPTER TWELVE

At the time David Short commenced his appointment in February 1984, the Department of Evangelism was heavily involved in its preparations for the regional missions at Liverpool in April and Hurstville in September. David was immediately involved in this work. He spoke evangelistically at three school and coffee shop meetings. There were also other speaking opportunities in other parts of the Diocese.

Diocesan Missioners had produced a regular Prayerletter since the time of George Rees. During John's time, as the staff of the Department gradually grew in number, each member was required to write a contribution reporting on the work immediately completed, identifying prospective work and nominating points for prayer. The requirement applied to catechists no less than to any other staff member. The nature of their work and its need to be strongly grounded in the regular community of prayer was no less important for them than for any other evangelist. In his first report, David Short wrote:

> Thank you so much for your prayer concerning the Fairfield Coffee Shops—God answered our prayers, often in ways we did not expect. For example, on Thursday night the electricity to the school was cut owing to an accident outside the school (the last thing you'd want) and yet it seemed to work to our benefit. Each night was different. Thursday was small and effective, Friday was large and difficult and Saturday was small and friendly. Above all, some of the kids were converted. Please pray for them at Fairfield High and for their follow-up.
>
> I have been very conscious that people have been praying and have sensed the Lord's help. Please pray for future opportunities (a list of which was given).[1]

David Short's second report gives an indication of the form his training took. He wrote:

> The last few months have been busy and profitable... The time I'm spending with John is proving invaluable. By hearing him each Sunday and quizzing him during the week, I'm learning a great deal.[2]

The training was that of a true apprenticeship. It was on-the-job training carried out by the trainee under the close personal supervision of a master craftsman. The major emphasis was on learning to speak evangelistically. The training consisted of three elements. First, the catechist would listen to John preach and the two of them would then analyse what John had done. Secondly, the catechist preached and a tape recording would be made of the address. Thirdly, John would listen to the tape and teacher and pupil would analyse the catechist's preaching. Any weak areas would be corrected and the same sermon would be preached again. The revised sermon would be re-analysed and made as good as one might hope for.

Each new appointee came with a clear understanding of the task that lay ahead. At the beginning of 1985, the Department's second catechist, Ian Powell, and his wife Michelle, wrote in the Department's Prayerletter:

> We're both very excited about working and training with John and the

Department of Evangelism. Could you pray that we are not too much of a burden to him and that God may even use us to serve and encourage him in his crucial ministry. We want to learn as much as possible about how to proclaim Jesus in a way that is of maximum benefit to the perishing. Ian is looking to having his preaching sharpened and refined by watching John and by having his sermons vigorously critiqued. Could you pray that John would be wise and brave to give us honest critiques and advice, and that we will be humble, quick to learn and slow to forget.[3]

Each year, the members of the new intake approached their work with humility, conscious of their human inadequacies and their lack of testing, but with an awe-filled trust in the Saviour Lord and with the heart-felt longing and nervous expectation of the evangelist. They longed to see people turn in repentance and faith to God through the proclamation of the gospel. Being adult students, they also expressed an apprehension about how they would cope with their lectures and study workload, their college exams and, in many cases, the prospect of impending marriage or impending parenthood.

Catechists were encouraged to be analytical about their work generally and about the form and conduct of the evangelistic meetings at which they spoke. John commented, "My hope is that they will learn to choose Bible passages that enable them to preach the gospel well; then to explain it with crystal clarity; then to urge people with warmth and persuasiveness. I hope they will gain a love for gospelling and a confidence to know that the gospel they preach will be the means of people being saved."

Catechists attended the weekly staff meetings of the Department at which their past work was reviewed, their future work was organised and everything was prayed over.

John has regularly enjoyed Bible-focused conversation with his fellow Christians. His conversation is often robust, suiting the seriousness of its object. Where it seems he may differ in his views from those that are being offered, and by way of seeking to engage and probe the mind of the person he is talking with as well as to sharpen his own mind, he has commonly employed an interesting technique. He has not immediately presented his own thoughts in contradiction or correction. Instead, he has conducted a cross-examination, often carefully constructed.

"Let me ask you this question..."

(Response)

"Well, let me ask you another question..."

(Response)

"Then I need to ask you this..."

(Response)

"Are you saying that on the basis of the verse in .... that says .... or are you thinking of another verse?"

Finally, he is prepared to express and explain his view. "Well, you see, in **my** judgment..."

Chapter twelve

The mere process of articulating a point of view before an intelligent hearer is often helpful in clarifying the idea. The shaping of the view by questioning its content introduces a level of objectivity into the discussion. The technique is one that has been well-applied as a means of training.

The training of young evangelists by John and by other members of the Department's staff often brought a mixed response from the trainee. The training was intensive and the necessarily personal nature of each appraisal was potentially wounding, particularly when the evangelists had approached their task thoughtfully and with great care and earnestness. It was sometimes painful to conclude that improvement needed to be made. A typical summation of the results of a year's tuition and practice was given in his final report by David McDonald, a catechist in 1989:

> One of the highlights for me this year has been getting into the Gospels. Before I came to the Department, I'd done very little preaching from any of the four Gospels. Chappo has encouraged me to preach from them so that I will be confronting people with the person of Christ. This has steered me away from the doctrinal/conceptual sermon with which I was more comfortable. It has also deepened my understanding and appreciation of the Lord Jesus. The subject of endless years of Sunday School lessons has been confronting me larger than life. I can no longer read about Jesus walking on the water, and go "Oh yeah, yawn".
>
> As I've had many talks critiqued by Chappo and Ian (Powell) a number of problems have surfaced regularly. I am a slow learner and it has sometimes frustrated me that I repeat mistakes. Yet, I reckon I've made a fair bit of progress with my preaching, especially in noticing what I do. These skills I will need to keep developing in the future so I don't get complacent.
>
> By far the greatest thrill this year has been the privilege of seeing God change people. It is exciting when someone writes a letter to say they, or their friend/s, became a Christian. Sometimes it is hard to believe you can make a difference, and we need to remember that the gospel is God's power to save those who believe. Please pray that more and more people will so

The Department staff members, past and current at July 1990. Standing from left: Phillip Jensen, Don Howard, John, Lucianno Ricci, Matthew Pickering, Ed Vaughan, Ruth Howard, Dudley Foord, Elizabeth Foord, Ray Galea. Kneeling from left: Brian Telfer, Carol Sawyer, Janet Kearsley, Cathy Hannon, Al Stewart, Stuart Robinson with his son, Jonathan.

believe and understand the gospel of Jesus that they are compelled to share it with others. As we pray that we ought to include ourselves, shouldn't we?[4]

"As Chappo always reminds the new boys and girls on the block, 'the first fifty years of preaching are the hardest' so keep on praying for us", wrote Peter Smith, a catechist in 1993.

1993 was a year that saw some changes in the appointment of catechists. All previous appointees before then had been men and all had been students of Moore College. In 1993, the only catechist who was a Moore College man was Peter Smith. Shaun Potts became the first catechist who was a student at the Sydney Missionary and Bible College and, more significantly, Lyn Yap became the Department's first woman catechist.

The ministry of women in the work of the Department had been a slowly evolving one. Women had first served the Department voluntarily in a secretarial capacity. Gradually, remunerated appointments were made, sometimes on a part-time basis, to deal with the office work. In October 1975, Patsy Dahl and Kay Lamport became the first women members to serve on the Board of the Department. In mid-1986, Janet Kearsley, the Department's secretary for the previous six years, replaced Howard Peterson in the administrative role of Outreach Projects Officer with responsibility for organising the conduct of regional missions. With Janet's appointment, the woman's role was expanded beyond a secretarial one. From July 1990 until January 1993, the Department enjoyed the services, as parish consultants, of the dynamic and irrepressible husband and wife team of Dudley and Elizabeth Foord. Both the Foords were theologically trained and both were well-known for the very considerable evangelistic and Bible teaching skills they had developed and applied with unyielding commitment over a lifetime of service. Elizabeth Foord was the Department's first woman evangelist. At the beginning of 1992, Sheila Spencer, a Moore College graduate and a former parish worker with St Stephen's, Willoughby, joined the Department's staff as its second woman evangelist. She had been a member of the Board of the Department since October 1988. At the time of her appointment, it appeared that it could only be for one year's duration. With the provision of further funding, however, that appointment was able to be extended in subsequent years. As a result of Sheila Spencer's employment, it became possible to undertake the training of a woman catechist and Lyn Yap's appointment was the result.

Without exception, the Department's catechists have developed into fine evangelists, strengthening their love for and commitment to the gospel and offering leadership in its cause in various parts of Australia and abroad. Several have later served on the Department's Board. Stuart Robinson had been the Department's sole catechist in 1986. In October 1991, he became the Chairman of the Board. In an article in the Department's Prayerletter in November 1993, he recorded that:

Working with Chappo, and being worked over by Chappo, was perhaps the single most influential facet of my ministry training. John was a gracious encourager, a relentless evaluator and a generous friend. The phrase—"State your point, explain your point, illustrate your point and apply your point" is burned into my mind for all eternity.

"Oh," John said dismissively when Stuart's comment was reported to him, "that's pure Spurgeon".

Where are they now?

Since working with the Department of Evangelism over two and a half years ago, Sandy and I have been ministering with Blacktown Anglican Church. More specifically, I have been given a brief to evangelise and disciple Maltese in the Western suburbs of Sydney. The ministry is called the Maltese Bible Ministry (MBM). The name is a bit of a misnomer because we have attracted a much wider range of ethnic groups, some of whom include Assyrian, Italian, Lebanese as well as Anglo-Saxon. (The ministry was later renamed the Multicultural Bible Ministry.) It has been exciting to see God bringing people into relationship with himself.

MBM meets each Sunday at 5 pm at Tyndale Christian School in Blacktown. We average about forty adults each Sunday—about a third of whom have come to Christ during the last three years. We also have six Bible studies meeting during the week.

The Department of Evangelism has played its part in the work. John, Steve (Abbott) and David (Mansfield) have spoken at MBM as have a number of catechists—Bill Salier, Rob Smith, Andrew Heard.

I am indebted to the Department (in particular, John) for sharpening my gospel focus and for making me a better preacher. John helped me to strip the sermons back into the clearest possible format. He also taught me the wisdom of knowing what to leave out of a sermon as much as what to say. The time with the Department as a catechist was invaluable.

Ray Galea

writing in the Department's Prayerletter in August–October 1993.

College teaching

In the years following his return to Sydney from the Diocese of Armidale, John received invitations from one or two Bible colleges to deliver lecture series for them, frequently on the theology and practice of evangelism. In July 1972, at the invitation of the Principal of the Queensland Bible Institute, that was his theme as he spoke in celebration of the Institute's 25th anniversary. In January the following year, he returned to give ten lectures at the QBI's Summer School of Theology on the sovereignty of God and evangelism. During Easter 1974, he spoke at the Adelaide Bible College Convention at Victor Harbour in South Australia.

John's first significant involvement in regular, rather than occasional, college teaching came with the commencement of a weekly evening course that he and Don Howard began at the Sydney Missionary and Bible College in February 1977. It was to train leaders for dialogue evangelism. The initial lectures were given an enthusiastic reception by a class of about 100 people. This course, practically based and designed to assist its students to present the gospel to contemporary society and to answer common objections to the Christian message, has continued to the present day.

John has consistently championed theological education. He has supported the work of Moore College, in particular. He was elected as a member of the Moore College Committee, the body that administers the College, in 1970 and has served as one of its members ever since. "The greatest need is for us to pray for those engaged in theological education," he wrote following "Connection '85", the regional mission in Warringah. "There is no doubt that the college is the key to sound education at the parish level."

Through the period of the mid to late 1970s, when Broughton Knox was Moore College Principal, John raised with him the possibility of introducing into the curriculum some lectures on evangelism. At first, John was unsuccessful, not because the Principal was opposed either to John or to teaching on evangelism, but simply because he felt, apparently, that students were already served with a sufficient breadth of courses and faced a heavy-enough workload. In addition, students and staff of the College went on mission each year. They engaged in practical evangelism then and supplemented their experience with morning sessions in which they reflected on and evaluated the events of the previous day. So, evangelism was not neglected. From April to June 1979, however, John and Don Howard did take an evening course on evangelism at the College for external students.

At the beginning of 1981, Broughton Knox invited John to lecture Fourth Year students for two terms of their year on the subject of evangelism. John was delighted. "It should be a very significant time as we talk about evangelism at the parish level," he wrote.[5] In the course, he taught the theology of evangelism and shared methods of parish evangelism then being used in different parts of the Diocese. John was invited to repeat the course in 1982 and 1983.

When in 1985, following Broughton's retirement, Peter Jensen succeeded him as Principal of Moore College, John again raised the question of college lecturing. John says:

I was concerned that efforts should be made to upgrade preaching. I have always been sensitive to the criticism of Moore College graduates that they were accurate in theology but boring in delivery. I have tried to break that stereotype. The early catechists we had at the Department were really so good and made such good headway that I went and spoke to Peter Jensen about working at

John and Peter Jensen.

College and trying to improve preaching generally. I think we still have a very long way to go to help preachers preach in an interesting way. It was mainly because of this that I joined the staff at Moore College.

At the beginning of 1986, Peter Jensen invited John to lecture to Third Year students for two terms each year in a course on evangelism. Entitled "The Minister and Public Evangelism", the course was one of practical instruction containing several parts. It dealt with preparing for the evangelistic event, looking at the elements of the event, evangelistic preaching, the making of an appeal and following-up inquirers and the newly converted. The course also included teaching concerning the use of several practical methods of engaging in evangelism. The students were, for example, taught how to use "2 Ways to Live" themselves and how they might teach others to use it.

By 1990, John was spending two days each week teaching, one at Moore College and another at the Sydney Bible and Missionary College. He was teaching courses on evangelistic preaching and evangelism generally.

At Moore College, John conducts a course for First Year students based on the material in his book *Know and Tell the Gospel*. It is the set text. He teaches a compulsory course for Second Year students comprising basic instruction on preaching generally. He explains how to put a sermon together. In teaching students this course, John engages in the close personal assessment of their preaching that is part of a catechist's training. He listens to a tape each student makes of a sermon they have preached and then evaluates it. "Do I need to tell you that this has put certain strains on my time and I would be glad if you would pray that I will know and do what is sensible," he wrote in the Department's Prayerletter in mid-1990. He also lectures Second Year students in an optional course called

John and David Cook.

"Evangelism". He runs seminars with Fourth Year students on the sermons they preach in the College Chapel. He teaches a one-year course called "Bible and Mission" for prospective missionaries.

John's work at the Sydney Missionary and Bible College where he spends one day each week, has been much the same, although it also has a Bible teaching component. He has taught Mark's Gospel to First Year students. He has taught the Catholic Epistles and Paul's Prison Epistles. He teaches courses on evangelism generally and evangelistic preaching and he conducts preaching and dialogue evangelism workshops.

During the years of his college teaching, John has not ceased evangelising. He has not withdrawn entirely from the on-going public ministry of declaring the mighty deeds of God. He believes that

he would lack the authority to teach evangelism if he were not himself engaged in doing the work of an evangelist. John has acknowledged that his formal teaching ministry is important and strategic. "To be able to teach evangelistic skills and preaching to others multiplies the numbers who can do it. To be able to teach them so they can teach others is even better. (*And then there follows this echo from deep within the heart of the evangelist.*) Please pray that I do not lose my vision of the importance of this. While I am teaching here I seem to be such a long way from the coal face."[6]

John has written:

It is good to be able to share with the students skills which I have learned over the years. They are so keen that they inspire me. We are truly blessed by God to see the way He continues to raise up leaders for His church in the future.[7]

Partners in the gospel

Our years of working with John were amongst the happiest years of ministry we have ever experienced. I still feel a sense of melancholy that the team did not last until death do us part.

In my last contribution to the Department's Prayerletter in December 1991, I commented that Chappo was the easiest boss I ever worked with. This is undoubtedly true.

I worked with John twice, once part time, and then again for four years full time. He always treated me with kindness and respect, my family with generous playfulness—hand weaving doll house mats, making peg dolls, bringing gifts home from overseas and Darrell Lea. My wife's opinions were actually sought and listened to with care. I enjoyed arguing with him. It was done with vigour and totally without spite. Good Christian debate. I have never known a man who was more ready to declare that he was wrong. (My humility has not yet extended to that high level.) He was my coach, partner, fierce competitor on the court and the links. John is still loved hugely by all the members of my family. We saw him in church the other day and the kids were thrilled. Shelly and I were too. John's sermon was one of the best I've ever heard.

Ian Powell
writing in September 1993 at the time of celebrating John's twenty-five years with the Department of Evangelism.

The next Director

As the time for John's retirement approached, he continued lecturing two days each week at the colleges. He felt that the Department of Evangelism needed a full-time Director. He was concerned that there should be a smooth transition to his successor in the Director's role. He suggested to the Board that he would like to step down as Director at the end of April 1993 after the special session of the Diocesan Synod convened to elect a new Archbishop of Sydney following Donald Robinson's retirement. Resignation from the position of Director would, at that time, leave a period of a little over two years before John reached retiring age on 23 July 1995, his sixty-fifth birthday. He proposed to complete that period under his successor.

In February 1992, a decision was made to invite David Mansfield to join the Department as Assistant Director with the intention that he be appointed as Director on John's resignation. David Mansfield was then the rector of the parish of Kiama. He accepted the invitation and joined the staff of the Department in December 1992. At the time of coming on staff, he wrote:

> We have all looked forward to this day for some time now. I think I can safely speak for all the new and almost new members of the staff when I say that it is a tremendous privilege to have the opportunity to work with and alongside John in the ministry of the gospel. When I was a kid I dreamed of running off Reg Gasnier in the centres for St George. Now a Christian and just a little more grown up, I reckon this is even more exciting.[8]

At the beginning of May 1993, David became the Department's Director.

How we thank the Lord for John!

I was seventeen and a Christian only a few months when I first met John. He had been invited to the Mowbray parish by John Turner to do a series of Bible studies on 1 John. I was rapt in his clear Bible teaching, relevant application and his warm, passionate, witty style. But it was in conversation over supper as he applied God's Word to an issue I was struggling with in my life that I was struck by his incisive ability to apply biblical principles in an uncompromising and yet deeply sensitive manner.

So many colourful memories spring to life as I reflect on the twenty plus years of friendship marked by those same qualities since that first encounter.

When students at Moore College, John took Steve Abbott and me golfing at Moore Park. I played a long iron on a fairway and took out a bird in mid-flight with my shot. As we watched the bird and ball fall out of the sky together, John dryly said, "I bet nothing like that's ever gone through his head before!"

Toward the end of College when I told John I was going to get ordained in Western Australia, his disapproval, somewhat lacking in subtlety, was something to be reckoned with. Only time was to prove how wise his counsel had been!

Fairly recently when Helen, the kids and I faced what was to that point the first real tragedy in our lives, John was immediately on the phone with support, comfort and wisely chosen words of realism and reassurance consistent with the gospel.

A truer friend and finer example of love for the Lord Jesus and this gospel one could not hope to have. How we thank the Lord for John!

David Mansfield

a member of the Department's Board from 1987 to 1992 and Director since May 1993.

A number of people counselled John against the transitional arrangement he proposed. They did not think it would work. They felt there should be a clean break because it could be difficult for his successor to assume full responsibility while John remained an active staff member. John had no such reservations. He expressed amazement that some were of the view that there could be difficulties. He was determined to conduct himself with total propriety. For his part, David Mansfield says:

> John has probably been the most significant influence on my evangelistic thinking. He has given outstanding evangelistic leadership. I hold him in very high esteem. I wanted him to keep working. I wanted him to pass on his expertise. At no time did I feel threatened or intimidated. John behaved himself!

John and a Moore College mission group at Dapto, 1977. David Mansfield is on John's right and Stephen Abbott is standing far right.

The transitional arrangements, while unusual, sprang from John's common sense. They were completely successful.

In conclusion

In the manner of the Acts of the Apostles, this record of John's ministry ends, yet his ministry continues. John has now reached the age of sixty-five and, on 31 July 1995, a significant chapter in his long and thoroughly

Staff meeting in John's home, 1993. From left: David Mansfield, John, Stephen Abbott, Janet Kearsley, Sheila Spencer.

distinguished work with the Department of Evangelism was formally concluded. It would, of course, be inconceivable to expect a man of John's convictions, gifts and energy to retire totally. While God gives him breath, this man who combines the mind of a theologian with the heart of a shepherd, in whom truth and love are transparently combined, will undoubtedly continue to be a true servant of the gospel in a lively and invigorating way, firmly resolved to know nothing "except Jesus Christ and him crucified" (1 Corinthians 2:2).

No time like now

On various occasions I have reminisced with John and we have remembered and become excited about some of the great events of the past when God's hand of blessing was unmistakably present. And I have said to him wistfully, "They were great days weren't they, Chappo!" Quickly he has smiled and agreed, but, just as quickly, he has also tilted his head at me as if to emphasise the point and added in a gently chiding way, "But these are great days, too, aren't they?"

Michael Orpwood
on the pleasures of writing biography.

CHAPTER TWELVE

1   Prayerletter No. 2 1984 (May—July).

2   Prayerletter No. 3 1984 (August—October).

3   Prayerletter No. 1 1985 (February—April).

4   Prayerletter November 1989—January 1990.

5   Prayerletter No. 1 1981 (February—April).

6   Prayerletter February—April 1992.

7   Prayerletter May—June 1993.

8   Prayerletter February—April 1993.

Senior Statesman.

EPILOGUE: INTO THE HARVEST FIELD

On Sunday 6 August 1995, John Chapman addressed a gathering of many friends from many places who had met in the Assembly Hall at Trinity Grammar School in Sydney to mark his retirement. This Epilogue contains the substance of the speech he made on that occasion.

Past, present and future

Today is a day to look in all directions—to the past, to the present and to the future.

Today is certainly a day to look to the past and to reminisce. Yet most reminiscences don't involve many people at a time and are often boring to the rest. Because of this, I will confine myself to two matters.

I was ordained on St Thomas' Day (21 December) 1957, so you will see that I lack two years to have been ordained for forty years. They have been wonderful years for me and, as I look back on them, I wish to place on record my profound gratitude to God who not only sought me and found me but who saved me and gave me His Spirit and made me His own.

At my Ordination Retreat, a series of meditations was delivered to us by the late Canon Bob Kirby on the verses in 1 Timothy 1:

I thank Christ Jesus our Lord, who has given me strength, that He considered me faithful, appointing me to His service. Even though I was once a blasphemer and a persecutor and a violent man, I was shown mercy because I acted in ignorance and unbelief. The grace of our Lord was poured out on me abundantly, along with the faith and love which are in Christ Jesus (1 Timothy 1:12–14).

I don't remember much of those meditations, but I have never forgotten the verses which summarise well how I feel when I look back over those many years in the ordained ministry. My service does not in any way compare with the author of those words yet they express exactly how I feel. I am so grateful to the Lord Jesus for His faithfulness and love over those years.

Yet, to look back to the past and to stop at ordination would be improper. My mind soars back through time until I see on a hill outside Jerusalem those many years before a young man unjustly executed. I hear again that terrible cry, "My God, my God, why have you forsaken me?" and I realise afresh that "all we like sheep have gone astray. We have turned every one to his own ways and the Lord has laid on Him the iniquity of us all" (Isaiah 53:6). I am caught again in the wonder of the death of the Lord Jesus which enabled me to come back to God and cry "Abba, Father"—a true son—fully forgiven and restored into fellowship with Him. When I look back to the past, I see it is the Cross of Christ that has both thrilled and motivated me. It has humbled me and brought me to this day. And I am profoundly thankful to God for that.

So much for the past. Let me return to the present. I wish to thank all those who have made this day so enjoyable to me. My special thanks to the Board of the Department of Evangelism for organising this "do"—to Dick Lucas for coming from England to be here and to help make this day really special—to Michael Orpwood for writing a biography—and to all of you, "Thanks".

Well, what about the future? How should we think about that? I have been greatly helped by a passage in Matthew 9:35–37:

Jesus went through all the towns and villages, teaching in their synagogues, preaching the good news of the kingdom and healing every disease and sickness. When He saw the crowds, He had compassion on them, because they were harassed and helpless, like sheep without a shepherd. Then He said to the disciples, "The harvest is plentiful but the workers are few. Ask the Lord of the harvest, therefore, to send out workers into His harvest field."

When God created us, He told us what His purpose was so we would reflect His character. "Let us make man in our own image," He said. God's purpose for us was that we should mirror His own person. However, sin entered the world and that image of God in us was marred. We have to wait until the perfect human, the Lord Jesus, comes before we see the image of God perfectly displayed in man again. Jesus is the image of God (2 Corinthians 4:4).

God also tells us that one of the reasons for which the Lord Jesus came into the world was to restore that damaged image of God in us. "For those whom God foreknew He also predestined to be conformed to the likeness of His Son, that He might be the first-born among many brothers" (Romans 8:29). Because of this, the

Lord Jesus is a model of how we should live in the world. At any given time or circumstance, we should act in the way Jesus acted. We should reflect God's way in the world.

This part of the Bible gives us a tiny cameo in the life of the Lord Jesus yet it has been an inspiration to me over many years. In this passage, there is a clear example of how we are to think and a clear command as to how we should act.

A clear example

When Jesus saw the crowd, he was filled with pity for them because they were like shepherdless sheep. Genuine love and compassion are wonderful traits. In Jesus we see them demonstrated again and again. But what we see here is an addition to the compassionate heart—the hard head. These two linked together are a very powerful combination. The reverse is fatal. Nothing is worse than the soft head and the hard heart! The Lord Jesus sees them with the eyes of God and they are lost.

Throughout the Bible runs the wonderful theme of God being the shepherd of His people and of the wonderful security which this brings. In Ezekiel, when the leaders of Israel will not lead God's people into godly ways, God says, "I myself will be shepherd to my people". I suppose the best example of this is Psalm 23. The psalmist lists the benefits of this relationship with God. He does not want. God leads him in the life situation in the path of righteousness. He satisfies him, leading him in green pastures and by still waters. He lifts him up when he is down. He restores his soul and, even in the face of death, he is still secure. "When I walk through the valley of the shadow of death," he says with confidence, "I will fear no evil". In the presence of his enemies, God comes to his aid and he lacks nothing. "Surely goodness and loving kindness will follow me all the days of my life and I will dwell in the house of the Lord forever."

But spare a thought for the people who do not have the Lord as their shepherd. Spare a moment for them, and pity them. What is it that they can say? And what is the truth of their position? Can you hear their cry? "The Lord is not my shepherd. I am in terrible want. No-one comes to my aid. I know nothing of green pastures or still waters. It is "every man for himself" in the world I live in. I flounder around in life desperately trying to make sense of it. When I face death, terrible fear grips hold of me, and in the presence of my enemies this fear intensifies. Goodness and loving kindness are total strangers to me. I have no hope at all when I look to life after death.

Pity the person who is shepherdless! We should have compassion on the multitude around us who are lost.

There is a clear example to follow. In this matter, we need the mind and heart of Christ. We need to know their condition. We need to love them and feel for them. We need to see them with the eyes of Christ. They are harassed and helpless, like sheep without a shepherd. This is a work that is done by the Spirit within us. We need to ask God to grant us His Spirit so we can behave as Christ has set us the example.

239

A clear command

One of the things I like so much about the Bible is that it is so uncluttered and so very easy to understand. Listen to the command of the Lord Jesus. "There is a great harvest but few labourers. Pray the Lord of the harvest to send out workers into his harvest."

What a great word of encouragement this is! The harvest is not meagre, it is plentiful. There is a great harvest. All around us are people without Christ who need Him. It is the gospel that will save them. This is the way He gathers in His harvest. The Lord Jesus is explicit about what we should do.

We are to pray that God will increase the number of workers. **Will you do that?** In this matter, will you obey God? There are not enough people witnessing, as a way of life, to the saving works of Jesus—not nearly enough.

If we are obedient to this command, there is no doubt in my mind that we will discover that we are the answer to our own prayers. It will dawn on us that we can swell the ranks of the witnessing workers by one more.

As I look to the future, it is my prayer that, however long it pleases God to spare me, my love for Him and my love for my fellow humans will grow more and more and that, as it grows, evangelising them will become a greater and greater delight. It is my prayer that the Lord of the harvest will send you into the harvest field too.

John in Dublin, 1994.

INDEX